HATTERAS JOURNAL

Meant to Be Wild: *The Struggle to Save Endangered Species through Captive Breeding*

Wind: *How the Flow of Air Has Shaped Life, Myth, and the Land*

HATTERAS JOURNAL

Jan DeBlieu

John F. Blair, Publisher   Winston-Salem, North Carolina

Originally published in hardcover by Fulcrum, Inc., 1987

———————————

*The paper in this book meets the guidelines
for permanence and durability of the
Committee on Production Guidelines
for Book Longevity of the Council
on Library Resources.*

Cover design by Debra Long Hampton
Layout design by Liza Langrall
Pen-and-ink illustration by Mara H. Bagnal

Library of Congress Cataloging-in-Publication Data
DeBlieu, Jan.
Hatteras journal / Jan DeBlieu.
p.   cm.
Originally published: Golden, Colo. : Fulcrum, 1987.
Includes bibliographical references and index.
ISBN 0-89587-214-5 (alk. paper)
1. Natural history—North Carolina—Hatteras, Cape.
2. Coastal ecology—North Carolina—Hatteras, Cape.
3. Hatteras, Cape (N.C.) I. Title.
QH105.N8D43   1998
508.756'175—dc21   98-14953

For Smith, my co-conspirator

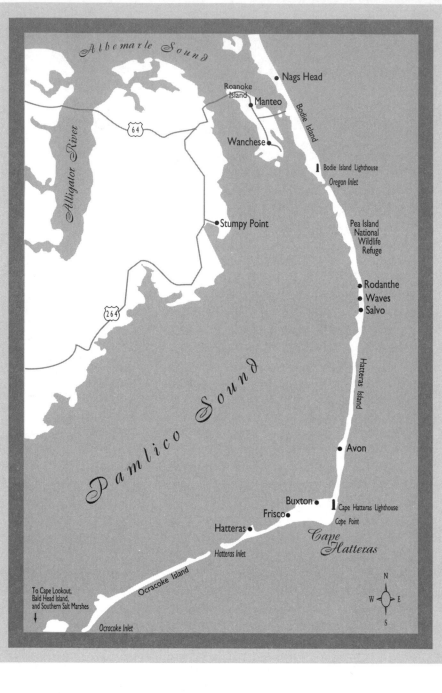

Albemarle Sound

Nags Head

Roanoke
Island
Manteo

Bodie Island

64

Wanchese

Bodie Island Lighthouse

Oregon Inlet

Alligator River

Pea Island
National
Wildlife
Refuge

Stumpy Point

Rodanthe

Waves

Salvo

264

Hatteras Island

Pamlico Sound

Avon

Buxton

Cape Hatteras Lighthouse

Frisco

Cape Point

Hatteras

Cape
Hatteras

Hatteras Inlet

Ocracoke Island

To Cape Lookout,
Bald Head Island,
and Southern Salt Marshes

N

W   E

S

Ocracoke Inlet

CONTENTS

ᴀ CKNOWLEDGMENTS

Wʜᴇɴ I ʙᴇɢᴀɴ the research for this book, I had only a perfunctory knowledge of coastal biology and a list of scientists and naturalists who might be of help. Of those, several gave their time so freely that my work was substantially reduced.

I am indebted, first, to the naturalists of the Cape Hatteras National Seashore, especially Kent Turner, Marcia Lyons, and Warren Wrenn, all of whom provided detailed information on the natural history of Hatteras Island, and who consistently tried to find answers to my rather obtuse questions.

Second, a number of scientists and biologists provided me not only with data and information but with ideas for topics and, later, with suggestions for improving the manuscript. These include Courtney T. Hackney of the University of North Carolina at Wilmington, Lee J. Otte of East Carolina University, and Michael L. Dunn of the North Carolina Department of Natural Resources and Community Development. I also received a quantity of information about barrier island wildlife from state and federal biologists, including Bonnie Strawser of the U.S. Fish and Wildlife Service; Robin Bjork, formerly of the University of North Carolina at Wilmington and now of the Florida Game and Fish Commission; and Jeffrey Ross and Beth Burns of the North Carolina Division of Marine Fisheries. Charles Don Edwards of the village of Waves kindly provided a great deal of material on the history of Hatteras Island families and customs.

The conception of this book was unusual, and I am especially indebted to Robert C. Baron of Fulcrum, Inc., for his willingness to support an unproven writer. In addition, I would like to thank E. Darby Junkin of Fulcrum for her timely words of encouragement and my editor, Pat Frederick, for her wit and well-chosen cuts and changes.

Finally, I owe my greatest thanks to my husband and parents for their patience and support, and to my friend Janet P. Walsh, without whose help my writings of Hatteras may never have found their way into print.

J. DeBlieu
Rodanthe, November 1986

HATTERAS JOURNAL

1

APRIL BLOW

FOR NINE HOURS last night a northeast wind railed against the Hatteras coast, stripping pants and socks from clotheslines and hurtling buckets across fields of flattened reeds. At the time the gale hit I happened to be at home nursing a pair of sunburned shoulders, but I might as easily have been on the beach, so completely did the squall take me by surprise. Certainly nothing about the water or sky that day had hinted at the bad weather to come. For more than a week the incessant Hatteras breezes had been pleasantly light, and during afternoon lulls the island had seemed like a sliver of land suspended between two layers of lucent and fathomless blue. A big blow was the last thing on my mind when, at 7 o'clock, I watched the sun slide behind the wax myrtle bushes in back of the house in a sky still tranquil and dotted with rosy swabs of clouds. A half-hour later the stepladder on the porch was knocked flat by a strong gust, and the lid to the barbecue grill flew upside-down into the neighbor's yard. I ventured out long enough to retrieve the grill cover and weight it down with bricks. Then I shut the door and planted myself in the kitchen with a book.

Through the windows I could see the feathery tips of cedar keeling to the southwest in the last minutes of foggy, blue light. Wind seeped through the wood-slatted walls of my old house, rippling the leaves of houseplants and rustling a stack of newspapers I had left in a living room chair. Where an hour before the house had been quiet, it was now full of clamor. The metal damper to the oil furnace squeaked on its hinges as downgusts pulled it open and shut. Panes of glass rattled, and outside the kitchen window a disconnected telephone wire slapped erratically against the side of the house. The slaps were just frequent enough to be irritating, and the rush of the wind just loud enough to set goosebumps on my arms beneath a heavy wool sweater.

This was the first storm of any consequence since I moved six weeks ago to the Outer Banks, a chain of barrier islands that juts more than twenty miles into the Atlantic Ocean off North Carolina. In early March I settled into a sixty-year-old frame house in the village of Rodanthe, a small but spreading town on Hatteras Island. From the attic in the back of the house I can see the shallow, briny waters of Pamlico Sound, and two hundred yards from my front door the chilly waves of the Atlantic Ocean wash a steeply sloped beach that is separated from the village by a single five-foot dune. The houses closest to the ocean are built on stilts. Mine is not. Last night, as the tea kettle boiled and the first drops of rain washed the front porch, it seemed that the crash of the surf grew louder and closer. The house creaked and sighed on its foundation, like a ship straining against its anchor. A beach ball rolled through my yard and lodged among the stubby, waving branches of a myrtle bush. At 8:30 the power went out.

In the continental United States no stretch of coastline except Florida is more vulnerable to hurricanes and northeast storms than the Outer Banks, the belly of the eastern seaboard that curls out just south of the Chesapeake Bay. The banks include two long capes: the unpopulated Cape Lookout and the more famous Cape Hatteras, comprised of Hatteras and Ocracoke islands and the southern tip of Bodie Island. Known to mariners for three hundred years as the Graveyard of the Atlantic, the Hatteras coast bears scars from storms that have flattened dunes and gouged new inlets in a single day. Floods occasionally wash out streets and lift houses off their foundations; in fact, local legend has it that several of the houses surrounding mine floated to their present locations during a spring storm in 1944. To weatherworn Hatteras natives, a puny northeaster like last night's was of no great concern. To me, a newcomer to the coast, the storm was exhilarating, bracing, good material for stories—but only as long as I kept a grip on my imagination.

My thoughts on the potential danger of this particular blow might not have been so vivid had it come at a different time. For the previous week and a half, though, I had spent most of my time reading articles and talking to naturalists from the Cape Hatteras National Seashore about the unusually severe erosion on the Outer Banks, especially on Hatteras Island just north of Rodanthe. Several evenings before, I had read a series of articles that had concluded it is a waste of time and money to attempt to stabilize the beaches of the cape as long as sea level continues to rise and storms continue to ravage the coast. To my surprise, the authors had agreed that it is not hurricanes that pose the greatest threat to the safety of island residents but the more frequent and long-lived northeasters that can develop in as little as twelve hours and churn up waves large enough to overwash State Highway 12, the only road to the mainland. Chances are that a major storm will one day demolish the settlements on the cape. And the possibility exists that the storm could flood the highway before residents realize the danger and have time to drive to safety.

As I sat in my darkened house and listened to the wind, it was difficult not to think of those dire predictions. Yet realistically I could conjure up no cause for great alarm. Despite the draftiness of my house, it has withstood enough storms to acquire an atmosphere of assorted personal histories; it is the kind of old, musty dwelling that would serve as a good home for ghosts. Its very longevity was testimony to its sturdiness, I decided, as the squeak from the damper again sent prickles up my spine. I briefly considered walking out to the beach to peek over the dunes at the surf, but settled instead on passing the hours before bedtime by baking a cake.

In the amber light thrown off by two kerosene lamps, I leafed through a dog-eared cookbook to a pecan upside-down cake that could easily be mixed by hand. Grabbing some unshelled pecans from a plastic bag under the sink, I began cracking them open, feeling cozy and snug. A particularly strong gust shook the house, and I thought of the shorebirds I had seen feeding on the beach a few days before, the earliest of the flocks that would soon come migrating through. In this kind of weather they would be huddled back in the marsh. The ghost crabs that had only begun to dig out of their winter burrows would have ducked back underground. Some animals were bound to die tonight, and if the ocean jumped the primary dune, most of the shrubs to the east of the highway would no doubt be choked by salt. I turned on the gas oven—for warmth as much as for the cake—and poured a yellow batter into a pan on top of a frothing mixture of butter, brown sugar, and nuts.

By 10:30, when I bit into the first moist piece of cake, my eyes had grown strained from the diffused, flickering light, and I was jumpy from the racket of the wind. Giving up on the evening, I made my way through dark rooms to bed, still acutely aware of the force of the gusts just on the other side of the walls. My last thought was of a series of tall, peaked dunes that line the road north of town. I wondered if they would still be standing by the storm's end. Probably, I thought. I'm probably making too much of this one brief blow.

The dunes I thought about as I drifted toward sleep are a favorite sight of mine on the straight and often tiresome road to Nags Head and Manteo, the nearest towns to Rodanthe on the drive north toward the mainland. In a landscape dominated by horizontal lines, the dunes rise steeply from the sandy hollows just east of Highway 12 and drop fifteen feet to the tideline in a nearly perpendicular descent. They are a tribute to the National Park Service's long struggle to limit the damage inflicted by storms on the Outer Banks. Covered with the shaggy stems of *Spartina patens*—a saltmeadow grass that resembles hay—they remind me more of camel humps than of dunes. In some areas, low, salt-tolerant shrubs such as wax myrtle creep up their backsides like soldiers overrunning a hill. The shrubs are in fact invading foreign terrain, for under natural conditions woody plants could not survive so close to the swash of high tides.

Sixty years ago the profile of the dunes resembled the more gradually sloped ridge of sand that fronts the beach at Rodanthe. Periodically, waves churned up by storms and pushed by northeast winds would spill over them, moving vast amounts of sediment into marshes on the western edge of the island and thwarting efforts to maintain a permanent highway from north to south. The immersion in ocean water killed all but the marsh grasses and left the island's profile even flatter than it is today. Compared to other barrier islands on the North American Atlantic seaboard, the Outer Banks were anomalies—unusually thin and unusually low, little more, really, than well-developed shoals colonized by a few hardy species of plants.

Coping with occasional overwashes had been a part of life on Hatteras Island for as long as anyone could remember. Nevertheless, there was strong belief among local residents that flooding had been less of a problem before English colonists cleared the island of large stands of cedar and oak in the eighteenth and early nineteenth centuries. Although no one knew for certain where the forests had stood, it was widely believed that they had covered most of the island, and a few large stumps remained as evidence of their existence. By the late 1920s, however, the only sizable woods left on Hatteras Island were near the town of Buxton, where the cape widens and arcs sharply to the southwest. Moreover, much of the island had been denuded by stock animals that ranged freely, grazing on saltmeadow hay. Gradually, people became concerned that without large areas of vegetation to trap and hold sand, the soil on which they had built their homes would eventually be washed into Pamlico Sound.

Studies of barrier island movement and sand transport only began to gain acceptance in the early 1930s, when the state of North Carolina organized a public works project to build three parallel lines of ocean-front dunes from the North Carolina-Virginia border to Ocracoke Inlet, the inlet that separates Cape Hatteras from Cape Lookout to the south. Few people were naive enough to hope the dunes would protect the islands from the most extreme storms, but many believed they would reduce the rate of erosion, help stabilize the beaches, and protect private property. The dunes were also expected to foster a favorable habitat at the center of the islands for woody trees and shrubs that would anchor sand and attract a greater variety of animal life— that would, in other words, make the islands of Cape Hatteras resemble wider, more stable barrier islands. After geologists conducted a survey to determine the optimum location for a dune line in relation to the tides and the slope of the beach, low fences were erected to trap blowing sand. As the sand began to mount, the new dunes were planted with cordgrass, sea oats, American beach grass, and wire grass, all of which propagate through rhizomes—creeping stems that grow underground and anchor themselves in loose, shifting soil.

The grasses thrived, and within two years a series of low but discernible dunes had developed along enough of the shoreline

to encourage additional work. In 1936 the federal government established the Cape Hatteras National Seashore and turned over the dune-building project to the Civilian Conservation Corps and the Work Projects Administration. Despite the hopes of federal officials, it was not until 1952, when private foundations donated $618,000, that the government appropriated funds to purchase land to operate the national seashore as a public park. Extending from the southern boundary of Nags Head to Ocracoke Inlet, the seashore encompassed seventy miles of ocean beach, the vast majority of which was undeveloped. Eight villages lay within its bounds, and the government agreed that the villagers' property would remain privately owned.

In the intervening years the seedlings had spread prolifically, transforming expanses of blowing sand into meadows of shaggy grass. The ridge of dunes had continued to build despite erosion by severe storms, including one in 1936 and another in 1944 that flooded entire sections of the cape. By the 1950s it was generally assumed that the dune-building projects would continue indefinitely and that the expense would be borne by the park service. That assumption was strengthened in 1952, when park service director Conrad L. Wirth wrote an open "Letter to the People of the Outer Banks" in which he proclaimed that his agency would "protect and control the sand dunes, . . . reestablish them when necessary, and hold them to protect the communities from the intrusion of the ocean." It was a tall order to fill, and one that would greatly exceed the amount of labor and financial support the park service director anticipated.

By augmenting the work that had been done during the preceding twenty years, Wirth believed the park service could establish a formidable system of dunes that would require little effort to maintain. During his administration the park service bulldozed sand into low ridges and planted millions of grass seedlings. The dunes on Hatteras Island rose gradually but consistently, some to the unprecedented height of fifteen feet. Majestic in stature and festooned in midsummer with the tawny tassels of sea oats, they seemed a triumph of modern technology; but as

they grew, the shoreline receded. The gently sloped beaches, once 150 yards wide, had steepened and narrowed to 75 yards. Undaunted, Wirth assured a congressional subcommittee in 1963 that additional work would stabilize the dune system and enable the beaches to build back out to the east. The cost of the work would probably exceed $5 million, he said, and would require another decade of concerted effort.

For the next three years the park service continued extensive plantings, concentrating on the shoreline of Ocracoke Island but also repairing breaches that opened in the dunes on Hatteras Island. Yet the beaches steadily receded. Finally, in 1966, the park service began pumping sand into severely eroded areas, and in 1968 George B. Hartzog, the new park service director, told the same congressional subcommittee he expected such beach nourishment projects to become common measures, despite enormous costs. (Fifteen years later a North Carolina Coastal Resources Commission task force would estimate the cost of beach nourishment at $1,000 per linear foot of shoreline. To be effective, the procedure would have to be repeated every five years.) By 1971 the park service was spending up to $500,000 annually to replenish sand in areas where ten feet of shoreline was being lost every year. And by 1973 construction had begun on a pipeline designed to carry sand from Cape Point to a badly eroded stretch north of Buxton.

Hartzog believed the federal government had a responsibility to slow the rate of erosion on national seashores as much as possible, even though geologists had shown that the barrier islands of the Atlantic were migrating rapidly to the west and that longshore currents tended to erode sand from the north ends of islands and push it to the south. Under the prevailing wisdom of the day—a wisdom that placed great faith in the ability of engineers to shape and mold the beaches—it sounded like wise and practical policy. But during the early 1970s, studies by Robert Dolan, a coastal geologist at the University of Virginia, and Paul J. Godfrey, a botanist at the University of Massachusetts, suggested what park service officials at Cape Hatteras had long before come

to suspect. In a series of papers published in respected scientific journals, Dolan and Godfrey argued that by eliminating overwash on the narrow islands of the cape, the park service had destroyed the mechanism by which sand is normally transported onto the shore and into the marshes. By trapping large amounts of sand, the carefully constructed dunes had hastened the narrowing of the beaches.

Dolan and Godfrey supported their argument with observations taken at Cape Lookout, the southernmost segment of the Outer Banks and the only area not included in the dune-building programs. In a paper written with University of Virginia marine biologist William Odum, the scientists noted that the beaches of Cape Lookout were still 125 to 200 yards wide, while some of those on Hatteras Island had receded to 30 yards. The beaches of Ocracoke Island, where dunes had been built only fifteen years before, had narrowed to about 75 yards.

How could the larger dunes have so drastically affected the profile of the shore? The scientists argued that they prevented the waves from spreading their force over a large area, which would have allowed sand to settle out on the beach and occasionally spill into the low runnels behind the primary dunes. Now, instead of dissipating on a smooth, gradual plane, storm surges traveled up a steep beach and slammed into a vertical sand wall. During the most severe storms, heavy surf bit into the sides of the dunes, scarping cliffs and carrying out to sea sand that would normally be transported to the marshes. At the same time, the protected valleys in back of the dunes had been colonized by shrubs and trees that were not adapted to immersion in salt water and that would certainly not survive a major flood.

The scientists said they had found no evidence to support the theory that large forests had once covered most of the Outer Banks. Instead, their work suggested that the islands had been inhabited primarily by plants that could survive occasional tidal floods. Finally, they pointed out that hurricanes drifting north up the coast can force water to pile up in Pamlico Sound, flooding the islands from the west. Before construction of the dunes, the waters would simply flow off to the east without causing much harm. Now the surges would leave the marshes under several feet of water, drowning plants and contributing to soil loss on the sand-starved western shores. Large dunes, they concluded, are ecologically unsuitable for the Outer Banks as long as sea level continues to rise and the barrier islands tend to migrate to the west. "Man has attempted to draw a line and prevent the sea from passing. The results have been unexpected and negative."

Park service administrators took note of the study and of several additional papers published by Godfrey and Dolan. In July 1973 they quietly decided to suspend a $4.5 million beach-nourishment project that had been authorized after a northeaster had overwashed the highway just north of Buxton. They planned to ask Congress to allocate the remaining $1.4 million from the project to study alternative measures for erosion control. Had the decision escaped wide publicity, it might have precipitated no more than a flurry of protest among Cape Hatteras residents. But in August a coastal geologist from Duke University named Orrin H. Pilkey, Jr., gave a presentation to journalists at a seminar on coastal geology and barrier island movement. An outspoken opponent of beach-erosion control measures, Pilkey said the federal government had finally realized the futility of trying to stabilize barrier beaches. "The park service hasn't announced it yet," he said, "but their new policy is to let Buxton fall into the sea." Despite the flippancy of the comment, its essence was true. Shortly after the suspension of the Buxton project, park service officials agreed they could do no more to protect private holdings within the national seashore.

Local reaction was swift and vehement. Business owners and politicians boisterously criticized the park service for reneging on the promise made by Wirth, and two North Carolina congressmen suggested that responsibility for beach-erosion control be given to the United States Army Corps of Engineers. Many Hatteras residents had been reluctant to surrender their land to the national seashore for fear that they would be giving up a source of substantial income and, inevitably, control over their way of life. Now it seemed their worst fears were being realized. Even people who agreed with the decision to discontinue erosion control criticized the manner in which it had been implemented. William W. Woodhouse, Jr., a North Carolina State University soil scientist, complained that "the Dolan-Godfrey theorizing has been seized upon as a convenient smoke screen to protect from view the cruel-sounding withdrawal of protection from private development. . . . Why not admit that the forecast of protection was an error? The cost has been excessive, it hasn't worked, and it's wrong anyway."

In a matter of weeks the issue gained national attention and was featured in the *Washington Post* and the *New York Times* and on national television networks. The park service decision affected not only Cape Hatteras but every national seashore, including Cape Cod, Fire Island, and Point Reyes. Surprisingly to the people of the Outer Banks, public sentiment came down strongly in the park service's favor. Consumer groups declared it a waste of money to continue fighting the forces of nature, and editorials upbraided landowners on the cape for expecting taxpayers to protect their interests. In the face of such criticism, local protest sputtered and eventually died. In its place grew a rift between park service officials and families whose residence on the cape predated the establishment of the national seashore. The schism has partially healed with time, but local sentiment is still dominated by a stubborn isolationism and by the belief that fair weather residents will never understand the hardships associated with living under the constant threat of a hostile sea.

More than a decade later many coastal scientists have begun to question whether ocean overwash is as important a factor in shaping barrier islands as Dolan and Godfrey believed. With the combined factors of sea level rise, sand movement, and storm frequency, geologists have found it difficult to predict how quickly a shoreline will erode. The equation has been complicated by a dramatic shift in storm and hurricane patterns, which seem to run in cycles of a decade or more. Ocean overwash is still considered an important geologic process, but in the past decade the Hatteras coast has been hit by few major storms. The ocean flooding common in the 1950s and 1960s has not occurred. Ironically, the beaches of Cape Lookout have steepened, and ten-foot dunes have replaced the sandy flats that first caused Dolan and Godfrey to question the wisdom of trying to stabilize a storm-battered coast.

Most scientists now believe that overwash has a much less profound effect on barrier islands than the constant opening of inlets, which tend to catch south-flowing sand and form wide deltas on an island's western edge. Eventually, as the beaches retreat to the west and the inlets shoal over, the deltas drain off and salt marshes form—a natural western extension of the island's shifting terrain.

Whether or not Dolan and Godfrey overestimated the importance of overwash, their work touched the lives of every resident on Cape Hatteras. Since September 1973 the park service has done nothing to stabilize the dunes or beaches, except for emergency plantings to prevent a section of Highway 12 on Ocracoke Island from being covered with sand, and a separate project undertaken in hopes of preserving the famous black-and-white-spiraled Cape Hatteras lighthouse. When the structure was built in 1870 it stood fifteen hundred feet from the sea, but in recent years storm surges have brought water within seventy feet of its base. Plans have been made not to curb erosion around the light house but to shape the pattern of loss so the structure will be left standing on an island all its own.

But the landscape of Hatteras will be left to its own devices. The rolling stretches of empty sand have disappeared beneath mats of sea oats and beach grass that resprout after floods and resume their laborious accrual of sand. Each year gnarls of myrtle and cedar creep farther into the marshes, displacing the *Spartina* grasses so well adapted to living in salty swash. And on certain stretches of Hatteras Island the fifteen- and twenty-foot dunes have succumbed to frequent batterings, leaving in their place wider beaches and ridges five feet high. As I slept, the dunes north of Rodanthe would be absorbing the shock of storm-whipped breakers that chopped at their bases, speeding their demise.

All night I remained dully aware of the wind rushing past the house in ferocious bursts. Near midnight the gale reached its greatest force—a mere forty-seven miles per hour—and a loud bang somewhere off the back of the house woke me from a light and nervous sleep. I responded by pulling the quilt closer to my chin. Whatever it was would have to wait at least until dawn. At 3 o'clock the lights flickered on and roused me again. Squinting and grumbling at myself for forgetting to turn off the bedroom ceiling lamp, I got out of bed long enough to walk to the kitchen and peer out the window at the motley collection of boards, bottles, and boxes of tools on my back porch. A piece of plywood had toppled on its side; that would account for the midnight crash. I turned out the lamp in the kitchen and started for the bedroom. Before I reached the doorway the bedroom light pulsed once and died.

I stumbled to a chair in the living room, rubbed my eyes, and looked across the road at the dark shape of the Chicamacomico lifesaving station, a landmark in Rodanthe and the most completely preserved of the seven stations established in 1874 on the Outer Banks by the U.S. Lifesaving Service—the forerunner of the Coast Guard. For eighty winters the stations were staffed by men who patrolled the shores around the clock to watch for foundering ships. Lifesaving surfmen rescued sailors from the sound as well as the ocean; many fishermen even consider the sound to be the more dangerous of the two. The sound can grow too choppy for safe navigation within an hour, and despite its shallowness—five feet or less in most places—heavy winds can force enough tide against the islands to raise the water level to ten feet.

Neither the sound nor the ocean could be treated as anything but a dangerous foe in this kind of weather. The thought made me cringe. For a moment I badly wanted contact with a neighbor, a weatherman, anyone who might be able to tell me if the road would flood and if the wind would blow all night and into the day. I resisted an urge to call the Coast Guard station at Oregon Inlet and wandered instead to the kitchen, feeling for the flashlight I had left on the table. In the feeble beam I could see dribbles of cake batter on the rim of the mixing bowl. There had been no electricity to pump water from the well, so I had left the dishes unwashed.

Near the mixing bowl were a notebook with some information on Hatteras weather and a park service pamphlet on the *Altoona*, a 102-foot schooner wrecked at the tip of the cape in 1878. The pamphlet explained that shipping channels off the cape are constantly reshaped by the juncture of the north-flowing Gulf Stream and a southbound countercurrent known as the Virginia Coastal Drift. Collision of the currents causes sand to settle out of the water and replenish the treacherous shoals that have beached hundreds of ships since 1565. The pamphlet did not mention what meteorologists call Hatteras-style lows, the weather systems that develop because of the unusual circulation patterns caused by the conversion of the currents.

A few days before, I had visited the federal marine weather station in Buxton to ask about weather systems around the cape and to find out what I could about the ceaseless wind that had chafed at my nerves all spring. It has been the presence of the wind more than any other factor—more even than the sulfurous water in my well and the ubiquitous salt and sand—that I have had difficulty adjusting to here. "You have to remember that we're out in the middle of the ocean," Wally DeMaurice, a meteorologist, told me. "There's nothing to knock the wind down, no mountains or tall buildings or trees. Any breeze that develops is going to have miles of open water to build up speed."

DeMaurice also explained that Cape Hatteras's unusually violent weather patterns are unlike any in the world except those off the east coast of Australia. In addition to the circulatory effects caused by offshore currents, the low-pressure troughs that develop here interact with cold-air masses that build up on the eastern side of the Appalachian Mountains. When conditions are right, the collision of the warm and cold air quickly spawns thunderheads and waterspouts, which can cause tremendous damage if they come ashore. "The bottom line is that even our not-so-violent storms can produce some extremely violent weather," DeMaurice said.

On one page of the notebook I jotted down several of DeMaurice's comments about the potential damage to the cape from hurricanes and northeasters. The previous fall, in October 1984, Hurricane Josephine had hovered two hundred miles east of Hatteras Island and had created an eight-foot storm surge that flooded Nags Head, severely eroded the tip of Ocracoke Island, and devastated a stretch of tall dunes only a half-mile north of Rodanthe. In the process Highway 12 had been buried under eight feet of sand. "It was a surfer's dream, because there were waves but no wind," he said. "But it did great damage all up and down the cape. The erosion was severe. Even a moderate storm can now create problems, and if we have a major storm—well, I'll leave it to your imagination.

"We've had more than fifteen years of unusually mild weather here, and people have gotten careless. They assume that they'll be able to ride out a hurricane or a storm like the Ash Wednesday storm of nineteen sixty-two. That one cut an inlet just north of Buxton. There's been nothing to equal it since. Seems to me it's only a matter of time before nature gets the best of us. I can't say exactly when it will happen; it may be years. I will say, though, that I expect us to have major problems with overwashes on Highway Twelve within the next five years. The island is just too badly eroded."

The warning was the last thing I had written. I tossed the notebook back on the table and picked up a fragment of shell that had been chipped and polished in its tumblings against the sand. Nothing the meteorologist had said particularly surprised me. Predictions of doom are commonplace on barrier islands, and most of the people I had met on Hatteras had grown inured to them. Some residents frankly consider the transient nature of the island to be part of its allure. Enjoy it now; tomorrow it may be gone.

I looked more closely at the shell. It was a thick clam, and its edges were tinted with a rusty shade common in many shells on the Rodanthe beach. Chances are it originally had been buried in the mud of Pamlico Sound and that hundreds of years later Hatteras Island had literally rolled over it, like a bulldozer, and unearthed it. The same would be true of the oyster shells strewn across the beach. The quartz gravel so abundant along the shoreline in the spring would have been dredged from riverbeds that existed eighteen thousand years ago, when a four-hundred-foot drop in sea level exposed the continental shelf and the rivers extended miles beyond their present mouths.

When it got down to it, anyone who looked would have a difficult time missing evidence of the island's movement to the west and south. A mile up the beach near a curve in the highway—the point where the dunes had been destroyed by Josephine—I had found the beach strewn with chunks of peat that centuries ago had formed the substrate of a salt marsh. Later I had chatted with a cottage owner who told me that in 1974 he dug twenty or more cedar and oak stumps from a quarter-mile stretch of ocean beach near his house. The stumps were the sole remains of a woody section that once fronted Pamlico Sound and had been smothered in sand as the island moved west. During a trip to Nags Head one day, I had detoured down a dead-end road at the northern tip of Hatteras Island. Photographs taken in the mid-1970s show the road extending another half-mile to the north. Now its terminus sits on a cliff that drops into Oregon Inlet.

For a moment I stopped thinking and listened hard to the wind. It seemed to be abating slightly, although it was possible that I had just grown used to the roar. The storm had blown long enough and hard enough to move some amount of sand to the marshes, but whether it would be significant I had no way of knowing.

Two weeks after I moved to Rodanthe a park service naturalist had told me that the layer of sand at the northern end of

Hatteras Island is unusually thin. I had found the statement difficult to believe; how could sand "thin" like a receding hairline? Yet Stanley Riggs, an eminent geologist, had confirmed it. Seismic readings have indicated that Rodanthe sits near the edge of the Pleistocene rock that forms the foundation of Cape Hatteras and the shoals offshore. Because the rock is unusually close to the surface here, the layer of sand and peat that covers it is unusually thin. As a result of this and other factors, the beach at Rodanthe is migrating more quickly than other portions of the cape, and the rate of erosion is unusually high. Some geologists believe that at one time Hatteras Island may have turned sharply inland here, much like the tip of land near Buxton known locally as Cape Point.

The Croatoan Indians of Hatteras might have called it Cape Chicamacomico, but if it ever existed it is long gone. In my hazy pre-dawn cognizance, I found it intriguing to be sitting on a rock topped with a thin cap of sand rippling briskly to the west. My house and yard likely would very be submerged in a century, perhaps a good deal sooner. An interesting thought—more interesting to me that night than the thought of living on a sedentary mound of clay. To reside here for any length of time would require constant accommodation to change; the alternatives, in comparison, seemed rather dull. Maybe it was the lateness of the hour or my hunch that the storm's wildness was near an end, but my nervousness had disappeared. At the moment I had no desire to be anywhere but in a candlelit kitchen on an ephemeral finger of sand.

By 6:30 this morning the wind had stilled, leaving the island in a white light baffled by moisture and fog. I woke at the sound of a passing car, then realized I heard nothing except the plaintive notes of a meadowlark that has taken to calling for its mate from a perch across the street. The damper had stopped creaking, and the telephone wire no longer slapped the side of the house. After a night of much noise and little sleep, the peacefulness of the morning carried the force of an intoxicant. Pausing only long enough to groan over the dirty dishes and the streaks of flour across the kitchen floor, I stepped outside and walked the two hundred yards to the beach.

Before I was halfway there I could see a line of oily foam where water had lapped over the truncated dune. The textured surface of the foam shimmered with pinks, purples, and blues, and it wriggled as I climbed toward it, a gelatinous roll laced with tunnels of air. Beyond, the beach was strewn with hundreds of frothy skeins, some pure white, some yellow from age. Most still curled to the west in the shape of the waves that had tossed them onto land.

Spray from the surf had turned the air milky and thick. I walked out to the water, picking my way around piles of foam as high as my knees. This must be what it is like, I thought, to be surrounded by corpses, the only survivor of a war. In the surf the battle still raged: bone-chilling breakers thrashed against shore, tossing up suds. But the tide had receded and the waves reflected the colorless sky. The stillness had caught me as completely by surprise as the beginning of the blow had twelve hours before. I might have been standing in the Arctic, so white and foreign was the scene before me.

Near the water three black-headed gulls poked at the sand, searching for small crustaceans. For them it was business as usual. An older couple I had seen before on the beach strolled toward me, and the woman waved. "Isn't it spectacular?" she cried. No one else was out. I turned south toward the dunes that border the Chicamacomico station. Weaving between foam and broken shells, I walked to a slough where heaps of froth drifted toward the sea in steady procession until an incoming wave knocked them back toward the dunes. Yesterday afternoon the slough had been nothing more than a thin runnel cut by the month's highest tide, and the beach and offshore waters had seemed familiar and warm, a collage of green, blue, and buff. Now the colorless tide swashed through an unfamiliar creek. Everything moved—the breakers, the seabound froth, the shimmers of color in the stranded heaps of foam. Everything but the milky air.

I remained on the beach only a short while, thinking that I

would return after breakfast and the luxury of a shower. But by midmorning when I ventured out again, the sky had deepened to blue and the mounds of foam had scattered in a light southwest wind. The beach was yellow, the sand clear of debris. No evidence of the storm remained.

2
A WELL-WEATHERED PAST

IN WINTER THE Hatteras wind sweeps in from the northwest, raking water through the marshes and the sedge-filled yards of houses off Pamlico Sound. By early sum-mer the prevailing breezes calm and swing southwest, bringing tropical air spiked with tangy scents of marsh and mud. In any season the wind can shift gently and temporarily to the south or southeast, or it can slam in from the northeast, driving a chill deep into sun-warmed sand.

The capricious presence of wind and wind-driven water have left their mark on every aspect of island life, from the scattering of plants on sheltered hillsides to the shifting, shallow channels between ocean and sound. In 250 years the arching strip of land between the North Carolina-Virginia border and the southern tip of Cape Lookout has fractured and fused at more than twenty points. Inlets that once served as main shipping lanes—Currituck, Roanoke, and Ocracoke—have closed or grown too shallow to use. The high triangle of unvegetated sand that forms Cape Point has migrated southwest, and the tip has been pinched and pulled sharp, then blunted and pinched again by tides. Yet as the northern beaches of Hatteras have eroded, the point has continued to gather sand, as if the hooklike protrusion snags a glut of south-flowing sediment while the rest of the coastline starves.

The violence of Hatteras weather and the instability of its inlets combined to discourage settlement on the cape for more than four hundred years. With the exception of the Croatoan Indians, a small tribe that lived in the vine-filled woods west of Cape Point, the Indians of the coastal plain came to the Outer Banks only occasionally to hunt and fish. By 1525 the North Carolina coast had been charted by Spanish explorers and visited by an Italian navigator, Giovanni da Verrazzano, who mistook Pamlico Sound for a wide sea that stretched to the Orient. But before Sir Walter Raleigh financed an expedition in 1584, no country had laid claim to the land.

When two British ships commanded by Philip Amadas and Arthur Barlowe reached the North Carolina coast in the summer of 1584, they turned north and sailed for 120 miles to search for a passageway to the protected waters of Pamlico Sound. Whether they entered Ocracoke Inlet, a break south of Roanoke Island known as Roanoke Inlet, or a harbor near the present-day settlement of Southern Shores is a matter of some debate. Once in the sound, they anchored, went ashore, and warily began looking for signs of human life.

Barlowe's log from this period contains glowing descriptions of low, sandy hills thick with grape vines and "the highest, reddest cedars in the world." It was early July, the most clement of times, when the sound flattens to a pale gray plane pierced by spikes of grass. The reedy marshes throbbed with the cries of "cranes, most of them white"—probably great and snowy egrets—and the woods abounded with deer, rabbit, and ducks. But no sign of humans could the explorers find.

Several days later three Indian men appeared in a log canoe and landed on the beach a short distance from the ships. After a brief meeting with Amadas and Barlowe, one Indian paddled out and began fishing. In a short time, with remarkable ease, he filled the canoe with fish "as deepe, as it could swimme" and left the catch for the boats. Perhaps a week passed before the explorers ventured inland to a village tucked in the dark forests on Roanoke Island, where they were fed fish and venison, fruits and melons, wheat cereal and a type of root. The Indians who received them so graciously were dressed in leather cloaks and jewelry of pearls and gold or copper. They were, Barlowe wrote, a civilized people, handsome, guileless, and kind.

In 1587 two British ships set sail for the North American coast, carrying 150 men, their families, and enough supplies to build a small permanent settlement. The expedition was led by John White, a noted artist whose detailed etchings of the Indians, plants, and animals of the Carolinas provided the British with some of their first glimpses of the New World. White's plans were to stop at Roanoke Island only long enough to pick up about fifteen soldiers stationed there at a small British fort. (He and Raleigh had agreed that the settlers could live much more comfortably on the sheltered shores of the Chesapeake Bay than the storm-battered Carolina coast.) But when the expedition reached Roanoke Island in late July, the admiral of the ships refused to sail on. Perhaps he and White had quarreled during the crossing, or perhaps the admiral hoped to capture a Spanish galleon that had been sighted in the area. No one is sure why the decision was made, but apparently it was irrevocable. White and the colonists were abruptly set ashore on Roanoke Island and left to fend for themselves. They found the fort leveled and a single skeleton nearby—the only remains of fifteen soldiers.

In the early weeks of the settlement it seemed the colonists might establish an uneasy peace with the Indians. According to White's writings, the Croatoans of Cape Hatteras began to teach the settlers the fishing techniques and the slash-and-burn method of farming so effective in the sandy coastal soil. The Croatoans and the Indians of Roanoke Island were branches of the Algonkians, a prolific coastal people that settled in villages and depended largely on agriculture for food. Among their crops were maize, beans, sunflowers, and a type of tobacco. White's sketches show Indians working orderly fields and using nets with handles to dip up fish, probably mullet and trout. They also fashioned fencelike barriers of reeds into pens with several connecting chambers—much like modern pound nets—in shallow areas of Roanoke Sound. On land they hunted deer and waterfowl with bows and arrows.

As the colonists constructed small log houses and learned the tricks of gathering food, their numbers began to grow. At least two of the settlers were pregnant, including White's daughter, Elenor, the wife of Ananias Dare. On August 18 Elenor gave birth to a girl, Virginia—the first English child born on American soil.

In mid-August a British flyboat found its way to the island. As White made plans to return to England for supplies, it appeared that his Cittie of Raleigh might comfortably survive the winter. His optimism faded, however, when the Roanoke Indians killed a colonist who had wandered away from the cluster of houses alone. When White embarked for England he left instructions for the settlers to carve a Maltese cross in a tree if they were forced by Indians to abandon the village. If they decided to move they were to carve out the name of their destination.

White never again saw his daughter and granddaughter. By the time he reached London the animosity between England and Spain had grown so strong that Queen Elizabeth ordered all ships to remain in port for defense against the Spanish Armada. He was unable to return to Roanoke Island until the summer of 1590, and then as a mere passenger in a fleet of three small ships. He found the colonists' houses torn down and the Cittie of Raleigh deserted. As a clue to their fate, the settlers had carved the word CROATOAN in a post at the entrance to a palisade that surrounded the village. The letters CRO had been cut into the trunk of a tree on the north end of the island near Roanoke Sound. There was no Maltese cross.

Had the settlers joined the Croatoans? White returned to the ship and implored the captains to sail south toward Cape Hatteras in hopes of locating the tribe's village. But Pamlico Sound was too shallow in most places for even small sailing vessels. Before a course could be charted, a storm broke the anchor cable of a ship, and high winds nearly pushed the vessel aground. As the weather worsened, the ships sailed for open seas. White's pleas went unheard; when the waters calmed, the ships turned east toward England.

A hundred years later, residents of Cape Hatteras would write of a few gray-eyed, light-skinned people living among the Croatoans. But by 1733 only eight Indians were reported to be on Hatteras Island, and by the end of the century the Croatoans had scattered among the Mattamuskeets of the swampy mainland. The fate of White's colony remains a mystery, a subject for speculation and vigorous historical debate.

To the British citizens who settled the banks of the Chesapeake, North Carolina had become, by 1650, a blight on the face of the New World. According to colonial records, the treacherous waters that so discouraged navigation provided a haven for the most unsavory of settlers, and Virginians referred to the area as "Rogue's Harbor." In 1681 Governor John Culpepper of Virginia complained to the Lords of Trade, "North Carolina is and always was the sink of America, the refuge of our renegades." Edward Randolph, a customs official, wrote in 1700 of North Carolina, "'tis a place which receives Pirates, Runaways, and Illegal Traders."

There is some evidence to back Randolph's claims that pirates were not prosecuted as vigorously in North Carolina as in Virginia. A ready market existed for stolen goods in the port town of Bath. Blackbeard, who lived on Ocracoke Island in 1718 and was slain in Pamlico Sound, is believed to have split his pirated spoils with North Carolina Governor Charles Eden and Eden's secretary, Tobias Knight. Throughout the colonial period Virginians also complained that Outer Banks residents helped themselves to the cargo of ships that foundered near shore.

Descriptions of Outer Banks settlers as an all-around rascally lot have been disputed by historians, who note that frontiers are generally colonized by poor but honest people anxious to obtain land. Indeed, interest in the barrier islands of North Carolina seems to have revived during the mid-1600s as Virginians began keeping horses, sheep, and cows. The settlers found most pastureland to be poor grazing; the best fodder on the coast was the cordgrass and saltmeadow hay that grew abundantly on marshy isles. Since fencing was expensive, the most desirable rangelands were those surrounded by water. By 1680 stock had been placed on the northernmost section of the Outer Banks, corn had been planted, and clusters of houses had begun to appear.

The first dwellings were built on high, wooded land on the west sides of the islands, as far as possible from ocean surge and the occasional floods of the sound. The earliest documented land grant, the island now known as Colington Harbor, was made to Sir John Colleton in 1663. Other claims would soon follow. But as legal documents bestowing land to the aristocracy were drafted in Virginia, the marshes and hammocks were settled by families of great self-reliance, if lesser fortune. Small towns began to appear on land ostensibly controlled by people who lived elsewhere.

Hatteras, with its unpredictable winds and surf, was one of the last sections of coast to be claimed. By 1715, however, a few houses had been built in the woods near Cape Point, in hammocks at the modern village of Hatteras, and on Chicamacomico Banks, an area that now encompasses the villages of Rodanthe, Waves, and Salvo. Clans whose names still dominate island life—Austin, Ballance, Gray, Hooper, Midgett, O'Neal, Scarborough, Stowe—established footholds and began fishing, hunting, and harvesting oil from beached whales. It is unclear whether the families' founding members were shipwrecked sailors, as legend tells, or whether they were English colonists who moved south from Virginia.

The pattern of settlement would continue to be dictated by the whim of the wind and sea, since residents of communities not in easy reach of shipping lanes lived with few imported goods. And colonial settlers had no way to keep an inlet open once it began to shoal. In the 1730s Old Currituck Inlet was reported to have closed and Roanoke Inlet to have become too shallow for the passage of large ships. The area's most navigable route to the sea lay just south of Ocracoke, where a community of pilots—men who guided ships through treacherous channels—built one of the first towns on the Outer Banks. Ocracoke Inlet served as a major entrance to Pamlico Sound until 1846, when a hurricane severed Hatteras Island to create Oregon Inlet and Hatteras Inlet, the two primary points of entry still in use today.

The seaports of the Outer Banks would always be at a disadvantage to the wider, more stable harbors to the north, and gradually the residents of the cape began to depend on occupations besides piloting. In the early 1800s red-cedar timbering operations brought an influx of money to Hatteras Island. A few residents had begun fishing commercially for shad and herring in the mid-1700s, and in 1842 Hatteras residents first employed haul seines to gather large quantities of bluefish from the surf. Mainland residents, anxious to escape summer outbreaks of malaria, discovered the healthful value of ocean air. The late eighteenth century brought hundreds of vacationers to Ocracoke Island and to Nags Head, which developed a reputation as a thriving, luxurious resort.

While the rest of the Outer Banks developed, the settlements at Chicamacomico Banks and Kinnakeet, fifteen miles to the south, remained isolated and difficult to reach by boat. A few families salted mullet or dried the brittle stems and waxy leaves of yaupon bushes to make tea. They traded the mullet and tea on the mainland for corn to be ground in one of seven windmills on the cape. But as late as the Civil War a visitor to Hatteras

Island would write that the residents "seldom see money, indeed they have no use for it."

The isolation of the cape was broken during the Civil War as Union and Rebel troops battled for control of Pamlico Sound. At the war's onset residents of Hatteras Island, in characteristic fashion, disassociated themselves from the mainland Confederate government by remaining loyal to the Union. Nevertheless, early in the war Confederate troops erected forts at Oregon, Hatteras, and Ocracoke inlets and staged raids on Union supply ships traveling off the cape. In August 1861 Union troops mounted a major assault and drove the Rebel troops north to Roanoke Island. Weeks later the Union set up a camp at Chicamacomico Banks.

From the Confederates' base, the Union movement north to Chicamacomico seemed a clear indication that federal troops were preparing to attack Roanoke Island, and the Rebels hatched an elaborate plan of defense. One October morning Union sentries sighted six Confederate steamships several miles offshore in Pamlico Sound. One vessel turned west, directly toward the Union encampment, and dispatched four companies of soldiers. The other five ships continued south, toward federal strongholds near the southern tip of Hatteras Island.

The Union troops panicked and fled south in hopes of reaching Hatteras, thirty-five miles away, before the Confederates could land. Six hundred soldiers marched along the beach with neither water nor food, their munitions weighing them down and the October sun kindling a deep thirst. Residents fled in front of the troops, fearing death at Confederate hands. By midafternoon soldiers and civilians alike had begun to drop in the heat.

A Confederate victory seemed assured, and the Rebel troops marched triumphantly south, capturing soldiers who had collapsed and ransacking empty houses. They halted for the night just north of the Hatteras lighthouse. Within hours, their luck abruptly changed.

The one factor the Confederates had neglected to consider was the shallowness of Pamlico Sound. The following morning the Rebel companies learned that the other steamships had grounded miles from shore, leaving them completely undefended. They quickly decided to retreat. As the troops reached an exposed stretch of beach five miles north of the lighthouse, a Union ship anchored offshore unleashed a barrage of fire. The number of men killed and wounded was never clearly determined. But as soon as the Confederates could make their way back to their ship, they sailed north, leaving Hatteras Island firmly in the Union's control. Later the battle became known as the Chicamacomico Races.

Hatteras returned to a sleepy state, but the depth of its isolation was never the same. After the war, island families became increasingly dependent on commercial fishing, an occupation that required at least occasional contact with the towns north of Oregon Inlet. Most of the fish sold commercially were salted or smoked, since rough water frequently delayed its transportation to market.

The first post office on the cape had been opened in 1840 at Ocracoke and the second at Hatteras village in 1858. In 1873 and 1874 the U.S. Government declared that three more post offices would be established on Hatteras Island—and that the communities served by them would receive new, government-designated names. The town known as The Cape was renamed Buxton, and Big Kinnakeet five miles north became Avon. Chicamacomico Banks—which perhaps was too long to suit postal officials—became Rodanthe, after *Rodantha manglesii*, a small violet or pink flower with a yellow center.

The *Rodantha* is also known as *Helipterum*, or Swan Lake everlasting. Its designation as the town namesake was, to many Chica-macomico residents, a source of continued irritation. A little-used bedding plant, it is sometimes dried for winter flower arrangements. Its range as a wildflower is limited to western Australia.

It has never bloomed on the Outer Banks.

Around 1722 the Lords Proprietors of Carolina granted nineteen hundred acres known as Bodie Island—said to have been named for the number of bodies washed up on its shores—to Matthew Midget or Midyett, a Frenchman of undetermined age. It seems appropriate that Matthew obtained a tract off some of the most treacherous waters in North America, for his progeny would become known widely as heroes for their efforts to rescue shipwrecked sailors.

According to family legend, in the first years of the eighteenth century Matthew and his brother John had made their way to London and learned the trade of ship carpentry, then, around 1708, signed on a ship bound for the coast of America. Months later the vessel sank off Cape Hatteras during a hurricane. Matthew washed ashore at Chicamacomico Banks, where Captain Thomas Paine, a local seaman, discovered him and carried him to safety. Within a few months Matthew married Paine's daughter, Judith.

A copy of Matthew's will names five sons and three daughters. Today the local phone book, less than an inch thick, lists 195 Midgetts and Midgettes. In an area flooded with newcomers, Midgett is not the most prolific family name, but it is certainly one that bears weight. In most Dare County communities, the Midgett surname is more common than the surname Smith. Island residents who have researched the family genealogy say more than half of the natives of Rodanthe, Waves, and Salvo descended directly from Matthew.

Matthew's brood presumably settled into the small, wooded hammocks of Bodie and Hatteras islands and began fishing and hunting alongside the cape's other bountiful clans. At some point the branches of the Midgett tree stretched so wide that family members began to intermarry. By 1874 the surname was common enough that the sevenman crew of the Chicamacomico lifesaving station frequently included six Midgetts.

During the last half of the nineteenth century, the shipping lanes off Cape Hatteras were some of the most heavily used routes along the eastern seaboard. Every week hundreds of ships rounded the cape on their way north with cargos of raw materials from the southeast United States and returned with merchandise from the manufacturing cities of the North. Ships grounded or sank at the rate of one or two a month; in 1889 alone, nineteen vessels were lost, and several dozen more sustained damage in mishaps off the Outer Banks. Lighthouses had been completed at Ocracoke in 1798, at Cape Hatteras in 1803, and at Bodie Island in 1847. But until 1874 the survival of people on foundering ships depended on the good will of island residents.

The establishment of lifesaving stations provided the Outer Banks with a new and steady source of income, but it was not for the faint of heart. When a ship sent up a distress signal, five or six men launched a narrow-hulled surfboat and tried to row out, often through crushing breakers. Once past the heavy surf, the crew would row toward the ship, picking their way around debris torn loose by thrashing waves. If the ship had grounded within three hundred yards of shore, the lifesavers might try to shoot a line over its boom with a lyle gun, a small bronze cannon. Once the line had been secured to the ship, the surfmen used a block and tackle to send out a "breeches buoy"—a round life preserver fitted with a canvas seat. With the line draped over the boom and the breeches buoy dangling beneath, the passengers and crew could be pulled to safety one at a time. In fair weather the surfmen kept watch on the horizon from a tower, but in rain, heavy surf, or fog they patrolled a seven-mile stretch of beach on foot. To prove they had covered their beats, the surfmen exchanged brass tokens with the crews of stations to the north and south.

Entries in the log book at the Chicamacomico station, though brief for want of paper, describe a life of Spartan quarters, equipment in ill repair, long hours of watching for ships, and little sleep. Initially the stations at Chicamacomico, Bodie Island, and Little Kinnakeet north of Avon—the first of ten lifesaving bases built on Hatteras Island—remained open only from December through March. By 1883 the stations were in full operation from September through May.

The rescue attempts were frequently heroic—and frequently

unsuccessful. A brief log entry describes the wreck of the 1,236-ton steamship *Strathairly* a mile-and-a-quarter south of the Chicamacomico station on a foggy morning in March 1891. Historians have pieced together a more complete picture through interviews and newspaper clippings. The *Strathairly* had grounded in the dark, and shortly before dawn, in a steady northeast wind that showed no sign of abating, the crew of the stranded ship attempted to launch a lifeboat. Just as the craft was lowered to the water the *Strathairly* lurched on its side, splintering the lifeboat and spilling two other lifeboats from its decks. A few minutes later the steamship began to break in two.

On the beach the lifesaving crew could hear the *Strathairly*'s distress whistle but could see nothing through the fog. The surfmen, guessing at the ship's position, readied the lyle gun and fired. The shot was short, and a strong current carried the line hard to the south. Breakers as powerful as the surfmen had ever seen—far too powerful to navigate—slammed against the beach. For hours the lifesavers could do nothing but wait for the fog to thin as waves battered the *Strathairly*'s decks. Around 10 o'clock the ship became visible from shore, and the surfmen fired. Three times the cannon sent lines toward the ship before one reached the rail. But when the sailors tried to pull it taut, it snapped under the force of the current.

Again and again the lyle gun fired, spitting out a slim projectile and a trail of rope. By midafternoon every line had been used without success. Finally, in desperation, the crew of the *Strathairly* jumped into the ocean and tried to swim toward shore as the current carried them south.

By then the wreck had attracted a crowd. When the swimmers reached the breakers, the surfmen and several residents waded waistdeep into the waves to pull them out. Sixteen sailors were dragged from the ocean; of these, only seven survived. The men of Chicamacomico worked until midnight to resuscitate one of the victims, then walked the beach until dawn to recover bodies of nineteen men. They laid the corpses in a boat room until coffins could be built the following day.

The Chicamacomico lifesaving crew was dominated by Midgetts into the twentieth century. By the early 1900s, the life-saving stations had obtained motor-powered, self-bailing surfboats, and their success had improved. In 1911 a three-story station with dormers, a watchtower, and a steep, graceful roof replaced the simple rectangular house built nearly forty years before. Shipping lanes off the cape were still heavily used, and with increasing numbers of vessels powered by steam, the number of wrecks had begun to decline. But the most spectacular and heroic rescue attempt would not come until the height of World War I, when three German submarines patrolled the North Carolina coast, setting mines and torpedoing ships.

Shortly after 4 p.m. on August 16, 1918, surfman Leroy S. Midgett, on watch in the Chicamacomico station, noticed a British tanker, the *Mirlo*, steaming north along the island. It was sunny, with a light northeast wind, but an offshore storm sent the surf hurtling toward the beach. The tanker rode smoothly across the swells, cutting a deep, fanshaped wake. As Leroy watched, the ship exploded and broke in half.

All hands were summoned as the two sections of the tanker drifted apart and the smoke from the wreckage changed from white to black. The *Mirlo*, a 7,000-ton ship, carried a full load of gasoline and oil, which spurted into the sea. The ship had been hit by either a torpedo or a mine, setting off a chain of explosions and scattering debris hundreds of yards. The *Mirlo's* crew of fifty-one men scrambled into three lifeboats and headed for shore. But before they reached safety one of the lifeboats capsized, throwing fourteen sailors into the oilslicked sea. The men clung to the hull as the water around them caught fire. A second lifeboat tried to circle back, but the spreading flames forced it to flee.

On shore the lifesavers were trying to launch their sturdiest boat and make their way past fifteen- and twenty-foot crests. Three times the boat swamped, forcing the crew to return to the beach. When finally the craft cleared the breakers, it carried six men—station Captain John Allen Midgett, Arthur V. Midgett, Clarence E. Midgett, Leroy Midgett, Zion S. Midgett, and

Prochorous L. O'Neal. Five miles offshore the lifesaving crew encountered a lifeboat with seventeen of the *Mirlo's* men.

The rescue that followed has become a Coast Guard legend. After learning that one of the lifeboats had overturned, John Allen began circling the wreckage looking for a route through the flames. The surfmen spotted the lifeboat's hull near the bow of the burning tanker as gasoline continued to explode, shooting fire a hundred feet in the air. The wind had increased, causing small circles of fire on the water to dance and flare and briefly part. Somehow John Allen maneuvered the surfboat around flame and floating debris to reach the capsized boat. Six sailors clung to it, their hair and clothes covered with oil. Surfmen pulled the sailors into their craft as the paint on its side blistered from heat. Within minutes John Allen had steered back through the flames.

Night was falling, and the lifesavers still had to land the forty-two survivors on the beach. Only the self-bailing boat from the station stood a chance of staying afloat in such heavy surf, so only eleven sailors could be ferried ashore at a time. There was nothing to do but shuttle the burned and blackened men to the beach in four trips, nothing to do but fight the breakers four more times. At 9 o'clock the last of the *Mirlo* crew reached dry ground. Only nine had been killed.

Three years later the British government awarded Gold Lifesaving Medals to John Allen Midgett and the five men who accompanied him on the *Mirlo* rescue mission. And in 1930 the Coast Guard gave each of the six lifesavers a Grand Cross of the American Cross of Honor—its most prestigious decoration.

In the seventy-year history of the Coast Guard, officials have awarded only eleven Grand Crosses.

In 1923 a twenty-nine-year-old Coast Guard surfman and his wife moved into a brand-new house northwest of the Chicamacomico lifesaving station. Part of the construction materials for the structure, including the floor joists and timbers for the framing, had been salvaged from a wrecked ship. The house was shingled with white clapboard, and beaded paneling, a hallmark of the era, covered most of the interior walls. On the second floor were two small bedrooms with low, sloping ceilings and an attic that overlooked Pamlico Sound. Highway 12 would one day lie between the house and the lifesaving station, but in the 1920s the major wagon and automobile routes on Hatteras Island were two sand roads and the wide, shrubless beach.

The couple had grown up on Hatteras not far from where they built their new home. Theodore Stockton Midgett was the son of a commercial fisherman. His wife, Ersie, a short, red-haired, and jovial woman, was the daughter of Efrica and Jethro Anderson Midgett, who ran a business delivering food and dry goods that they brought to the island by sailboat. At the time Stockton and Ersie built the white house, Hatteras Island was still little more than a sparsely vegetated bar of sand. There were no paved roads, no running water, no electricity, no dunes. Construction of the Oregon Inlet bridge was forty years away. With no reliable weather forecasting system, the island's residents stayed continually prepared for major blows.

Stockton's work with the Coast Guard took him to Ocracoke Island or Morehead City for months at a time, but he was able to spend at least part of each year with his family. His children remember him as a kind, energetic man who liked to take them fishing and involve them in projects. And his projects were frequently lucrative. In the early 1930s he bought a half-ton dump truck that he leased to the state for construction work. When New Inlet opened five miles north of Rodanthe in 1933, he and his eldest child, thirteen-year-old Harold, were hired to haul materials for a wooden bridge to span the two shallow channels. (A portion of the bridge still stands west of Highway 12, although the channels closed in the mid-1940s) New Inlet had been cut by two hurricanes that occurred within weeks of each other that fall. The second storm also flooded the first floor of the white house. Stockton and Ersie knew another storm could hit at any time, and they decided to move the structure to higher, more protected land a quartermile east, just north of the Chicamacomico station.

A few years later when the Civilian Conservation Corps set up a base camp in Rodanthe to headquarter their dune-building project, Stockton realized the crews of men needed a source of food and supplies. In 1936 he built a general store just west of the white house. At first he intended to turn the store's operation over to his sons, Harold, Anderson, and Stockton, Jr. But the boys soon tired of staying inside to clerk and put up stock. Within two years the storekeeping had been delegated to Ersie, who was quick at figuring prices and balancing books. Stockton had other plans for his sons. In the fall of 1938 he went to Baltimore and came back with a franchise for the island's first transportation system, a bus line from Hatteras village to Manteo. The afternoon he returned he took a short stroll around Manteo while he waited for Harold to pick him up. A half-hour later when Harold arrived, Stockton was dead from a heart attack on the grassy lawn of a motel.

Harold was eighteen, Anderson was thirteen, Stocky, Jr., was ten, and the only girl, Joyce, was six. With the profits from the community store, the family members knew they could get by. But Harold and Anderson were determined to start running their new business as soon as they could. To help drive their first "bus"—a brand-new Ford station wagon—they recruited their young brother, Stocky. Once a day the station wagon made its way from Hatteras village to a ferry at Oregon Inlet, then on to Manteo and back. "We called the route one-O-one—a hundred and one different ways," Stocky recalled. "At low tide we drove the beach. At high tide we drove the bank—the top of the beach, where the dunes are now—or the inside road, which consisted of several different tracks. There were always more people than we had room for; most of the time we'd put 'em on the running boards and in each others laps, and sometimes on the hood. If we got stuck, which we often did, everybody got out and pushed."

The modern world had begun to discover Hatteras Island. In addition to the debut of public transportation, 1938 brought electricity to Hatteras village with the formation of a municipal cooperative. Electricity meant running water, indoor toilets, refrigeration. Slowly residents began to enjoy more luxuries and to have more contact with the outside world. Occasionally a hurricane or a strong blow would disrupt the island's development, but storms were accepted as sporadic, shortlived dangers, like tornados in the Midwest. Yet the damage they wreaked could be widespread and sudden. In 1944 a major hurricane pushed eight feet of water through Rodanthe. As Ersie, Joyce, and Anderson sat in the wood-frame house, a sudden blast of wind twisted the structure and sent it sliding twelve feet off its foundation. When the eye passed overhead, the family rushed to the home of a relative—only to have that house picked up beneath them by a surge and floated fifty yards, tossing and lurching in the waves. The receding tide left the relative's house perched on top of Anderson's brand-new Ford.

And still the pace of progress quickened. In 1948 the electric cooperative extended its service to the north section of Hatteras Island, and the state paved the first portion of Highway 12, a twenty-mile stretch between Hatteras village and Avon. In 1952 the surfaced road reached the length of the island. Although easier to drive than the beach, it was frequently overwashed or covered with sand, and the Midgett brothers' vehicles continued to get stuck. One evening as Stocky was driving back from Manteo in a school bus loaded with people, he suddenly found himself driving through water. "The sea had backed up right behind the dunes, and one of the dunes broke through," he says. "Water came rushing through like a funnel. I had on a pair of leather boots, so I climbed around on the fenders trying to get the hood up without getting my feet wet. By the time I dried off the engine, the front wheels of the bus had settled down through the highway. And before we could do anything else, the rear wheels fell through. The bus started settling down just like you'd put a casket in a grave."

Passengers piled out of the vehicle and climbed a dune while Stockton started north, walking and swimming toward the nearest Coast Guard station. An hour later when he returned with help, the bus had disappeared. "When the tide fell, the highest point of the bus was the left front corner. It was about eighteen inches above the surface of the road. I called my brother to tell him I'd lost the bus. He wanted to know if I'd been off drinking someplace."

The bus line's business declined with the completion of the bridge over Oregon Inlet in 1963. By then, however, the brothers had opened a garage in Hatteras village, and Stocky had been licensed to sell real estate. "I'd be working on a car, and I'd wash my hands in a gas bucket and off I'd go to meet a customer." Single-story cottages, set above the sand on eight-foot stilts, began to line the meadows on the ocean side of Highway 12.

The bridge brought increasing numbers of tourists, especially anglers eager to test their skill at Cape Point, where the Gulf Stream makes its closest pass at the eastern United States. Perhaps because of its storms, its distance from major cities, its overwashed, pot-holed road, its quirky electric blackouts, and its long reputation as Rogue's Harbor, Hatteras became known as an outpost for the sturdy and stout-of-heart. Through the 1960s and early 1970s the few people who settled on Hatteras year-round were looking for solitude and a life free of city ways.

By 1972 Stocky and Anderson had built something of a real estate empire on the Outer Banks. Their childhood home had been resided with bright yellow shingles several years before, but it was still drafty in the winter. It was time, the brothers decided, to build their mother a thoroughly modern brick home. The yellow house was moved back to the west of Highway 12. After raising a family there, Ersie would not see it torn down.

Ersie died in 1977. Her tombstone in the family graveyard in back of the brick house, her last home, bears a photograph of a white-haired woman with cats-eye glasses, a wry, toothy smile, and wrinkles gathered in deep folds at the corners of her mouth. Stockton, Sr., cleanshaven and much younger, looks out at the world from the next tombstone over. Their mementos—photo albums, children's report cards, a rocking horse—fill the attic of the yellow frame house, the house where I live.

The beaded paneling has been covered with a half-dozen coats of paint, and the window frames and doorjambs, once squarely fit together, have slanted at crazy angles since the hurricane of 1944. In the evening I eat at a low kitchen table built from Coast Guard crates around 1920 by Stockton, Sr. The wood is glossy from use, and the words SOUTH BROOKLYN, stenciled in faded black paint, line a plank on top. A plank on the bottom bears the words COAST GUARD STORE, 58TH ST FIRST AVE.

Midgett Realty now controls a substantial portion of land on Hatteras Island, perhaps the majority of land in private holdings. Residents have come to depend financially on tourism and real estate, although many men fish commercially or work for the Coast Guard. Yet here, on a stormy night, the resort town of Nags Head seems twice as far as the twenty-five miles that separate it from Rodanthe. A different system of time operates on Hatteras Island. I call it island time. It is a way of life in which you learn not to make very firm plans, because at any moment something unexpected—a storm, a shift of wind, a blackout that prevents you from drawing water or gas—may force you to change them. Power outages, caused mostly by the accumulation of salt spray on wires, are still frequent enough to make electric clocks virtually worthless. The road, although raised and repaved in 1983, still washes over once or twice a year. A lack of dependable technology breeds a liberalness with days and nights. Few people care to know the exact time; it is enough to know the time within ten or fifteen minutes. Island people do not guard their hours as jealously as city people, perhaps because—in years past, at least—lost time did not mean lost money.

Every day some work will get done and some will be left for tomorrow. You cannot force life to unfold at a faster pace; you will drive yourself crazy if you try. This relaxed philosophy is born not from laziness or lack of character but from knowing that the island world can change at any moment, and not always for the better.

A few weeks after I moved to Rodanthe, I heard a story that captures what I have since come to regard as the essence of

Hatteras Island. The moral, if the story has one, is that no person, no matter how wise or strong, is completely safe in the waters of the cape. The tale's other elements—a mystery and the simple, unwavering faith of an island woman—seem to me to describe the capricious forces that spring from the constant battering of wind and sea.

Virginia O'Neal, the town postmistress since 1967, has a kind, jowly face, a sweet smile, a stout build, and the easy, gregarious nature of a woman who has spent two decades doing business with neighbors and friends. With no children of her own, she is an adopted aunt to most of the village's youth. When introduced to newcomers, she often invites them to services at the Fairhaven United Methodist Church, which she has attended for more than twenty years.

In 1946 Virginia married Oscar O'Neal, a Rodanthe man then in the early years of a career in the Coast Guard. She had grown up in West Virginia and had met Oscar during a visit to an aunt's house in Baltimore, where he was in boot camp. After their marriage the O'Neals moved frequently as Oscar was transferred to different Coast Guard stations along the East Coast. When he retired in 1965 the couple settled down in his boyhood home. Once reestablished in Rodanthe Oscar began to fish, sometimes commercially, sometimes for fun. Local residents describe him as youthful and handsome, with dark hair and an athletic build. He was known as an unusually strong swimmer. Occasionally he swam from the beach straight out four hundred yards, around the end of the Hatteras Island fishing pier, and back to shore.

In February 1969 Oscar went fishing on a day that was sunny and not particularly cold, between 45 and 50 degrees with a light wind. He had set some gill nets about a mile and a half from shore in Pamlico Sound, and that morning he had gone out early in a flat-bottomed wooden skiff to see if the nets had snared any shad. Two hours later a fisherman from Salvo found Oscar's empty boat putting along more than a mile offshore, its propeller tangled in net.

When a waterman disappears on the cape, Coast Guard

surfmen, relatives, and neighbors all participate in the search. For two days island residents scoured the waters near Oscar's nets and the marshes where his body might have washed up. Oscar's disappearance seemed curious, given that he was a good swimmer and physically fit. But the temperature of the sound was less than 50 degrees; if he had fallen overboard he might have collapsed from hypothermia. By the third day the searchers began to concede that if Oscar were found at all he would be dead.

Virginia, suddenly cast in the role of a widow, could do nothing for her husband but pray and walk the marshes. A devout Christian, she appeared to accept her loss with silent strength. But on Sundays she frequently asked one or another of her friends to search a section of marsh with her after church, even if the area had been searched before. And she began to hear Oscar calling her, " 'Ginny, Ginny,' real softlike." She developed a strong intuition that Oscar's body would be found, by her, when the time was right.

In early March Oscar's cap washed up in a marsh several miles south of Oregon Inlet. A short time later Virginia dreamed that Oscar's body would be discovered when someone spotted the bottom of his boot sticking up through some mud. His wallet would be in his back pocket.

March and April faded into the warm hope of a Hatteras spring. On the first Sunday in May, Virginia went to church as usual. In the middle of the service she began to hear Oscar calling her name, soft and insistent. It occurred to her that she should check a stretch of marsh just south of the old wooden bridge at New Inlet. After the service she asked Oscar's cousin, Lennie Midgett, to walk the marshes with her one more time. Virginia describes what happened next simply, as if events could have unfolded no other way.

"We made our way out to the water, which took a little while because there weren't any paths through the brush. Lennie saw something out off shore a little ways that she wanted to check, so she waded out. I just kept walking along the shore. A little ways down I saw the bottom of a boot. I called to Lennie and said, 'Come here; I found him.'

"She said, 'Oh Ginny, you didn't; you're fibbing.' I had her take my hand and we went back to him. He was lying face down. There wasn't so much as a hole in his clothes that I could see from the back.

"I checked his back pocket. His wallet was right there."

Lennie ran back to the road and flagged down a car for help. A short time later, when two of Oscar's friends arrived, they found his body on a sandy flat where a high tide had washed him perhaps only a few days before. He lay on his stomach with his arms stretched in front of him. The skin on his fingers had dried and cracked to the bone. One of his boots was gone, as if in a final effort to swim he had kicked it off. Virginia stood only a few yards away, clutching the wallet.

"We had twenty-three good years together. It was terrible not knowing what had happened to him all that time. In that sense the day I found him was one of the happiest of my life."

3

ᏗOUNDED BY SEA

 JUST AFTER DAWN on a cloudless mid-May morning, I hike north on the beach to a set of tall, crumbling dunes. There is a southwest wind, still gaining force, that catches foam and occasionally hurls it back over the shoulders of a breaker the way a woman might toss a long braid. The beach's pitch is steep; to find the most level walking I stay on high sand, away from the line of tides. A bank of fog hovers on the eastern horizon and— for the fourth straight morning—obscures the sun's emergence from the sea. I have yet to see a true sunrise on Hatteras. By noon the fog will have burned off, but I would lay money down that at daybreak it will be back.

I walk this stretch often in first light, which in May sneaks across the island between 5:30 and 6:00. Twenty-five miles east of the mainland, in a landscape of white sand and glare, the term "early" takes on particularly harsh meaning. By 6:15 bright yellow sunshine slips through curtains and floods under doors. By 6:30 a good portion of the island population is up, dressed, and well into their work. To me it is worth the pain of rising in the dark to be out for the early morning light. Just past sunrise it strikes the Hatteras sand with a gilding intensity that is lost as the sun ascends. For a few minutes the reeds and grasses take on an orange sheen that makes it seem as if they are lit from within, like a candle or a Japanese lamp. A soft, diffused glow kindles the air; warm molecules of light surround every stem, every fleck of sand. And then the radiance fades, as quick and fleeting as a final drop of kerosene being bled from a wick.

It is just before 6 o'clock, and the early glow has dimmed. The knife-shaped shadows begin to shorten as I pass the boundary for the Pea Island National Wildlife Refuge. The dunes I am heading for climb abruptly and fall to the edge of Highway 12 near the northern loop of three long, slow curves that Hatteras residents call the S curves. At the southern edge of the curves is a ridge of low, unvegetated sand that often sifts into the road— the reason for the sudden crooks in the highway's unswerving plunge to the south. North of the curves the sand is shaggy with sea oats and saltmeadow hay, and the dunes are higher and steeper than anything within a mile. I hoist myself up to a small ledge with my arms, scrambling for footing in cascading grit. Sand lodges beneath my fingernails and seeps into my shoes.

Morning is my favorite time here, but it is not the only time I come. The panorama from the top of the dunes is always impressive, if only for its limitless scope. Neither trees nor buildings block my horizons; in any direction I can see to the curve of the earth. Half of my view is taken up by a sky that deepens in blue at its top and thins almost to white at its edges, the other half by water and a narrow, undulating strip of sand. There are no cozy thickets in sight, no protected coves. No oil rigs mar the eastern horizon; no mainland hovers on the west to anchor Hatteras to the rest of the world.

I could sit here all day, twirling sea oats around my fingers and burying my feet in cool sand; just sit and think about landscapes, seascapes, and the psychological consequences of living where the two collide. Between boundless horizons my own possibilities seem boundless, and my most pressing problems wither in size. I once read that many primitive cultures associate wide spaces with freedom and adventure, while forests, valleys, and sheltered coves evoke feelings of security and warmth. If so, it makes sense that the first people to come here were intrepid souls looking for a place where they could live unencumbered by traditional law.

A sense of freedom abounds, but at the sacrifice of comfort. For all practical purposes I am sitting in the middle of a desert. Nothing flourishes here that needs much fresh water, or that lacks hardiness and the determination to survive. You cannot escape the salt, the sun, the rotten-egg stench of marsh, the mosquitoes and greenhead flies. The coast is not a place where you can easily ignore the elements. Storms can be seen for miles advancing like spreading stains. The sea sloshes dark and broody beneath a pastel dawn, or flaccid and green below thunderheads. The wind, when it cannot be felt or heard, imposes its presence by jostling bushes and whipping whitecaps on the sound. And yet the clearness of the light, the constant swish of the surf, and the yield of the sand underfoot spark a sensuousness that strips aside the discomfort I would normally feel in such a barren and hostile setting.

Each element—earth, wind, water—wields a double-edged sword of pleasure and pain. The sand that molds itself so comfortably around your feet and body becomes, in high wind, a brutal, solid sleet. A heavy breeze steals your breath, but a light one whistles through your nostrils and virtually does your breathing for you. The surf can chill you with its violence, or it can lick the beach in a soothing, two-count rhythm. I walk on the beach to relax. Before I moved here I did deep breathing exercises instead. I would sit with my eyes unfocused and draw in deeply, imagining the air rising to my brain and seeping into my bloodstream before I exhaled through my mouth, long and slow. As my mind began to clear I would picture myself on a sloping beach with ocean waves swirling over my feet. The rhythm of my breath became the roar and fizz of a gentle surf, a body of water alive and breathing.

The waters around me are alive and breathing, but the vitality within them easily escapes the untrained eye. Today the surf is green and muddied by the southwest wind. The waves collapse quickly, flattening and spreading without force, lolling onto the beach. To me their docileness is calming and therapeutic. Others who have spent more time at the ocean's edge would undoubtedly view them with a more critical slant. They are no good for surfing, because they do not hold a vertical face. They may swarm with fish, but only fish that can subsist in murk—in other words, fish that hunt for food by smell. As schools migrate up and down the coast, experienced anglers study the clarity and turbulence of the surf to figure out what species have ventured close to shore, and where. In early summer clear waters bring in the yellow-speckled Spanish mackerel, a species that feeds by sight. In fall and spring rough waves attract the hard-fighting and hefty red drum. A gap in the breakers may mark a breach in the bar—a cut-through, in fishing lingo—that serves as a passageway to sloughs twenty feet off the beach. A knot of gulls or an oily slick may reveal the location of a school of bluefish. For more than two weeks, though, the fishing has been unusually slow. It is likely that nothing swims near the beach now but crabs.

The life with which the water breathes today is largely microscopic. Green surf tends to be rich with phytoplankton, the one-celled, free-floating plants that sometimes hook together in short strands and that form one of the primary links in the ocean food chain. Although they are usually too small to see, their absence is readily apparent. In the winter the waters off Hatteras turn sapphire, the color of barrenness and killing cold. As the sun's elevation climbs in the spring, its rays pierce more deeply into coastal waters, widening the zone in which plants can live. At the same time the midlevel waters begin to heat. The stratification that has existed for five or six months—a warm surface layer above the ocean's chilly depths—begins to dissolve. Bottom waters mix and boil to the top, bringing with them clouds of nutrients. The effect is the same as when a garden is doused with manure. Phytoplankton reproduce and bloom in the largest orgy of the year, in numbers so great that the water is suddenly tinted green with chlorophyll. Immediately planktonic animals increase at a frenzied pace, in turn providing food for larger marine animals and fish. This process does not occur simultaneously at all latitudes. For weeks masses of cool, blue sea bump against swirls of warm, green water and squeeze against the coast. Today's emerald surf means this annual cycle is well under way, although I wouldn't be able to see any clues if I were to slop some water in a jar.

I am not sure I will ever learn to read the contents of the water by studying its surface the way practiced fishermen and biologists can. I might become better at reading subtleties in the landscape—the high spots and hollows, the gradual shifts in habitat and species. In terrain so devoid of obvious landmarks, a change in elevation of a foot becomes a distinguishing trait. Initially the dunes and swales of Hatteras looked to me to be virtually the same, but I have slowly begun to discern variations. To the west of these dunes the island plunges into a narrow strip of myrtle and ends in an even narrower strip of salt marsh. The shape of the marsh is jagged, like the edges of a jigsaw puzzle, where waves have undercut its peaty soil. At less than a half-mile in width, this stretch is one of the lowest and most unstable segments of Hatteras Island. Yet plants compete ferociously for space. The dune where I sit is so thickly grown with saltmeadow hay and sea oats that I have a difficult time extracting my feet when I clamber down its slope to the road.

Just west of the highway the grasses are crowded out by myrtle, a species with waxy leaves that slow the loss of moisture, rubbery branches that bend easily in high winds, and extensive roots that suck moisture from the quick-draining sand. It cannot stand many dousings with ocean water. Since the dune-building projects of the 1950s reduced the frequency of ocean flooding, the myrtle has adapted so well it now pushes far into the marsh. A half-mile north of here, in fact, the wildlife refuge has begun burning fields of myrtle and turning under the soil to encourage the growth of grasses that provide food for waterfowl.

Every inch of the island is subject to takeover by resilient plants; the more protected the terrain, the more fierce the battle for space. In a wide section just south of Salvo, two sets of dunes separate the highway from the beach. The greater stability and higher elevation have enabled a stand of pines planted in the 1930s to survive, although the trees on the eastern edge of the grove are shorter because of their exposure to salty spray. Even farther south, in the high dune fields west of Cape Point, a buffer of hardy, salt-resistant trees and shrubs protects a diverse pine and hardwood forest from ocean winds. In the thickest part of the woods grow swamp dogwood, red mulberry, American holly, and American hornbeam—none of which can tolerate salt. Briars and rattan vines cascade from the trees.

The forest has grown up on ancient dunes that at one time may have been part of a separate island. Now, however, they form the highest portion of the cape, the shoreline least susceptible to erosion. Buried within the dunes lies the bulk of the Hatteras Island water supply, a lens of clean, fresh liquid balanced on top of a salty underground sea. Fresh water and nutrients leach quickly through sandy soil and are never in plentiful supply on a barrier island. But except for the beaches—the harshest, outermost zones—plants crowd into every square inch, seeking moisture and cover from salt, chopping the island into a montage of ecological zones.

Within each of the habitats are zoological zones with bounds that depend on such subtle factors as wave action, temperature, the amount of shade, blowing sand, and moisture in the ground. Were I to take a walk in shallow surf right now, I would come across stretches where my feet would be bumped by mole crabs—half-inch-long, gray animals shaped like footballs with legs and curling antennae. As adults, mole crabs develop hard shells tinted with pale blue. They live at the rim of the surf, riding the tide up and down the beach and burying themselves in sand with each receding wave. As water slides over their burrows they extend their antennae to catch algae and bacteria. Mole crabs congregate in large groups; one patch of sand may swarm with them, but a similar patch two yards to the south may be empty. Why they choose one area over another is not clear.

At Coquina Beach, north of Oregon Inlet, the spring sand is flecked with tiny burrowing clams known for their colorful streaked shells. Coquinas show up sporadically in the swash in front of the Cape Hatteras lighthouse and in great numbers on the flat beaches just south of the Outer Banks, where, like mole crabs, they slip into the sand between waves. They travel up and down the coast, collecting plankton and moving on. At Rodanthe, though, they never appear. The beach is apparently too steep for their taste.

An invisible crosshatch, vertical as well as horizontal, determines the bounds by which the animals and plants of Hatteras live. This is the case in any terrain, but on the coast a variety of zones can be easier to discern because of the rise and fall of the tide. Last week I waded out in the surf by the jetties at the Hatteras lighthouse in hopes of seeing animals and plants that normally live below the surf. It was the day after a full moon—a day when, because of the lunar pull, the tides run unusually high and unusually low. These twice-a-month pulls are called spring tides and occur after each new and full moon. In April or May, spring tides become particularly full, flushing organic debris from the marshes and filling the sounds with a pulse of food for young animals and fish.

Although the tide had receded farther than normal, cool spring waves washed the bottom of the jetties and moistened the air. I pulled off my shoes and waded in, hesitating between waves, aware that my jeans and sweatshirt were about to be soaked. With every breath I took in lungfuls of wet, salty air. My feet clenched in the cold. In a few minutes my calves began to ache.

Strands of green weed were scattered across the top edge of

the concrete wall I chose to examine. A foot or more down in a band exposed to heavy spray, a slimy weed, probably *Cladophora*, grew in wispy beards. Two feet below in a zone normally wetted by breakers was a weed with long, coarse strands made up of tubular pieces strung together, end to end. This plant (an *Enteromorpha*, or hollow green weed, I later discovered) occupied most of the wall. I could see air bubbles in some of its tubular strands. Toward the bottom of the jetty grew a branching red weed with thick leathery leaves, a species I had not encountered before. The red weed was almost always under water; it crept high up the wall as the jetty extended farther into the surf.

I ran my fingers through the tubed weed. Deep in its strands I pinched down on four thin, slippery creatures, which I quickly stuck in a jar. Two tiny crabs—black-fingered mud crabs, I think—eluded my grasp by skittering into the vegetation. I continued to comb through slimy hollow strands, shivering as waves slapped against my legs. Pulling a fistful of plant from the wall all at once, I spotted three more brown, long-legged creatures, all of which danced deftly into snarls of vegetation. I gave up, took the four organisms I had managed to capture, and retreated to the beach.

The most pronounced feature of the sticklike animal I had collected was a pair of bulbous sacs hanging from the middle section of its spindly body. Through a magnifying lens I could see seven elongated body segments, five pairs of legs, and two antennae. On the second pair of legs, gnathopods—soft, claw-shaped legs—dangled like tears. The animals' bodies were translucent and beautiful in the way of a water spider or a delicate fern; it was hard to believe anything so frail could be alive. They kept rising up and throwing themselves forward with the searching enthusiasm of inchworms.

I took them home to my kitchen table. From a field guide I discovered them to be a form of amphipod—that is, a crustacean with seven body segments and no shell—called *Caprellas*, or skeleton shrimp. A second book informed me that skeleton shrimp live among fine weeds and fouling organisms on rocks and pilings in sounds and ocean surf. I would not have found any among the coarse red weed at the jetty bottom. Some species have the ability to change color, chameleon-style. The sacs, "which droop like transparent raindrops," carry eggs. By chance I had collected four females.

I read on. Skeleton shrimp live deep among grasses and in hydroids, the delicate branching animals commonly mistaken for seaweeds. They cling fast to their hosts with their back legs and let their bodies sway in the current, like wisps of weed. This trick enables them to withstand the force of breakers. Most of the time they keep their front legs pressed against themselves, "folded as in prayer," but ready to grab any copepod or other morsel that comes drifting by.

"These peculiar little amphipods are often abundant," the book finished. ". . . Unlike any other amphipods, form and behavior suggest miniature praying mantises. . . . slow and methodical in movements." I looked at the three surviving creatures, which, sure enough, rose up and flung themselves forward in methodical rhythm. Miniature praying mantises, eh? Funny how nature mimics itself in the shape of its plants and creatures, in the complex and wonderful orderings of life.

Late in April the beach at Rodanthe began to fill with holes I knew to be the entrances to ghost crab burrows. Anyone who has spent time on the middle and southern Atlantic coast has seen these sandy shelled crabs that retreat to underground chambers in the hottest part of the day. Long thought to be scavengers—the garbage collectors who clean the beaches of dead organisms—ghost crabs are really adept predators who feed on mole crabs and coquinas. Field guides frequently describe them as an evolutionary link between animals of the land and the sea, since they cannot swim but must wet their gills with ocean water at least once a day. Their genus name, *Ocypode*, derives from a Greek phrase meaning swift-footed. This seems especially appropriate for a crab that can run as quickly as five feet a second. Their most engaging feature is well-developed eyes, which protrude a half-inch above their shells on shiny black stalks.

In winter, ghost crabs close off the entrances to their burrows, then dig out all at once in the spring. Or so it seems. One afternoon I noticed a very small ghost crab cowering in my shadow near the swash. Its half-inch-wide shell was speckled in a pattern of pale blue and brown that made it difficult to spot among the gravelly spring sand. I stomped my feet; it dashed off in a mad zigzag. Within two days the beach was riddled with holes, but the crabs remained out of sight.

A few nights later I was driving back from Nags Head, tired and not very alert. It was just past midnight. The air was damp and still with the oppressive weight that heralds a shift in the wind. I wanted nothing more than to crawl into bed; in my mind I could already feel the give of the mattress and the coolness of the sheets. In the distance I saw the flat sheen of the signs marking the first loop of the S curves. Only a little over a mile to home. I was starting into the first turn, sighing relief, when eight squat, alabaster shapes with deeply bowed legs appeared in my headlights and jolted me awake. I was driving too fast; they disappeared beneath my truck before I had gotten a good look. Were they ghost crabs? They could not have been anything else. The shapes had been scattered across the highway, with several in the southbound lane, and it seemed likely that I had hit one or two. I continued on my way home, resolving to go back the next morning and examine the carcasses.

At daybreak a thin haze obscured the sky, but patches of blue showed through as I pulled onto the highway. At the northern segment of the S curves, the asphalt was streaked with skid marks. To my surprise there were no road kills, no crushed claws or sprawling legs. I parked my truck and walked back to the curves, almost trampling two shiny black eyes that protruded from a burrow in the shoulder. The crab ducked inside as I stepped around it.

Quietly I mounted a steep dune and peered over the top. On the beach thirty-odd ghost crabs busied themselves with pushing sand from the entrances to their burrows and skittering back and forth to the surf. They ran sideways on butter-colored legs with their ivory claws in front of them, tips down. Most of them glided across the sand in a straight path to and from the sea, but a few moved in short bursts toward the north or south, darting in and out of holes. At the sight of me they froze with their eyes turned in my direction.

I topped the dune and crouched in full view of the crabs. The sand was littered with chunks of cocoa-brown peat, cracked and crusty from the sun. From behind several of these, eye stalks protruded like periscopes. I kept still despite a twinge of uneasiness; when I looked to the left, I was painfully aware of the beady eyes that studied me from the right. After three or four minutes a few crabs turned back to slinging sand from the burrows. Others resumed their dancing to the surf. I lowered myself slowly from a crouch to a sitting position.

Suddenly on the fringe of the colony two large crabs ran toward each other, raised high on sinewy legs, and rammed together. They pushed hard against each other with their claws for twenty seconds before one lowered itself, folding its legs beneath it, and backed away. The victor advanced aggressively on tiptoe, its claws pushed out, as a half-dozen crabs peeked from burrows or blocks of peat. The losing crab continued to inch away, nearly flattening itself against the sand. A quick movement at the edge of the colony caught my eye. Another two of the largest crabs collided and pushed with what appeared to be all their might, stepping sideways for balance, flailing their legs. They separated after perhaps ten seconds, waving their claws at each other the way an angry man might shake his fist, and parted.

Around me more shoving matches began. I had never heard of crabs mounting such violent and short-lived challenges, and for no obvious reason. The matches were sporadic and usually ended with no clear victor. In the background the surf pummeled the beach, its roar the morning's only sound. A large orange sun backlit the crabs, shining through their brittle legs and giving their silent antics the quality of the surreal.

I began trying to keep track of individuals to see what they did after each skirmish, but they moved among others so swiftly that I lost them. Could this be a courtship ritual? If so, the victors paid no attention to their intended mates. The clashes were brief, though they seemed ferocious, and the crabs involved came away without visible harm. Was it a series of territorial disputes? This struck me as unlikely, since the crabs dodged in and out of different burrows.

The sun's glare was growing painful, and my sunglasses were in the truck. I stood up as slowly as I could. Three dozen ghost crabs froze. See you later fellows, I thought. Maybe same time tomorrow.

But I did not return the next morning, or the next. On the third day when I drove to the S curves and sneaked over the dune, the tide washed within a yard of the ghost crabs' battling grounds. All the burrows had been closed over; the beach was empty and still.

I went home, dissatisfied and restless. My curiosity had been piqued, and by the most common animal on the beach. After breakfast I called Thomas G. Wolcott, a North Carolina State University biologist who had conclusively refuted the belief— widely accepted since the first studies in 1908 on the species' behavior—that ghost crabs scavenge the majority of their food. Wolcott had noted that relatively few dead organisms and windrows of grass wash up on North Carolina beaches, certainly not enough to support thousands of crabs. During the summers of 1975 and 1976 he had spent night after night capturing ghost crabs to see what they were eating. He also cemented radio transmitters to the shells of crabs so he could monitor their movements. He concluded that ghost crabs subsist chiefly on mole crabs and coquinas, although they consume decaying material in the absence of live prey. The research won him recognition as an authority on the species.

Wolcott had not seen many matches like the ones I had witnessed. But he had read studies suggesting that the encounters were only ritualistic challenges. By pushing against each other the crabs could determine which would win a full-scale fight. Wolcott could not say for sure what issue the pushing matches were supposed to resolve. "They could be mating displays, since the crabs mate in the spring," he said, "or they could be territorial displays. Ghost crabs don't like to dig holes. After one is through feeding for the night it finds itself a hole. A large crab will drive out a medium-size crab, which will in turn find a burrow with a small crab it can drive out."

When a crab leaves its burrow for the night, it may walk nearly a mile and scramble for a burrow at the approach of dawn, like children in a game of musical chairs. The conflicts I witnessed may have been the last challenges of the night. "But," Wolcott added, "very little is known about ghost crabs. I've been surprised at just how little scientific work has been done on the three dominant invertebrates on sandy beaches—namely, ghost crabs, mole crabs, and coquinas. They just move too much. They're extremely difficult to study."

To complicate matters further, ghost crabs apparently shed their shells, mate, and incubate their eggs below the sand. No one has ever reported seeing them molt, although they must. Few people have seen them copulate. Rarely do gravid crabs appear on the beach, even at night. Scientists have not even been able to determine conclusively where the crabs spend the winter. Wolcott believes many of them burrow deep into secondary dunes, where the water table is lower than on the beach.

"You have to understand that it's much easier to look at the community structure when you can get at the critters," he finished. "In a rocky tidepool, a lot of animals are sessile or nailed down. You can watch how they feed; you can measure their growth and biological changes over long periods of time. One might think it would make more sense to study organisms about which little is known. But science does have its fads."

I hung up with a feeling of smugness, and on a morning soon after I returned to the S curves to watch the crabs. Eighty years ago marine scientists conducted the first studies on ghost crab behavior, yet even now the species manages to grow, mate, and release eggs without being bathed by the spotlight of science. It has become almost a ritual, these frequent hikes to the dunes north of the S curves, and I have been rewarded with glimpses of fighting crabs a dozen more times. On my walks I sometimes dig mole crabs out of wet sand with my toes. They boil to the surface by the hundreds as waves slip over them; they seek refuge far down in the surf, below the depth where ghost crabs can feed.

Science has its phases and so do I. Since the night I encountered the crabs on the highway, I have been examining the surf and the fall of the beach more frequently, and with a critical bent. I find it entertaining even to watch the daily changes in the sand. For weeks the beach has been patchy with gravel, ancient riverbeds dredged up by storm-churned surf. The beach profile has steepened; a hazardous dropoff swallows swimmers who venture ten yards into the surf. This is as the textbooks say it should be in spring, after winter waves have bitten into the berm and carried much of its sediment to offshore bars. If theory holds, and it probably will, by September the sand will have been brought back in, and the beach will descend gradually enough for easy swimming.

In early March I nailed a block of untreated wood to a piling on the Rodanthe pier near the low-tide line. I had read that a buoy placed in the ocean in April, when the water is rich with larvae, will grow oysters and other organisms by fall, but a buoy put out in the fall will grow virtually nothing for a year. Since it was April, I decided to see what I could cultivate on a piece of wood. I nailed a square, three-inch-thick block about a foot above the sand on a wave-battered piling. A week later, after a rush of heavy surf, the block was four feet above the sand. In a matter of days the rough breakers had badly eroded the beach. The next week the surf calmed, and ten days later my block was nearly buried. If any organisms were clinging to its sides, they were still too small to discern. But the block had served a purpose I did not foresee.

Curiosity sends me to textbooks and field guides for answers to questions that, it seems, no one of scientific bent has ever answered. I used to think that studying natural science was something like building a wall. In some sections, bricks of knowledge have been fit tightly together with a mortar made from data and observations, but in other sections only the scaffolding stands. The bricks will be filled in later with careful, logical work. Now I think of science as a free-form, undisciplined art. Our knowledge of the natural world is like a big canvas. In some places the picture is minutely detailed, with brilliant brushwork, but much of the canvas is completely empty. Every once in a while somebody manages to splatter paint in just the right place and fill a in some of the gaps.

Is this an eccentric way to view the world? Maybe, but the fact remains that the most common phenomena, such as the pattern of shells on the beach, can defy explanation by knowledgeable people. It is not unusual to find a wide strip of utterly bare sand near a swath so full it looks as though the shells have been brought in by truck. One week I asked four naturalists and a geologist to explain the uneven distribution. All any one of them could offer was a guess that shells tend to be tossed up in certain patterns because of the changing shape of sloughs and shoals. The explanation makes sense and I am willing to buy it—but no one I have talked to claims to know for sure.

If you pick among the shells like a rock hound, you will also notice that certain things tend to show up in droves. In March I kept stumbling across the bulbous shells of purse crabs, tiny pouches with dark purple specks and three spines on their rears. For several weeks I collected them and stuck them randomly on shelves and window sills. Then they disappeared from the wrack. Last month the purple and yellow shells of lady crabs were strewn through the weeds on shore. A week later I found no lady crabs but dozens of the long brittle shells of razor clams and the smooth, spiraled cones of knobbed whelks. There were no signs of the fleshy animals that once lived in them. More recently the helmet-shaped shells of horseshoe crabs have been around for the asking. The crab shells are small and empty, as if they were shed in recent molts. And it would make sense that crabs would molt all at once, since their eggs hatch in great numbers in a short span of time.

I began asking questions of the national seashore's most knowledgeable staff. Is it common for razor clams to die and wash ashore in great numbers in the spring? For whelks? Do crabs molt all at once? One naturalist shrugged. Another said she had noticed that certain species tend to be common on the beach around the same time every year. The previous day she had seen a number of parchment worm tubes washing up near the Cape Hatteras lighthouse. More fuel for the fire; a parchment worm occupies one tube all its life.

A toast to mystery, to lack of explanations. Late in the day, after I returned from a talk with the naturalists, I went for a walk on the beach. A flotilla of high, flat-bottomed clouds hovered in the eastern sky as I began hiking quickly to the north. Before I had gone a quarter of a mile, I slowed to a normal pace, and then to a stroll. Beside me the ocean curled its tongue, exhaled in a roar, and admonished me to relax. Someday I will probably discover why the empty shells of razor clams come to the beach all at once, but there is no real rush. This is Hatteras Island, not New York or Nags Head. We are living here, all of us, on island time.

4

eNESTING IN THE SPOILS

 LATE SPRING, THE season of romping and romance. For two months the birds of the coast have been in their flashiest plumages and their most flamboyant moods. Near a marshy creek one day I spotted three large shorebirds marching up and down a stretch of sand. Each bird had a hood of black feathers, a white belly, startling yellow eyes rimmed in red, and a long orange bill. They stepped along single file with their necks stretched out and their bills pointed down, piping out short, high-pitched trills. First they marched to the north, then about-faced and marched to the south. Every few minutes one bird halted, pumped its neck up and down, and snapped open its unwieldy bill as if taking huge bites of air. They looked, in a word, ridiculous.

North, about face, south, pipe-pipe, pump the neck up and down, pipe-pipe. This was the courtship ceremony of the American oystercatcher. Two males and a female, perhaps in a ménage à trois. Oystercatchers mate for life, but sometimes an established pair will adopt a second male that stays around until the year's brood has hatched and fledged. Three players in the avian game of love.

Later I noticed two black-headed laughing gulls only a few inches apart on the beach. They stood stock-still, eyes trained on each other, until one tipped its head back and pointed its dark red bill straight up. The second mimicked the motion. The first gull again tipped its head back, then down; the second followed suit. For maybe thirty seconds they kept up, craning their necks toward the sky, until the first gull sauntered up to the other's backside and mounted. Then he began squawking maniacally and flapping his wings for balance. Laughing gulls are not known for their discreet affairs.

In shallow, grass-rimmed ponds, spindly legged herons goose-step after their mates in a yearly game of hard-to-get. Rufous-sided towhees perch atop thickets while the male serenades; boat-tailed grackles hop through fields, the male spreading his wings and tail and occasionally emitting the classic wolf whistle—a two-note call, long and low. Terns dip and bob above the sea in a courtship flight, then the male brings an offering of fish as the female opens her mouth and begs to be fed, like a newly hatched chick. They stand together when the female has eaten, close but not touching. Sometimes they stretch their necks and circle each other, as if admiring their choice.

Mixed among the terns are black skimmers—dark-backed birds with white faces and thick, orange bills tipped with black. In flight a skimmer flashes its white underside and moves far with each beat of its long, tapered wings. To feed, it glides above calm ponds and bays, cutting a shallow path through the water with the long bottom section of its bill. As it finds minnows and small crustaceans, it closes its bill and swallows. The motion is as smooth and fluid as if it is skimming foam off the water with a straw.

Standing together on the beach, all facing the same direction, skimmers look too top-heavy to be so graceful in the air. Their legs seem short for their long bodies and heavy bills. Yet their shape is an integral factor in their courtship maneuverings. The wooing begins with a frenzied flight, and perhaps with the male bestowing a symbolic gift—a five- or six-inch-long stick. Just before mating he squats beside the female in the sand, his bill and tail feathers pointed up, so that his body forms a U. He begins to pivot on his breast, shoveling sand from behind him with thick webbed feet.

Several days later the female lays her eggs in one of the shallow depressions formed as her mate turned round and round.

Walker Golder slipped down the side of a dune, plopped a straw hat on his head, and turned around to hand me a long wooden stake. In his other hand he twirled the butt end of a fishing rod as pitted and rusty as if it had spent the winter buried in sand. "This is a special scientific instrument," he joked. "I just happened to find it the other day on the beach at Cape Point." A small orange flag swayed from the crown of his hat, and his light-blue chamois cloth shirt was splattered with thick white droppings. My own shirt would soon be in the same condition. Already a welcoming party of terns and skimmers had taken wing and was headed in our direction. A few minutes before, I had stuck a feather in the band of a baseball cap, which I now pulled tight against my skull. With luck the terns would peck at the feather instead of my scalp.

We had entered a stretch of beach that in other circumstances would have been forbidden territory, a nesting colony of skimmers and common terns, with a few gull-billed terns and least terns mixed in. The area was closed to foot traffic, but Golder had been hired by the Cape Hatteras National Seashore to conduct a periodic census of tern and skimmer colonies on Hatteras and Ocracoke islands. On this day in late June, the peak of the nesting season, he expected to find as many as six hundred nests in a single hundred-yard stretch north of Rodanthe.

The black-capped, slim-bodied terns are the daredevils of the beach, the birds that fold their wings and dive straight down for fish, often from heights of fifty feet. Although their slight build makes them appear rather frail, they defend their colonies of nests by mobbing any person or animal that comes too close. An intruder can usually count on being surrounded by dozens of swooping, swirling birds and—without a feather or flag to draw their fury—pecked vigorously on the head. Certain species, including the common terns circling toward us, were known for their feisty defense.

"Okay, now there's nothing to this," Golder said with an air of relaxed command. At the age of twenty-two, he is something of a prodigy. As an undergraduate at the University of North Carolina at Wilmington, Golder had been uninspired by his course work and preferred to spend his time surfing—until he had taken a class in ornithology his sophomore year. In the two years since, he had logged hundreds of hours of field work with nesting birds.

"Okay," he repeated, "we're going to walk back and forth across the colony counting only the eggs that are still in the nest. We'll each take a stick and drag it behind us to make a line in the sand. That'll mark our transects, so we'll know what we've already covered. We'll look for least tern eggs, which are the smallest and usually right out in the open near the edge of the colony. Then gull-billed eggs, which are easier to spot because the nests tend to be made of big mounds of shells." Despite a distinct Southern drawl, he spoke quickly. Apparently this was a speech he often made. "The common terns tend to line their nests with a little bit of shell or grass, and they lay brownish or greenish eggs. There's a lot of color variation. The skimmers' eggs are a lot whiter; you'll be able to tell them with no problem. Ready?"

I followed him to the tideline at the south edge of the colony. He positioned himself about ten feet north of me and started toward the dunes, dragging the fishing rod behind him. Fragments of brownspeckled eggshell were scattered across a patch of gravelly sand. "Those were probably washed over by that storm last week," Golder said. "Look here—here's a least tern nest with a couple of eggs." He pointed at the sand with the rod.

I stared at the patch he indicated. All I saw were a couple of sun-bleached cockles and some ground-up shells. After an embarrassing stretch of silence I noticed a shallow depression holding two oblong brown eggs, each only slightly longer than a thimble. I had been expecting something larger and more obvious; the eggs blended so well with the large grains of sand that I might have missed them completely. "I can see why you don't want people coming through here," I said.

"Yeah. Be pretty careful where you step."

Above us the terns chittered loudly, dipping toward us but pulling back before touching our hats. On my first slow pass through the colony I found one small hollow, or scrape, with two eggs. A third egg lay several feet from the nest. I reached the dunes, skirted the strip Golder had checked, and started back to the sea.

On my second and third transects I found no eggs at all. It was a day of light breeze, and a band of sweat coated my forehead beneath my cap. Patches of brown-, black-, and buff-colored sand began to dance in front of my eyes. "I think I may be missing some nests," I confessed.

"You'll see them if there are any to see. I've only found two myself."

When we had worked our way through a third of the colony, I began to find piles of gravel and shell with two or three blotched, tannish eggs deposited in neat hollows—the nests of gull-billed terns. Where gull-billed terns, least terns, and skimmers are plentiful, each species tends to form large colonies by itself. Here, though, the petite least terns and the shy, unaggressive skimmers often nest alongside common terns, which, because of their habit of divebombing intruders, help protect the young of the entire colony. Gull-billed terns sometimes steal chicks from the nests of least and common terns and feed them to their own young. For that reason, they are barely tolerated by other species and tend to nest along the colony border.

Nearby, the greenish eggs of common terns had been laid in scattered scrapes, and fat chicks, fluffy with mottled black and tan down, pressed their bodies against the sand. The youngest chicks lay very still, depending on camouflage for protection, but three older chicks bolted, waddling toward the surf on skinny, orange legs.

Toward the middle of the colony the number of nests in each transect tripled. Some were next to tufts of grass or near pieces of driftwood, which helped block the wind. Skimmer chicks flattened themselves against the sand, their chins propped on the edges of their nests as we passed quietly overhead. The skimmer eggs, a rich cream color sprinkled with a confetti of black, were slightly larger than the tern eggs and nearly matched the mottled black and white down of the chicks. The terns began to hit my feather. I hunched my shoulders and kept my head down. We needed to hurry so newborn, featherless chicks would not be exposed to too much heat and sun.

At the north end the number of nests quickly thinned. In the last four transects we found only two gull-billed tern nests and a single least tern egg outside a scrape. The terns continued to carp at us with high-pitched cries, but the skimmers were already settling back down.

"Things look kind of bad for that colony," Golder said as we made our way back to his truck. "I won't know till I count up the figures, but it seems like there were only about 250 successful nests in there. That's less than half what I expected. It's been a bad year for the birds, especially the ones that nest on the open beach. I've been here a little more than a month. In that time I've already counted sixteen days of severe weather, meaning days with driving rain and blowing sand. When the wind really starts to whip out here, the birds can't stay on the nest. They've got to get up and move around, or they just get pelted with sand. And if they leave their chicks out in the open for any length of time the mortality rate is incredible.

"Then there have been overwashes, which bury nests in sand. A bad overwash can just about wipe out a colony. A lot of the birds nest again later in the season if they can find a suitable place. But what with the overwashes and the heavy winds this year, some of these birds may try two or three times and still not hatch a successful clutch. If that happens a couple of years in a row, especially to the common terns and skimmers, we may have cause for some worry."

If not for the empty beaches of the Pea Island National Wildlife Refuge, the colony where Golder and I counted nests would likely never have formed. No one knows how many terns, skimmers, gulls, and herons nested on the East Coast before the heavy development of barrier islands, but it is believed the Atlantic coastal bird population was several times larger during the mid-1800s than it is today, perhaps by four or five times. Settlers wrote of great flocks that filled the mudflats and sky during spring and fall migrations, and hunters of plover, snipe, woodcock, and curlew in New England frequently brought home thirty birds apiece. Common terns, always the most numerous terns of the East, were reported in 1879 to be nesting by the hundreds of thousands on the sandy spits of the Massachusetts coast. And Hatteras residents say their grandparents shot snipe from flocks that once crowded the fields between towns.

The abundance of waterbirds only guaranteed that their slaughter, when it came, would be indiscriminate and swift. As the passenger pigeon began to disappear in the last half of the nineteenth century, professional hunters found a new source of money in the migratory waterfowl that traveled predictable routes. From 1880 to 1900 marksmen reduced the flocks of curlew and plover that migrated along the Atlantic—once so plentiful their flight was said to darken the sky—to a few reclusive bands. Egrets and herons, beautifully plumed during breeding season, were slaughtered by the thousands to satisfy the whim of fashion, which in the 1870s turned to using lavish arrangements of feathers in hats.

Waders were not the only birds sought for the millinery trade, but they were the most popular, and hats adorned with their plumes reached the height of international fashion. When the herons and egrets began to vanish, the milliners restyled their creations with the heads and feathered skins of several species of gull and tern, especially the tiny, light-winged least tern. By 1900 conservationists began to fear for nearly every species on the Atlantic coast.

In 1905 the formation of the National Association of Audubon Societies accelerated the campaign to save species threatened with extinction. Thirty-three states passed laws that protected nesting colonies, and in some areas the Audubon societies hired wardens to patrol sanctuaries. Nevertheless, large numbers of birds continued to be killed illegally. The federal government finally put an end to the slaughter in 1913 with the passage of legislation barring the possession of non-game birds except for scientific research. By the end of the 1920s the government had also outlawed the shooting or trapping of curlews, turnstones, dowitchers, and plover. The Eskimo curlew was all but extinct, and flocks of golden plover never again would darken the sun. But for several decades the birds of the coast lived in relative peace.

In the late 1920s the U.S. Army Corps of Engineers began cutting the Atlantic Intracoastal Waterway, a project of unprecedented proportions—and one that inadvertently provided a wealth of new nesting sites for many coastal birds. In North Carolina alone engineers cut 308 miles of channel and dredged millions of tons of sediment from coastal rivers and bays. At the same time, local governments dredged channels and inlets to keep shipping lanes open near growing port towns. The sand, shells, and silt were deposited in neat piles to form circular islands. During the 1950s and 1960s as oceanfront development began to crowd ground-nesting species from the beaches, the birds moved their colonies to spoil islands, which generally were out of the reach of predators such as bobcats and raccoons and were ignored by humans.

The spoil islands tended to be higher in elevation than the natural beaches and less susceptible to storm overwash and tidal floods. If left alone they would have been colonized by a succession of grasses and, much later, woody shrubs. Even the first thin cover of vegetation would have made it difficult for skimmers and terns to dig their shallow nests in the sand. But the channels and inlets continued to shoal over, and periodically the dredges returned to dump more sediment on the island crowns. Just as windrows of salt-tolerant grasses began to appear, a new load of sand would bury them. Through the 1960s the spoil islands remained ideal habitats for colonies of terns and skimmers; at a time when the birds might have suffered severe ecological stress, they actually prospered.

The corps of engineers, an agency that frequently has evoked the ire of conservationists by building dams and jetties or dredging wetlands, had come to the rescue of a half-dozen fragile species. Its timing could not have been better, for the skimmers and terns were facing pressure from a number of fronts.

When coastlines become crowded, the stocks of bait fish and shellfish gradually shrink, and terns and skimmers must spend more time searching for food. However, the growth of seaside resorts can enhance the diets of herring gulls and laughing gulls, which scavenge trash from dumpsters, steal bait from anglers, and occasionally snatch tern and skimmer chicks from the nest. In the late 1950s and early 1960s laughing gulls prospered, and flocks of herring gulls grew and expanded their nesting range from the northeastern states and mid-Atlantic states to Pamlico Sound. The one advantage still held by terns and skimmers was a wide choice of nesting grounds. But that advantage was not to last.

As soon as silt and sand are deposited on top of a spoil island, they begin to slide slowly downhill under the forces of gravity, wind, and tide. The constant erosion retards the growth of plants and can cause the bases of the island to grow wider and wider, like a spreading volcano. In the 1960s coastal biologists began to complain that the hundreds of spoil islands in the bays and sounds of North Carolina were covering substantial acres of clam beds, oyster reefs, and the stringy green eelgrass that serves as an important habitat for crabs, scallops, and shrimp. The biologists

voiced a special concern for eelgrass beds, which had been deci-
mated by a blight in the mid-1950s and were only beginning to
recover.

In the early 1970s, as federal and state governments adopted
a range of regulations on the dredging and filling of wetlands,
the corps of engineers began building dikes around the spoil islands to keep the sand and silt from spilling into marshes and
sounds. With the bases of the islands stabilized, salt-tolerant plants
such as cordgrass and sea rocket spread and grew too densely for
terns and skimmers to make their shallow scrapes in the sand.
Gradually, laughing gulls and herring gulls—aggressive birds that
nest in grassy meadows—invaded the islands that had been diked.
The crown of some islands remained bare where dredges occasionally deposited more sand. But the sediment so important to
nesting birds was no longer considered spoil. The barrier islands
of the Atlantic were clearly eroding, in places alarmingly so, and
any clean sand was now a valued commodity. Ornithologists knew
it would be only a matter of time before the dredges were per-
suaded to dump their material elsewhere.

If the terns and skimmers were to have an adequate number
of places to nest, they would have to receive special attention.
In the mid-1970s several ornithologists began lobbying for the
corps to leave certain islands undiked. Among them was James F.
Parnell, a biologist from the University of North Carolina at
Wilmington and one of the country's eminent authorities on the
birds of the Atlantic barrier islands. In 1975 Parnell and Robert F.
Soots, Jr., then of Campbell College, published the results of a
four-year study on the use of dredge spoil islands by various species of birds as patches of sand gave way to grasses, shrub thickets, and small trees.

Soots and Parnell concluded that the vast majority of birds
that nest in colonies had moved to spoil islands. They found
that vegetation on the islands tends to establish itself near the
tideline. As the grasses spread around an island base, terns and
skimmers build their nests toward the crown, giving up their
former colonies to gulls. Once dredges stop dumping on an

island, the bare sand disappears in only a matter of years. The seaside grasses so well suited for nesting by gulls and pelicans can be expected to grow prolifically for more than a decade, the study found. Islands untouched for thirty-five or forty years develop thick shrubs used by nesting colonies of egrets and herons.

Soots and Parnell also discovered that no one had made precise counts of the numbers or distribution of birds nesting in North Carolina. They followed their 1975 study with a meticulous census of colonial nesting birds in 1977 and a second census in 1983. The results led them to several tentative but alarming conclusions.

Parnell punctuates his predictions about the population of colonial nesting birds with notes of caution. "When you get right down to it," he says, "I don't think anyone can say for sure what's going on. Things may be fine and dandy, or we may be entering a new period where things aren't so fine. With only two censuses to compare, we can't be completely sure that the decreases aren't just counting errors. But I'm beginning to see a few things I don't like. One, it looks like the colonies are getting bigger, and there are fewer of them. I'd rather see them fairly well spread out. Any time birds nest in large groups, they're subject to catastrophe, whether it's disease or a storm or one feral cat in the colony. For another thing, it looks like not as much material is being placed on dredge islands now, although no one has done any studies to see exactly where the spoil is being put.

"You talk about getting complicated. Things used to be," he sighs, "very simple. The corps dumped wherever they wanted, the birds had plenty of places to nest, and that was that. But I can't blame the fisheries people for fussing at the corps; I've been fussing at them myself for years. Now it's a matter of trying to figure out how to give sand to the beach communities, how to keep from covering up the bottom of the estuary, and how to save some nesting sites for the birds—all at the same time."

The solution, Parnell believes, is for ornithologists, fisheries biologists, and corps engineers to agree that certain islands will be preserved as nesting sites for specific birds. He and Mark A.

Shields of the University of Wyoming have drafted a management plan that is regarded by many coastal biologists as innovative and timely. It is also the first of its type. The goal of the plan is to use dredge spoil to keep plants from growing on some islands and to cultivate vegetation on others, thereby attracting certain species of birds to the same sites each year. For example, undiked spoil islands near inlets will be maintained for terns and skimmers, with clean sand being deposited on them at least every five years to keep the vegetation down. "When you dredge an inlet, you usually end up dumping very coarse sand, and if some of it runs back out it's not so bad," Parnell says. "If you have a lot of silt, like you do around river mouths, it stays suspended in the water. That's when you want to dike. There tends to be more fish near inlets anyway, so it makes sense to try and concentrate the birds there."

If the state maintains a number of sandy-topped spoil islands, the terns and skimmers will be more likely to nest in small, widely dispersed colonies, thereby increasing their chances of survival. At the same time, the birds that nest among grasses and shrub thickets will continue to have a wide choice of sites—as long as dredges are prevented from burying the vegetation. No sediment will be deposited on the islands during nesting season.

The plan requires such careful scheduling of dredging and dumping that the North Carolina Wildlife Commission may establish a committee of ornithologists, fisheries biologists, and corps engineers to oversee it. In addition, biologists will conduct extensive statewide counts of bird nests every five years to monitor population trends. "If we're going to make this work, we have to keep track of how the birds are doing," Parnell says. "We can't just assume everything will be dandy for years to come. There are always catastrophes that occur in nature—a storm or an oil spill or something that throws a monkey wrench into things for a while. But with this plan in place we should be able to keep enough balance, so that when a catastrophe occurs, the birds can recover."

By July the excitement of courtship is long past. Pale blue eggshells and downy feathers litter the myrtle thickets at the Pea Island refuge, where in early spring herons and egrets fashioned messy wedge-shaped nests from reeds and twisted twigs. The chicks they hatched were blind and featherless, with greenish-yellow skin and gangling legs. At the peak of heron nesting in May, the rookeries were full of stringy young birds perched unsteadily on slippery boughs. The sounds of the colony, a collection of caws, grunts, squawks, growls, and hisses, added to the overall impression of a tenement—a crowded, dingy, and dirty dwelling tucked in the thickest hammocks of the marsh. Now, though, all that remain are the carcasses of chicks that fell from their trees and starved.

Most waterbirds are still tethered to the chores of hatching eggs, feeding chicks, frightening off predators. Terns wheel and dip above any person who wanders within a hundred yards of their colony's edge. Where a month ago sandpipers filled exposed mudflats, they stay in secluded spots now, always keeping their chicks in sight. It is a season of tedium, of constant hunting or fishing, constant guard and care.

One morning I drove to a muddy field where I have often seen black-necked stilts, to me the most enticing bird of the marsh. The stilt has a needlelike bill and hot-pink legs that are longer in proportion to its body than those of any other bird found in North America, except perhaps the flamingo. In flight the legs trail straight behind the bird like bright ribbons. The slim body is mostly white, but the bird looks as though a black cloak has been draped over its wings and black. A line of black drips around each eye. The effect is one of almost comic elegance, as if the stilt is dressed up for Mardi Gras.

Stilts are considered rare in North Carolina. On Hatteras Island they nest only near the brackish ponds of the Pea Island refuge, which are kept at levels especially well-suited to the needs of wading birds and ducks. Stilts sometimes lay eggs on bare mud, but they may also build elaborate mounds of twigs and marsh grass in the middle of a pond. If the water level of the pond begins to rise, the parents will hastily shove more twigs underneath the eggs to keep them dry. The ornithologist W. Leon Dawson, having observed this process, reported in 1923 that the eggs are "mauled about and soiled in the mud; but the day is saved. I have seen a stilt. . . squatted on a truncated cone of vegetation eight inches in height and as broad across the top, a veritable Noah's ark of safety."

By stealing through myrtle and grasses, I hoped to glimpse some eggs or chicks without getting close enough to frighten the parents. I scrambled down a short bank and skirted an algae-covered pond. Clumps of saltmeadow hay dotted the field, giving way to patches of gray mud etched with the tracks of herons and coons. Coons, especially, like to eat eggs; slowing down, I studied the bleak soil for signs of shell. The bitter smell of hydrogen sulfide seeped from the ground.

Across the marsh, grasses and shrubs nestled tightly together, weaving a textured mat of yellows, browns, and greens. Cattails and saltmeadow hay lolled against each other, rubbing blade against blade. Reeds stood stiffly erect, pinpricks of dark green next to the silky strands of hay. Yellow asters swayed on slender stems. I hadn't walked a hundred yards before a pair of willets announced my presence by swooping toward me and crying out a shrill pip-pip-pip. I could forget about stealing up to a nesting stilt; the willets' calls were plenty loud enough to alert any bird within a quarter-mile. Momentarily at a loss, I halted and dropped to a crouch among the hay. Thirty yards to my left was a stilt I had completely overlooked.

The stilt craned its neck to examine me and lifted itself into the air with quick wingbeats, its legs trailing behind. Instead of fleeing, it circled toward me with a series of sharp, squeaky barks. Two other stilts rose from some reeds and joined in. Without realizing it, I had ventured close to either a nest or some chicks. I stood up and looked around in vain. When I did, one of the birds landed in a muddy patch twenty yards from me, fluttered its wings, lifted one leg shakily, and dropped delicately to the ground. It sat hunched over, its pink legs folded like a carpenter's rule beneath it. If not for its incessant bark it might have been playing dead.

Many coastal birds, including oystercatchers, simply skulk away from their nests as if abandoning them in despair. Other species engage in what is known as distractive display to lure predators away from nests or chicks. Stilts can appear to have broken wings, broken legs, and sometimes both. I had never before been the object of a feigning bird, and now I stood frozen, trying to figure out how to react. The shrieks and pecks of terns may be effective at keeping intruders at bay, but as soon as I saw the stilt collapse I forgot all about any young that may have been hidden nearby. The exquisite markings and plaintive cry commanded my attention; although I knew the bird would simply fly, I was tempted to move closer.

Even from a distance stilts appear almost brittle, as if the long legs could snap like glass pipes beneath their weight. Now, so close I could see individual feathers, the bird on the ground seemed far too fragile to survive in a harsh world of predation, of competition for food and space. The stilt's obvious fright and distress only increased my impression that it is one of the world's most delicate creatures.

A number of behavioral biologists believe distraction display in nesting birds evolved from two conflicting but powerful emotions—the urge to protect the nest and the impulse to flee. Several chapters back in the history of nature, certain birds became so distraught when danger approached that they in effect suffered nervous breakdowns; unable to cope, they fell down or became ill. This theory is not universally accepted. But somehow a wide range of ducks, shorebirds, and songbirds developed ritualized and very successful techniques for drawing predators from their young. A few colonial nesting species, including black-necked stilts, work in groups to distract predators that are not very close to nests. The two birds swooping around me and the "fallen" stilt were part of an elaborate community effort. Once a nest is discovered, however, the stilts are powerless to defend it. Most of the birds fly off, leaving the parents alone to witness the loss of their eggs and chicks.

Certain species have even learned to use different tactics for different situations. The American avocet, a close cousin of the stilt, can feign a broken leg, although not as convincingly as the stilt. But when an intruder approaches a nest, the avocet flies close by, swinging its sharp, upturned bill in a threatening motion. The killdeer, a ringed plover of the marsh, will pretend that its wing is broken when threatened by a man or a dog. But when a cow or horse approaches a killdeer nest, the parent bird will fly repeatedly at the animal's face to drive it away.

None of this came to mind, however, as I watched the stilt. I had been captivated, enchanted, despite a lack of wind and a gathering heat. When after several minutes I had not budged, the stilt stood up, hobbled a few steps, and dropped back to the ground, yapping and yapping, its eyes fixed on me: Look, you fool, I've got a broken leg; I'm yours for the taking. The other two stilts circled nearby, crying out with their repetitive bark. The charade might have continued indefinitely, but after several minutes I began to worry that the stilts' eggs and chicks lay unprotected somewhere nearby. I backed away from the scene, keeping low to the ground. As I did a glint of sunlight hit the feigning bird's eye. For that moment the image of frágileness shattered. The eye stared back, a deep blood-red, calculating, cold, and thoroughly unnerving.

In the spring of 1983 a U.S. Fish and Wildlife biologist flying over the Pea Island refuge noticed three pairs of brown pelicans nesting on a tear-shaped spoil island west of Oregon Inlet. The sighting was noteworthy, since brown pelicans never had been known to nest north of Ocracoke Island. During the previous five years, however, the pelican population had been rising, and ornithologists were hopeful that the species finally had recovered from a brush with extinction.

The near demise of the brown pelican and several other large birds had been caused by the widespread application of pesticides in the 1950s and early 1960s. The greatest harm came from the use of DDT, which accumulated in the soils and groundwater and was ingested by insects, plankton, and plants. The concentrations of DDT increased with each step in the food chain, until it began to affect the physiology of carnivorous birds. Ospreys, pelicans, and peregrine falcons began laying eggs with thin, brittle shells easily broken in the nest. In less than a decade brown pelicans disappeared from Texas, and their numbers dropped precipitously in Louisiana, Florida, and South Carolina. No data were ever compiled to show that the pelicans in North Carolina had been affected adversely by DDT, but on Ocracoke Island the pesticide was used with great frequency to control mosquitoes. Many families even owned small foggers that they used to spray their yards several times a week.

Now, with DDT out of use for more than fifteen years, the brown pelican is once again common along the southeast Atlantic coast. The three nests at Oregon Inlet indicated that the birds were producing so many healthy clutches that they were under pressure to expand their range. In 1984 sixty-six pelican nests were built on dredge islands just inside the inlet.

But would the chicks hatched at Oregon Inlet have a good rate of survival? And would they return as adults to raise their own young on the islands? In mid-July of 1985 John Weske, a Maryland ornithologist, decided to spend a morning banding pelican chicks at Oregon Inlet. Each summer since 1976 Weske has banded royal tern chicks in every known colony in Virginia and North Carolina. A soft-spoken, spare man of fifty, he is known on Hatteras as kind and dedicated, with an unusual passion for the study of birds. In 1984 alone he banded seventeen thousand royal tern chicks in North Carolina and another five thousand in Virginia. It is his hope to band an entire generation of royal terns and Sandwich terns so he can monitor mortality rates, breeding ages, and patterns of nesting.

The pelican colonies at Oregon Inlet had attracted Weske's curiosity, although he did not have the resources to conduct a full-scale study on them. "Since it's a new colony, we don't know it'll survive and what will happen next if it does," he says. "Are these birds pioneers that will eventually expand their range into Virginia? Do they stick around here during the winter, or are these same birds going to stick around here at all? It's worth taking a couple of mornings out to see if we can get some clues."

At 6 a.m. on the morning of Weske's trip to the pelican colony, I found him launching a small aluminum skiff at a public dock. Three workers from the Pea Island refuge waited in a wide, flat-bottomed boat, and seven teenagers from the Youth Conservation Corps lounged on a wooden dock. We cast off and glided across the milky green surface of Pamlico Sound. Fifteen minutes later we anchored the boats off a steep, sandy bank. Behind us the silhouette of the Oregon Inlet bridge threaded the horizon.

There was still no sign of the pelicans, but the telltale smell of guano wafted toward us on a faint southwest wind. Acidic and sharply bitter, it increased in intensity as I followed Weske through a soft wall of reeds. The ornithologist tromped along well ahead of the group, his red baseball cap just visible over the vegetation. Suddenly a convoy of adult pelicans lifted quietly from the center of the island, wagging their tails with each wing beat and tucking their bills against their chests. By the time I reached the edge of the colony, Weske had conducted a quick survey of the site, and the chicks had set up a clamor of throaty, tremulous calls that sounded something like the scared whinnies of horses. They certainly did not sound much like birds. Thick brown reed stems, dry and crunchy underfoot, littered a wide clearing, and on mounds of rotting twigs crouched small, downy chicks too young to run and hide. The older chicks had scattered through the reeds; their cries were ugly and unsettling. I felt a momentary pang of guilt.

Weske and three of the teenagers walked toward the reeds, flanking a group of chicks. I moved tentatively after them as the birds screamed louder and scrambled to find an escape. A long-armed boy reached for one of the fleeing chicks and closed his fingers around its yellow, snapping bill. Pinning its wings together just above the crook, he handed the chick to me and reached in for another. I grasped the bird's wings at their base and lifted, surprised when its body went limp and its legs dangled below. The young chicks still in the nest looked like small dollops of flesh, lopsided and plump, with folds of veined yellow skin. But at only a few weeks of age they were two feet tall, with long, sinewy limbs. I hoisted the bird over a small bush as gently as possible and carried it to the clearing, where Weske disbursed pliers and alloy bands.

The young pelican moaned softly as I set it on the ground. Except for mottled brown wings, it was white and downy, and its yellow bill had a prominent hook on the end. Below the bill, a pouch hung in folds of pale colors—yellows, greens, streaks of vermilion, and creases of white. The pouch was surprisingly thin and smooth, like fine velvet or silk. Letting loose of the bill, I stroked it gently and ran my hand down the nappy breast. The bird responded by stamping its feet and raising small puffs of dust.

Weske dropped to a crouch beside me and stretched the chick's right leg to the side, then slipped an inch-wide band around it. The chick moaned again and tried to flap its wings. I studied the leg, which was covered with a scaly, yellow skin brindled with white. "Some of these bands seem really tight," Weske said, wincing slightly as he tightened his grip on the pliers to close the band. "But pelican legs don't get any larger. They actually decrease in diameter as the bird grows. The important thing is to make sure the ends of the band meet. If it's not closed all the way, or if it's crimped, the bird runs the risk of getting tangled up in fishing line and perhaps drowning." He gave the pliers a final squeeze, inspected his work, and moved on.

I carried the bird back to the brush and set it down. It paused for a minute as if confused, then ran off with a series of squeals. Nearby, eight chicks had taken a stand in a twisted myrtle bush and were snapping their bills viciously as two timid girls maneuvered for a grip. One of the girls shrieked as a chick bit her on the thumb. I tried to close my hand around the bill of a large bird, but it deftly avoided me at the same time it nipped the edge of my hand. I reached aggressively into the bush and caught the wings of the largest bird, lifted it, and plopped it down in the small circle of chicks and volunteers that waited for bands. It struggled to free itself and made a rumbling sound in its throat.

Next to me was a boy who, during the ride to the island, had told me of his hope to become a veterinarian. He seemed almost mesmerized by the young bird now in his charge. Pinning the wings together lightly, he stroked its breast instead of holding its bill. "Maybe if I'm just nice to you, maybe this won't be so bad," he said tenderly. The chick began to snap its bill and squawk. There was no getting around it; in the minds of the birds, our intrusion was very likely the worst event of their lives. The chick I held continued to moan and look at me with soft brown eyes. I had the power to do with it what I pleased. It probably expected to die. A hard-nosed scientist would have called me sentimental, would have pointed out that it was to be released unharmed, and soon. The shiny numbered band on its leg might produce data to aid the survival of the species. I knew all the scientific reasons for banding young birds. At the moment, though, none of them seemed to matter.

Less than five minutes later I returned the banded chick to its bush and ran to catch another that had fled to the colony's edge. Above, the adults soared round and round in a loose circle, sprinkling us with bursts of waste. I stepped around piles of regurgitated fish and combed through grasses for unbanded birds. The acid smell intensified as the day warmed.

A particularly ill-tempered chick, too young to band, sat in its nest and snapped its bill again and again as if crazy with anger and fright. With each snap it reached far out of the nest and jerked its head back, recoiling its long neck and flapping its tiny wings. A yard away three hatchlings with puffy faces and luminescent purple skin leaned against each other, too weak to stand. The raucous cries resounded from all corners.

We combed the entire colony twice, corralling every bird old enough to wander from its nest. By 10:15 we had banded ninety-two birds and Weske was walking the rim of the colony, tirelessly peering among brambles in a final search. Never had the term "beating the bushes" so aptly applied. The rest of us, scratched and covered with sweat and dirt, waited passively in a clearing. Weske returned to the group. "Do you think we got them all?" he asked. "I think we got them all." A girl next to me nodded in vigorous agreement.

As we pushed off for the ride home the adult pelicans tightened their circle to a funnel. With each pass a few more dropped to the ground to soothe their young and regurgitate fish. By the time we reached the channel that led to the public dock only a few birds remained in the air. The rest had settled like dust from the still air of a summer day.

5

ᏦHE SWAMP ON A HILL

THIRTY MILES NORTHWEST of Rodanthe on the thinly settled banks of Pamlico Sound, the fishing community of Stumpy Point sits among creeks, marsh grass, and a tangle of cat briar and evergreen shrubs. Around the settlement the sand and clay soils of the coastal plain are overlaid with a thick, brown hash of mud, muck, and decaying plants and trees—organic peat. In boggy areas the peat is overgrown with sphagnum moss and a shrubby hedge so dense that a person dropped in its midst would be unable to see more than five feet in any direction. The name given to this country is "pocosin," an Algonkian Indian word that means, roughly, the swamp on a hill.

H.O. Golden moved to Stumpy Point and began shrimping just after the end of World War II. He remembers the waters of

Pamlico Sound as clear and blue and the oysters and shrimp as abundant. Back then the runoff from heavy rains was soaked up by the spongy plants and mucky soils of the pocosins and released slowly and evenly into surrounding creeks. The rain trickled through stands of *Juncus roemerianus*, a grayish, needle-tipped marsh grass that looks like porcupine quills. Eventually the rain seeped into shallow tidal creeks—the primary nurseries for most of North Carolina's shrimp, crabs, and fish.

On a hot July afternoon there is little sign of activity in Stumpy Point, a town of salt-box houses, grassy yards, and neat cords of firewood. The community's only road loops from Highway 264 along the banks of the sound, past the Holiness Church Incorporated, the Rock Church, the Shiloh United Methodist Church. Around a bend the road parallels a narrow, black canal and ends at a tackle shop and boat ramp. The town is typical of the conservative, rural communities of the North Carolina mainland. Residents stock their freezers with fish, shellfish, venison, and wild duck. They heat with wood stoves, grow their own vegetables, and look to the Lord to provide.

Since the mid-1970s the prayers of Stumpy Point watermen have frequently gone unanswered. Most years the quantities of oysters and shrimp have fallen far short of what the town needs to prosper. But in this summer of 1985 the shrimp have filled the nets and holds of Pamlico Sound trawlers in numbers not seen for more than thirty years. Boats that normally bring in between a hundred and three hundred pounds of shrimp have returned to the docks with up to a thousand pounds. Even on the worst days the catch has been double that of a less prolific year. The sudden turn of fortune, H.O. Golden believes, is due largely to an unusually dry spring, when little rain water cascaded out of the canals that have been cut deep into the pocosin swamps.

"The fishing still isn't what it could be if we didn't have such a problem with the water," Golden said, settling back in an easy chair and taking a long draught from a towering glass of tea. Now in his sixties, he talks slowly and rather softly. His opinions on the water quality of Pamlico Sound are spoken with no trace of the argumentative. As he sees things, it is an indisputable fact that the fishing communities of Pamlico Sound have suffered great losses ever since timber and paper companies drained the swamps on the jagged peninsula that lies between the Albemarle and Pamlico sounds.

Golden lives with his wife and daughter in a wood-frame house next to the Methodist Church. In midsummer a thick cedar tree, laden with pale blue berries, shades a swing in the front yard, and hummingbirds stretch their ruby throats to sip from a glass feeder. Across the street the muddy waves of Stumpy Point Bay slap a grassy bank. I had stopped to see Golden on a Sunday, which in Stumpy Point is still a day of rest.

We sat sipping tea, ensconced in overstuffed chairs. There was a flatness to our conversation as Golden described the forty-year deterioration of Pamlico Sound. He has repeated the story so often to reporters and state officials that it has lost some of its punch, even though it is a story of financial woe. During stretches of silence a clock ticked loudly from somewhere deep within the house.

Golden had not planned to shrimp this year, but decided to rig his nets when his neighbors began predicting a banner catch. "I used to shrimp nearly every year," he said. "I quit around—I guess it was somewhere around 1975—because it got to the point where it was hardly worth taking your boat out. Used to be we'd all get a good portion of our yearly income from shrimping."

How much shrimp could he catch in the 1940s?

"The boats were much smaller back then. In nineteen forty-five most of the trawlers were only about thirty-two, maybe thirty-six feet with light-power gas engines and flat nets about forty feet long. You could average a thousand pounds a day without much trouble. Some days you'd get twenty boxes—two thousand pounds. Some of these boats nowadays are a hundred and twenty feet, with four nets eighty feet long. I'm fishing a forty-foot boat this year, and I'm averaging about five to eight boxes a day. My best day I got twenty boxes. That's trawling daylight to dark."

Stumpy Point residents earned a reasonable living from

shell-fishing through the 1950s, Golden continued. But in the early 1960s the West Virginia Pulp and Paper Company cut hundreds of miles of canals and roads through the inland swamps, harvesting pulpwood for their mills. "That hurt the area more than anything. At the time it was done, of course, we didn't have any idea of the way ecology worked and how the runoff from those canals might affect the small marine animals. Then in the seventies a lot of land was drained for agriculture, and more canals were cut. The canals go back into the swamps for miles. Let me show you something, if I can find it."

He got up, crossed the room to a tall hutch, and took out a cardboard box that overflowed with papers. "I've been collecting this stuff for years," he muttered, pulling out documents and sorting them into piles. "Here." He spread a creased map of the peninsula on the kitchen table. The land was incised with thin straight lines that reached far into the interior of the peninsula. Each line represented a canal. The creeks where they emptied were some of the richest fish and shellfish nurseries in the state. "You can see how all the storm water from way inland comes out right around here," he said. "In the spring the amount of runoff is quite high. And that's when the development of the small marine animals is most critical."

He stopped talking suddenly, as if mulling over his next thought. The clock ticked on. "You always hate to see someone else having a bad time of it," he said at length, "but we're catching shrimp this year because we haven't had much rain. I know the farmers are suffering, and I'm sorry. But fishermen, we're not like farmers. A farmer has to put a lot into something to get something out of it; but nature would take care of us by itself if the water were just okay."

In Pamlico Sound, where the fresh water of rivers meets the skirt of the salt sea, a settling-out occurs like that when oil and water are combined in a jar. The dense salt water sinks to the bottom, leaving a fresh film on top. The layers mix some with the stirring of tides, but in years of little rain the salty wedge pushes far into the marshes, increasing the range of shrimp, crabs, and other estuarine animals. Conversely, when storm runoff pulses into a brackish creek, it abruptly changes the level of salinity, a key factor in the survival of marine organisms and fish. The stress caused by freshwater intrusion is greatest in the spring, when the marshes and creeks are filled with the young fish and shellfish of the year. If the young survive the influx they may be forced into deeper, more open water, where they become easy prey.

During the past ten years ecologists have come to suspect that the freshwater swamps known as pocosins play an integral role in controlling the flow of rainwater into coastal rivers and bays. Conservationist groups claim that in North Carolina pocosins are being cut, drained, and converted to farmland so quickly that the balance of life within Pamlico Sound is being altered be-yond repair. Many coastal fishermen echo Golden's complaint that their annual catches of fish and shellfish have decreased dramatically since the early 1960s. The farmers counter that the poorer fish and shellfish landings may have been caused simply by overfishing—a persuasive point, given that each year coastal fishermen use bigger boats and longer nets to catch as much sea-food as they possibly can.

Until recently pocosins were studied very little, in part be-cause the mucky soils and the thick cover of shrubs and vines make them difficult to explore. In the winter and spring—the wettest seasons—the surface soils are saturated, and mats of moss cover the lowest ground; but in the dryness of summer and fall, the water table drops, leaving a layer of spongy, air-filled soil. Depending on its elevation, a pocosin swamp may contain a rich variety of ferns, orchids, and insect-eating plants scattered among the bushes, or it may be dominated by squat pond pines and a uniform layer of evergreen shrubs.

Judging from the term they coined for the freshwater swamps, the Algonkian Indians must have had some understanding of how pocosins regulate the flow of water into brackish creeks. Most wetlands draw water from tidal flooding or from rivers and creeks that run through them. Pocosins, however, must catch and hold rainwater to nurture the moisture-loving plants in their midst. They do not drain directly into rivers or lakes, and they frequently have higher elevations than nearby waterways. Hence the name "swamp on a hill."

The possibility that extensive draining and clearing might affect the web of life within Pamlico Sound did not occur to the farming and timbering operations that first set out to develop the swamps of the Albemarle-Pamlico Peninsula. Indeed, early colonists viewed swamp drainage as a public service, since it was believed that escaping gases caused yearly outbreaks of malaria. Land had become scarce as settlers spread through Virginia and North Carolina, and by the 1780s speculators began to eye the peninsula's cedar swamps and pocosin bogs.

In 1784 a group of Edenton businessmen received permission from the state to drain Lake Phelps, twenty miles from the Albemarle Sound, and to establish rice paddies on the rich lake bed. The lake was surrounded by forests of white cedar and bald cypress so thick that it had not been discovered until 1755, fifty years after colonists first settled the area. The elevation of Lake Phelps was higher than the Scuppernong River to the northeast, and a canal dug by slaves enabled the rice farmers to flood and empty the paddies with ease. During the same era, the governments of Virginia and North Carolina financed the dredging of a canal between the Chesapeake Bay and the Albemarle Sound. The new waterway drained much of the Great Dismal Swamp just south of the Virginia state line.

Small farms began to dot the Albemarle-Pamlico Peninsula in the early 1800s as settlers discovered that the organic muck within the swamps continued to produce abundant crops year after year—well after the sandy soil of the coastal plain had worn out. After the abolition of slavery, however, the coastal region came to depend increasingly on timbering as an economic mainstay. Virgin stands of cypress and cedar—many filled with trees six feet or more in diameter—had been cut in the Great Dismal Swamp, but small stands remained on the Albemarle-Pamlico Peninsula. Timbering companies had the resources to drain the swamps and float the lumber out. From the 1880s through the first third of the twentieth century, logging crews cut thousands of acres of wet, vine-filled woods. A portion of the cleared land was converted to agriculture. As reforestation came into practice in the 1930s, the timber interests sold their holdings to paper companies for the cultivation of second-growth pine.

Three decades later the West Virginia Pulp and Paper Company began to harvest timber from several tracts in Dare, Tyrrell, and Washington counties. The company was not the only enterprise to dig canals and build roads during the 1960s, but its operations were the most extensive. Its officials talked of cultivating cedar on the cleared acres, and the canals were cut partly for future irrigation. But the reforestation plans never materialized. Gradually shrubs, sweetgum, and pond pine filled in the empty fields.

Occasionally in hot, dry weather, fires started in the cleared fields, and abandoned logs served as kindling. During major fires the peat soil exposed by the lowered water table smoldered for months at a time. When at last the fires went out, the spores of ferns and wetland forbs—dormant since the land was drained—sprouted and began to spread.

A map of the canals cut before 1974 on the Albemarle-Pamlico Peninsula shows only scattered patches of open, undrained land. An intricate system of waterways dominates the landscape. Along the banks of Lake Mattamuskeet, to the southwest of Stumpy Point, canals slice diagonally into swamps every quarter- to half-mile. If the elliptical lake were a giant eye, the canals would be crow's-feet—a set of wrinkles so close together that the skin of the earth has been marred beyond repair. All empty, ultimately, into Pamlico Sound.

In late 1972 stirrings in a distant corner of the globe set in motion a chain of events that eventually would affect the estuaries of North Carolina. That winter a warm equatorial ocean current known as El Niño wandered unusually far south along the west coast of South America, displacing the cold Peruvian current. The current disrupted the ocean's nutrient flow and dev-astated the year's catch of anchovies in Peru, the largest pro-ducer of protein meal in the world. Near the same time, the U.S. Department of Agriculture agreed to sell major quantities of grain to the Soviet Union and Eastern Bloc countries, opening a new market for American farmers. As the price of soybeans and grain rose, farmers searched for more acres to put into production.

The following year Westvaco—formerly the West Virginia Pulp and Paper Company—ran an advertisement in the *Wall Street Journal* offering for sale its entire holdings on the Albemarle-Pamlico Peninsula. The ad attracted the interest of Malcom P. McLean, a Winston-Salem, North Carolina, trucking and ship-ping magnate and a director of R.J. Reynolds Industries. Within a year McLean purchased 289,000 acres from Westvaco and be-gan negotiations to buy another 85,000 acres adjacent to Westvaco land. By 1975 he owned a third of the peninsula.

McLean's was the largest of several new agricultural domains owned by major corporations and wealthy investors. In 1972, 35,000 acres known as Mattamuskeet Farms was purchased by the John Hancock Mutual Insurance Company and American Cyanamid, a New Jersey chemical manufacturer. Two years later Japanese and Italian interests bought more than 50,000 acres on the peninsula, and in 1977 John Hancock purchased an addi-tional 26,000 acres of cleared land. In a matter of years, a region of impenetrable forests and shrubs gave way to a patchwork of farm fields, any one of which stretched for five or six miles. The new landscape was one of expensive tractors, combines, and irri-gation systems, of food production on a corporate scale. The hold-ings gave investors a hedge against spiraling inflation and, when the farms lost money in their first seasons, provided substantial tax write-offs.

McLean's plan was to begin with row crops, then raise cattle and hogs in herds large enough to rival the great midwestern ranches. He named his empire First Colony Farms. Some of his land was already cultivated, but thousands of acres were covered with swampy vegetation. A tract of cleared land just south of

Lake Phelps contained mucky soils and submerged trunks and limbs that could ruin large tractors and harvesting machines. But could such rich deposits of peat be put to other uses? As corn and feedgrains appeared in other fields, McLean's staff tinkered with the notion of harvesting peat to burn for generating electricity or making methanol fuel.

When a ton of moist peat burns, it produces between six and seven million BTUs of heat, substantially more than the output of wood. Peat gives off less ash and sulphur than coal, but it is much bulkier; to save on shipping costs, it must be burned near the harvest site. In 1977 and 1978 administrators at First Colony Farms approached several electric utilities about building a peat-fired generating plant on fifteen thousand acres of McLean's land just south of Lake Phelps. Meanwhile, First Colony engineers experimented with techniques to drain the peat fields, shred the submerged wood, and dry the mucky soil.

In 1979 Peat Methanol Associates, a company formed by an energy corporation and a chemical manufacturer, approached McLean with a proposal to convert peat to methanol fuel. The associates offered to build a conversion plant large enough to process a half-million tons of peat a year, enough to yield about sixty million gallons of methanol. The plant was expected to employ eleven hundred people during construction and three hundred once it began making fuel. As the first peat-mining project on the East Coast, the investors eventually received a promise of $465 million in loan guarantees and price supports from the Synthetic Fuels Corporation, a federal agency started under President Jimmy Carter.

"When PMA started talking about all this," said First Colony Farms president, Hobart Truesdell, "they elicited all kinds of comment from people in the area, and nobody seemed to object. PMA seemed very organized. They held little coffee groups in various towns to talk to people about the proposal, and no one seemed to have much negative to say. They informed the commissioners in the various counties that might be affected. They were left with the impression that the communities here wanted the money and jobs the project would bring into the area. Then in the summer of eighty-one [Governor] Jim Hunt announced the program and endorsed it. All of a sudden people became interested. This was a new fuel, and there was a lot of concern awakening about pocosin destruction. Well, things got kind of tied up after that."

The problems that delayed Peat Methanol Associates grew from seeds sown nearly a decade before, when the North Carolina Division of Marine Fisheries decided to take routine samples of shellfish and fish in primary nurseries. In 1973 state biologists began running test trawls once a month in marshes and creeks where young marine animals were believed to be the most abundant. The organisms collected were counted, measured, and thrown back, and the data was recorded for comparison with later years.

Most of North Carolina's primary nurseries are concentrated on the western edge of Pamlico Sound, and are rimmed with expanses of black needle rush. The sheltered creeks and quiet marshes appear as pristine as any coastline in the East. But by 1976 the biologists had found relatively few marine animals in waters that should have been teeming with life. The creeks that seemed the least productive were those nearest the mouths of drainage ditches and canals.

In 1977 biologists Robert A. Jones and Terry M. Sholar of the state Division of Marine Fisheries selected three nursery areas in eastern Pamlico Sound and set out to examine the waters' salinity and the distribution of young organisms, especially brown shrimp. The state had recently passed a regulation to protect the estuaries where commercially valuable species begin to mature. Two of the sites Jones and Sholar selected were major outlets for canals that siphoned runoff from farmland and from Lake Mattamuskeet. If the area had not been ditched, most of the runoff would have flowed north into the Alligator River and eventually into the nearly fresh Albemarle Sound. A third site was buffered by an undrained pocosin swamp.

From 1977 through 1980 Jones and Sholar took bottom salinity readings and trawl samples in the study areas three times a week during May, June, and July. In late summer and fall they reduced their sampling to twice a week. They also gathered data on meteorological elements that can affect the shape of the estuarine salt wedge, such as tides, rainfall, and the direction and speed of the wind. An area that was unaffected by drainage canals was added to the study in 1978.

The samples confirmed what the biologists had come to suspect. Creeks left in their natural state had a very stable level of salinity, and they contained substantial populations of young shrimp, blue crabs, southern flounder, and spot. But in the creeks that received runoff from drainage canals, "the salinity patterns were extremely erratic, to the point where they had to be affecting the young of the year," Sholar recalled. "One year when it was unusually dry we did find a good number of shrimp in the altered sites. But in wetter years there was a statistically noticeable difference in productivity."

The study suggested that some of the state's most important seafood nurseries—areas that nurture as much as 80 percent of the state's yearly commercial catch—might be affected drastically by runoff from drained land. "There are all sorts of opinions on what this means, but they're still just opinions," Sholar said. "We don't have any solid data to show that the numbers of mature flounder or crabs or shrimp have definitely dropped off since the peninsula was ditched and drained. This was very much a preliminary study. But it found that, yes, the drainage ditches have impacts we need to look at more closely."

In 1981, the same year Jones and Sholar published their findings, Duke University ecologist Curtis J. Richardson edited a book of scholarly papers on pocosins. The book was the first attempt by scientists to examine the role of pocosin swamps in the coastal ecosystem, and it raised serious concerns about their widespread destruction. In the lead article, Richardson and two other Duke University ecologists noted that nearly 70 percent of the pocosins in the United States are found within North Carolina. By comparing a 1962 study of pocosins with satellite photographs taken during 1979, they examined the pattern of land clearing and development on the Albemarle-Pamlico Peninsula. They concluded that a third of the region's pocosins had been cleared completely and that an additional 36 percent were either partially developed or were owned by companies that would very likely clear them. Only 5 percent of the bogs lay within state and federal preserves.

The study's findings dismayed many coastal scientists, and they were reported widely in North Carolina newspapers and magazines. Although the figures would be disputed later, they became a rallying cry for conservationists, even as Peat Methanol Associates pressed on with their plans to mine peat.

In January 1983 three environmental activists came to Stumpy Point to tell fishermen about the plans to mine peat from the First Colony tract. Perhaps the most persistent of the group was Todd Miller, a resident of the small community of Ocean and the lone staff member of a new nonprofit corporation called the North Carolina Coastal Federation. The federation had been incorporated the previous year to fill what its founders viewed as a serious gap between scientific research, public policy, and the awareness of watermen and coastal residents. "There were a lot of citizens up and down the coast who were active on certain issues but who weren't really working with each other," Miller said. "Our idea was to have the federation act as a kind of clearinghouse that could make citizens groups more effective."

For nearly a month Miller and two friends spent the bulk of their time talking to the watermen of western Pamlico Sound about the plans to mine peat from First Colony Farms. Miller suspected the independent-minded fishermen of the area would be reluctant to join a cause. His fears were quickly realized. "The first week was pretty bad. We'd talk to people and they'd act interested, but you knew they weren't going to tell the first person about it. They felt that First Colony had done whatever it wanted for so long, things just weren't going to change. But after people found out the federal government had promised almost a half-billion dollars to back up the peat-mining project, it wasn't hard to get them involved."

Within a few months residents of Stumpy Point had organized a lobbying committee and begun soliciting support from surrounding towns. At a meeting in April with the state Environmental Management Commission, more than six hundred commercial fishermen voiced objections to the peat-mining plan. Their greatest concern was that removing the peat would drastically increase the amount of storm runoff pulsing into the sound through the drainage canals. They dismissed as unbelievable claims by engineers that a pumping system would have the capacity to control overflow from even the heaviest rains. And they objected to plans by Peat Methanol Associates to farm the tract after the peat had been taken out. The amount of fertilizers and chemicals flowing downstream, they said, would only worsen the quality of estuarine waters.

The coastal fishermen were not the only people worried about the ecological impact of the First Colony plan. Early that spring a governor's task force of scientists and engineers had recommended that all peat-mining ventures be required to file a water-quality plan with the state. The task force members had echoed concerns that the peat-mining project would be unable to consistently control the flow of storm runoff. Peat Methanol Associates hired a Gainesville, Florida, engineering firm to draft the plan. In April 1983 the engineers recorded unusually high levels of mercury in a canal near the site where First Colony had run experiments on peat-mining techniques.

The findings halted further development, and in the fall of 1983 Peat Methanol Associates asked the federal government for increases in the project's price supports and loan guarantees. In the interim McLean's staff attempted to counter what they regarded as a rash of inaccurate publicity by hiring Philip S. McMullan, a Durham consultant, to write a documented study on land-clearing trends on the Albemarle-Pamlico Peninsula.

McMullan's hundred-page report, published in January 1984, asserted that the Richardson study on pocosin destruction was based on a number of faulty assumptions. The consultant argued, first, that Richardson had overestimated the amount of undisturbed pocosins that existed in 1962. He also concluded that, because the satellite maps did not show enough detail to distinguish between pocosin bogs and swampy woodlands, the Richardson study had greatly overestimated the rate at which pocosins were being cleared. Finally, he found that Richardson had underestimated the percentage of pocosin bogs owned by the public and by conservation groups.

But the McMullan study was issued too late to aid Peat Methanol Associates. Early in 1984 the Synthetic Fuels Corporation refused to grant the firm additional loan guarantees and price supports. In February of that year the investors announced that they were disbanding and would no longer pursue their plans to mine peat. The group's breakup left First Colony Farms with thousands of acres of untillable land.

One humid summer afternoon I stood ankle-deep in sphagnum moss as two graduate students stabbed a stainless-steel blade into the soft earth. Attached to the blade was a steel rod several yards long. By pushing on the rod the men could sink the blade to calculated depths and torque a crosspiece to cut out a plug of peat. All day they had been tromping the woods of the Dare County mainland to measure the depth and content of the peaty soil. Mud covered their jeans and hands, and their boots were immersed in a sinkhole of moss and peaty soup. As the blade was brought up to the surface, a third graduate student marked a plastic bag with the large numerals, "D3 6–6 1/2" (Dare County site three, six to six-and-half feet). The sharp edge, dripping with muck, was swung back to reveal a central chamber and a dense log of peat.

We were five miles southwest of Stumpy Point in a Carolina bay, an elliptical pocosin found on the Albemarle-Pamlico Peninsula. Dried sphagnum moss cracked and flaked like damp, decaying newsprint beneath my feet. Nearby, the thin plumes of ferns and the lime-green heads of pitcher plants nodded in the breeze. The pitchers had invaded an old bulldozer road known as the Bombardier Trail, where in 1977 rescue crews had searched fruitlessly for a downed plane and its pilot. We had taken advantage of the trail to hike a mile into the bog, scrambling through briars and scrub. Next to the path the pliant limbs of *Zenobia*, a hardy, waxy-leafed shrub, pressed together in a tight maze. The *Zenobia* reached only four feet in height; rolling densely across the low fields, it reminded me of the brush common on tundra and high-altitude meadows.

Beside me Lee Otte, a geologist from East Carolina University, fingered a bag of viscous brown peat. A few minutes before, the peat had been pulled up by the core sampler from three feet underground. Otte and three graduate students—Mark Purser, Dave Mallinson, and Chee Saunders—are scholars of both geology and botany, a combination that is particularly useful in pocosins, where vegetation trapped in peat begins to fossilize, leaving clues on the succession of plant life over thousands of years. In the following days they would sift through their samples and sieve out the seeds, stems, and root material within. Their findings would then be catalogued for a study on the evolution of plants within pocosins, marshes, and forests underlaid by peat.

In the past decade Otte has been in more of the state's pocosins than perhaps any other individual. Beginning in 1979 he and Roy Ingram, a professor at the University of North Carolina at Chapel Hill, conducted a statewide survey of peat deposits for the North Carolina Energy Institute. They found the thickest and most abundant deposits—as deep as twenty feet—to be in Dare County and the Croatan National Forest west of Morehead City. In 1981 Otte published a definitive study on the evolution and vegetation of North Carolina pocosins. During the study he attracted the help of Mallinson and Saunders. The men spent weeks chopping through six-foot stands of *Zenobia* to take samples of peat.

"If you can imagine walking headlong through somebody's hedgerow, that's something like what it required," Otte said. "In an hour we could cut a two-foot-wide trail for about a hundred feet. Think about what it would be like to take an hour to walk twice the length of your house. After eight hours of that we'd look like we had spent the day in a catfight. We talked to one old-timer down in the southeast corner of the state who had the best description of pocosins we've found. He said, 'It's so thick in there my hound dog has to back up to bark'."

That day we had already visited two other sites, a brackish marsh of sawgrass and a cool woodland of sweet gum, red maple, and bayberry. At each site the steel blade had been inserted into the ground at half-foot intervals, deeper and deeper until the peat had given way to a grayish strip of clay or sand. "We go until we hit bottom—the point at which the site was not a wetland," Otte said. "The deepest deposits are old creeks and riverbeds that have been backfilled by mud and peat. You can measure the peat depths at different spots and get a pretty good idea of what the area was like before the most recent sea-level rise."

From the second site in the interior of the Albemarle-Pamlico Peninsula we had driven east along Highway 64 and turned south toward Stumpy Point. The roads were rimmed by blackwater canals and a continuous rat's nest of scrubby branches. Before long we had reached a stretch of road marked with deep slits from bulldozer tread. The students had taken off through the brush, stepping high as the spongy moss sank under their weight. Otte— soft-spoken, long-legged, and thin—had paused to photograph a blooming pitcher plant, then had caught up with the others in a few easy strides. Now we were in one of the wettest and largest pocosins in the state. It is owned by First Colony Farms.

Purser jammed the peat sampler into the ground again and twisted the crosspiece, bringing up a plug of peat that was slightly browner than the last and full of small fibers, probably decaying wood. He stuck his finger in the sample, tasted it, and spit. "Got a ways to go," he said. I smeared a small bit of the sediment on my tongue. It was pure peat, smooth, slimy, and cool. The presence of gritty particles would have meant the sampler was nearing a layer of clay or sand.

"Look at this," Otte said, holding up two bags of peat. They were cool to the touch, as though they had been pulled out of an underground cave. The first, taken from a depth of a foot and a half, appeared black and dense next to the brown sample taken from three feet. "You have to look close to see a color change, but this is enough of a change for us to consider it significant."

"Do you think First Colony could ever get permits to mine this?" I asked. Shortly after the demise of Peat Methanol Associates, First Colony had announced new plans to mine peat and convert it to electricity.

"It's a prime peat area," Otte replied, "but I would hate to see them try to take the peat out. It's one of the most untouched pocosins in the state. The same with the pocosins in the Croatan National Forest. I think it's a different story with the land First Colony wants to mine near Lake Phelps. That area has already been damaged extensively. There should be white cedar on that land, but that was logged off a long time ago.

"I've got the same questions a lot of people have about mining peat. Is it worth risking a lot of ecological damage to generate a little more power? But geologists tend to look at natural cycles from a much larger time frame. We've already had so much ecological damage in this country from logging and farming and industrial development that I have a hard time singling out peat mining as the only culprit.

"First Colony may find out that it's too expensive to mine peat and do it right. Then what? Suppose the peat catches fire. To me it seems there's not much difference between mining the peat off and having a fire burn it off. The end result's the same. Then, if the land is left alone, it'll grow up with red maple or pocosin. In twenty years you won't be able to tell there was ever anything there."

A light breeze ruffled the bushes, as refreshing as a long, cool drink. Purser had just hit solid clay sediment at seven feet and was taking apart the rod. The students, still energetic, collected their gear and began roaming the small clearing, poking at pitcher plants and the tiny, hairy pods of sundews scattered through damp depressions in the moss. Another group might have found the terrain bleak, but to us the green leaves and waxy, white, bell-shaped flowers of the *Zenobia* had a subtle beauty beneath the deep-blue sky. Saunders, a dark-haired, talkative man with round wire glasses, stuffed the peat samples into the pockets of a field vest and turned to me before lunging back through a wall of brush. "Everyone else we know jogs for exercise," he joked, and disappeared.

"In the spring," Hobie Truesdell said, "on days with low humidity and winds out of the southwest, you're always out watching your land and you hope everyone else is watching theirs too, because you know there are going to be fires. Sometimes only twenty acres will burn. Sometimes we'll have a disaster."

We were sitting in the small aluminum building that serves as the office of First Colony Farms. Outside, a twelve-story grain silo overlooked miles of dusty earth planted with corn and beans. The silo is the only structure of size in the countryside south of Creswell, North Carolina, where incomes tend to be modest and the unemployment rate is frequently one of the highest in the state. On my drive from Manteo I had passed country homes with brick chimneys and broad porches, with swing sets on grassy lawns and ponies in fenced mud yards. Thirty miles from Manteo I had taken a side road south to where a wildfire had burned unchecked for two weeks the previous spring. In all, ninety-six thousand acres of swampland and farmland had been ravaged, and in areas of deep peat the soil continued to smolder. At the height of the blaze, the ash and smoke had traveled as far west as Rodanthe, carried eighty miles on ceaseless winds.

At First Colony Farms, the fires had destroyed about 600,000 tons of peat in the experimental mine fields but had been contained before reaching large fields of cultivated land. In midsummer the countryside near the silo showed no sign that anything had ever been amiss. Fields of corn stretched for miles in three directions. The pale-yellow tassels stood stiffly erect, rows fading to ridges, ridges rolling toward a single band of trees on a dusty, distant horizon. Rough gravel roads and interconnecting canals sliced through the fields. In Truesdell's office a large map showed the tract and several around it to have been drained for the first time in the 1830s.

As president of the farm, Truesdell does not have an abundance of time. Nevertheless, for several months he has met with virtually anyone who has questions about the new plans to mine peat, convert it to electricity, and sell it to local utilities. The plan bears similarities to the one proposed by Peat Methanol Associates, but Truesdell believes it is fairer to the state's fishermen and is environmentally sound. A short man with sandy blond hair and a rather high-pitched voice, he routinely provides a long-winded and detailed explanation of the peat-mining plan. The day I arranged to see him he talked for nearly three hours, moving smoothly through peninsula history to the mechanics of peat mining and its effects on water quality, air pollution, and wildlife. The entire mining procedure, he said, was designed to have the least possible impact on the environment. Moreover, the project engineers revised their plans several times to alleviate new concerns voiced by fishermen and conservationists.

If the state grants the necessary permits, engineers will construct a fifteen-hundred-acre lake to contain storm runoff and the water that would have been absorbed by the peat. At least some of the water will be used to cool generators in the plant. Whatever does not evaporate will be pumped slowly into canals —a vast improvement, Truesdell maintained, over the pulses of rain that now cascade into Pamlico Sound. "We can buffer the peak flows in every case. Our modeling has shown us that," he said. "The fishermen have a very legitimate concern about what this will do to their nurseries. Their livelihood is at stake. But if we can control the amount of runoff in heavy rains, and if we can give them some fresh water when there's too little, we're doing them a favor."

Mining is a misleading term for the procedure used to harvest peat. Instead of digging caverns in the earth, the "miners" scrape away layers of soil and turn it to be dried. The peat is excavated inch-by-inch over such large distances that it is difficult to discern any change in elevation at all, even in fields where several feet of soil have been removed.

Under the long-range plan, no more than eighteen inches of peat will be excavated in a year. It will be mixed with limestone or sand and burned in a fluidized boiler that recycles the smoke as many as twenty times to remove much of the ash and sulfur given off by conventional boilers. As the peat is harvested, strips of trees will be planted through portions of the site for wildlife. Eventually the mined fields will be planted with timber. Although the company had originally intended to farm the land, officials changed their plans after receiving complaints from coastal fishermen.

From Truesdell's point of view, the end result will be not much different than if engineers had set about to mitigate the problems caused by two centuries of land clearing and draining; not only will water quality improve but the mining will give area residents an income from a tract of land that would otherwise simply burn.

"We've lost the equivalent of one-and-a-half million dry tons of peat—about ten percent of our resource—from wildfires," he said. "The ash from those fires either went up in the air or precipitated out into the water. Last spring there were hawks cruising the edge of the burning fields to pick off small mammals as they fled. Twenty percent of the deer population died outright, and some deer were burned so badly they were deformed. It seems to me that when you have something like that happen, you have an environmental catastrophe.

"I've had people tell me that all the ditching and draining that's gone on here has caused these fires. That's ridiculous. It may be true that fires are more common now. But there are records of fires from way back. Peat soil burns. In a hundred and fifty years the peat that's out there now won't be there. It will either have eroded away or it will have burned. What we're trying to do is use it constructively. And we think this is a constructive use. Let's take a ride." He stood abruptly, pulled on a jacket, and walked out.

A light drizzle was falling, and in the grayness of the afternoon a dull glare had settled over the fields. We got in a late-model Jeep and set out across washboard gravel roads, raising plumes of dust even in the rain. Truesdell continued to talk but changed the subject to the friendliness of the area's residents. "I've always liked the country," he said. "It's a good place to raise kids, a good place to get to know your neighbors. We'd like to give the people here some more jobs." He turned down a road that was blocked by a gate and got out to unlock it.

Beyond were fields of grated coffee-colored soil. Shallow ditches, each cut in the shape of a V, ran the width of the field before us. This was the experimental site where First Colony had begun excavating peat. The damp earth was full of twisted chunks of wood, and in places large limbs and roots had been raked into piles as high as twenty feet.

In the middle of the field sat several large pieces of machinery, idle in the rain. Attached to a large combine was a wheel six feet in diameter with gaping sawlike teeth that could pulverize wood buried in the top fourteen inches of peat. "Between ten and fifteen percent of the peat weight is submerged wood," Truesdell said. "We can't pick it all out, so we incorporate it by shredding it as much as we can."

He drove slowly, silent for the first time. For some reason I found myself thinking of strip mines and mountainsides left bare of timber by clear-cutting crews. The peat fields were not as ugly as all that; they looked more like a large construction site, a future parking lot, than anything else. But they were dismayingly empty of lush, organic life. Once this was a swampy forest so thick that it took settlers fifty years to discover a seven-mile-long lake in its midst. Some conservationists believe that if the peat fields were abandoned the canals that drained them would back up with litter and the bogs would slowly return. It struck me as somewhat ironic that it had required the utmost in modern technology to transform a swampland into a desert.

I stared out the window, trying to imagine the site as a dense, vine-filled forest or a pocosin bog with rolling hedges of *Zenobia*. "What grew here before it was cleared?" I asked.

"A little pond pine, some fetter-bush, nothing very tall. It had burned, remember, so not much was left."

There was nothing else to see. Truesdell turned the truck and circled back through the gate. A few minutes later he detoured down a side road and pulled into the driveway of a house on the banks of Lake Phelps. The straight, blackish-gray trunks of pond pines rose from a dark-red earth. The rain fell more quickly now, and the surface of the lake, lusterless and gray, wriggled beneath the pelting drops.

Inside the house Truesdell picked up a jar of dark crystals from a small living room table. The crystals resembled freeze-dried coffee. "This is where we put up our out-of-town guests," he said. "I just thought I'd give you this—it's milled peat. It originally had the consistency of grease."

As we drove back to the office, he said, "The argument that I'm making—and I'm making arguments to you—is that I think we've come up with a program that's okay. But if you don't like the project, I want to know why. I'm not particularly interested in talking to someone who says, 'There's no way you're going to do anything but unmitigated harm. You are evil personified.' And no matter what we do, it seems some people are still going to feel that way."

The rain that drenched First Colony Farms fell also on Stumpy Point and western Pamlico Sound. For two days it continued unabated, muddying the marshy creeks and the waters of Stumpy Point Bay. By then, though, little damage could be done. The shrimp had moved south to deep water.

H.O. Golden will continue to speak out against peat mining as long as there remains a possibility that the projects can be blocked. Because of financial troubles at McLean Industries, First Colony's parent company, there is speculation that the farm will abandon its plans or, more likely, lease or sell its peat fields to an outside interest. In addition, a Chicago entrepreneur has asked the state to approve peat mining on a low tract of land southwest of Stumpy Point. The breakup of Peat Methanol Associates, which initially appeared to be a decisive victory, turned out to be only the first skirmish in a prolonged war. There are many who believe that eventually peat will be mined in North Carolina. But the Coastal Federation, the Stumpy Point Civic Association, and a coalition of other groups have sworn to fight the proposals from as many fronts as they can.

Since 1982 Todd Miller has seen his fledgling Coastal Federation blossom from a loosely organized group of friends to a small but potent lobbying force with an annual budget of $100,000. Before any peat mining is approved, Miller believes, the state should write a comprehensive management program to protect the waters of Pamlico Sound. Maryland and Virginia drafted a plan to limit agricultural and industrial runoff into the Chesapeake Bay after parts of the estuary were found to be depleted of oxygen. "The water quality in Pamlico Sound is already poor," Miller said. "It's been years since any big tracts of land have been stripped, and yet the nurseries have continued to deteriorate. We still don't know the extent of the damage that's been done. Why add to it?"

Golden is clearly tired of the fight. Although First Colony Farms has launched an extensive public relations campaign and made several concessions, he and his neighbors remain convinced that the peat mines can only hurt the ecology of the sound. The state has adopted regulations that will use mathematical models to examine the environmental stress caused by each mining venture. Golden flatly dismisses claims that the models will protect the primary nurseries from further harm. "It doesn't matter if all of their fancy models are right or not," he said, "because once these operations get rolling they can do pretty much what they want. They can make it look real pretty on paper, but the state doesn't have the finances to keep as close a check on things as it should."

Even if peat mining were outlawed throughout North Carolina, even if the peat fields and farmlands were abandoned, as the most radical conservationists think they should be, Golden believes the Pamlico Sound fisheries will never be as rich as they were when he married and moved to Stumpy Point. "There are lots of sources of pollution—pulp mills and factories, a phosphate plant in Aurora—it would all have to be cleaned up. The estuaries just can't flush all the pollution out."

From my house on the other side of the sound, the controversy over peat mining seems distant and futile, one of those dilemmas with too many facets to be resolved to anyone's satisfaction. It is tempting to forget about it, although the effects of the mining, if there are any, will also play havoc with the commercial fishermen of Hatteras Island.

It seems to me the dilemma hangs on two diametric, dearly held, and irreconcilable beliefs: first, that the spread of pollution is unstoppable and bound to wreck the lives of honest, hardworking people who depend on nothing more than the cycle of the seasons; and second, that technology has advanced so far it can reweave the fragile web of ecology, and still turn a profit. Extreme positions, but they are classics of twentieth-century life. The questions they raise affect lives and livelihoods in every nook and cranny of the globe.

6

𝒯HE BACKYARD MARSH

A FEW HUNDRED yards west of Highway 12, Hatteras Island ends in jigsaw lobes of marsh grass and thick, slippery mud. This rim of land is flat, its top overswept by waves, its base undercut by the back-and-forth rustlings of Pamlico Sound. In places the marsh slides gradually into crescents of sand and down to the wave-ridged bed of the sound. But most of the western edge drops off abruptly, a meandering, two-foot bank that bows first to the west and then to the east, as jagged and fickle as if it had been cut out with a knife.

One warm spring afternoon I sat on a small rock in back of my house. The rock was near the edge of a marshy point that bulged farther into the sound than any point within a quarter-mile. Around me were the blunt stems of *Spartina alterniflora*, a lush salt marsh cordgrass that had been shorn off the previous winter by a layer of ice. Farther back the sediment was obscured beneath windrows of *Spartina patens*, the saltmeadow hay that covers the island's tall, sloping dunes and grows on less frequently flooded terrain.

From my seat on the rock I could examine the ground in some detail. It was the color of chocolate—smooth, slick, and soft enough to hold the footprint of a gull. Triangular patches of a flossy green weed grew close to the rock but disappeared at the edge of the bank. Occasionally I heard the gurgle of water seeping through cracks. Nothing much seemed to be going on around me, yet I was in the midst of one of the most productive ecological settings on the face of the earth. Scientists estimate that an acre of salt marsh produces between five and ten tons of leaves and stems a year, nearly as much as an acre of wheat that has been genetically engineered to grow quickly. And that is only the vegetable matter. Throughout the shallow waters, the puddles, and the slick sediments of the marsh are billions of tiny worms, crustaceans, lichens, and algae, some with life spans so short they do not live to see the rise and fall of a single tide.

I had discovered the marshy point only an hour before, after weeks of searching for a path through the wax myrtle and briar in back of my house. Many of the islands off the southeast coast are lined with wide marshes, where cordgrass stretches for acres. On Hatteras Island, however, woody thickets press the cordgrass into a single thin zone on the western shore. Several times I had tried unsuccessfully to cut a path from the house through myrtle and poison ivy. Finally I decided to explore the terrain off a pothole-filled road a half-block to the south.

Past the Rodanthe Community Center—once a single-room schoolhouse—the road ended at two fish houses and a string of docks built on a creek. Cube-shaped wire crab pots were stacked like building blocks on the road edge, cutting off the only route to the marsh south of the creek. To the north a muddy set of tire ruts wound into a clearing filled with oil cans, rotten boards, and rusty cars. Not nice walking, but passable. I picked my way around refrigerators, stoves, piles of wood, and cascades of broken glass. My unexpected approach scattered three cats that had been sunning themselves on the hood of a corroded Chevrolet.

In the midst of the junkyard sat a pitted school bus that had once served as somebody's home. Tattered curtains flapped in broken windows, and a plywood door creaked in the breeze. A sandy road gave me an easy path through the debris, but it was spooky to walk among cars and appliances abandoned by people I didn't know. The road ended in a V-shaped clearing hedged by a single row of myrtle shrubs. I stepped over a mangled bicycle, pushed past a myrtle branch, and found my backyard marsh.

A narrow beach ran north for thirty yards and ended in the marshy table that jutted into Pamlico Sound. Curled around the inland edge of the beach was a ridge of dried, stringy eelgrass that compressed beneath my weight. I stepped onto the soft mud of the marsh and walked out to the point. Most of it was covered with swirls of saltmeadow hay, with the kinked, red and green stems of glasswort interspersed. The point was narrow but untouched. Beyond, the marsh cut sharply to the east, then extended west in a sweeping emerald arc. I brushed the mud off the rock, sat down, and stretched in the late afternoon sun. I had found a spot where I could settle in and, even better, where I could return to watch the seasons of the marsh.

I looked west to the empty horizon. On either side of me the bank cut sharply inland, so that I was surrounded by water on three sides. The sound spilled over the edge with soft lapping noises, like waves slapping the bow of a moving boat. With nothing but blue water in front of me, I felt as though I were moving west against the tide, afloat on a small mudberg.

Near the edge of the point the ground curled toward the water as if on the verge of collapse. The mud was mottled with the round burrows of fiddler crabs, but the crabs did not appear. A school of minnows started at my shadow and swam off, flashing silvery sides. The whorled, bluish shells of marsh periwinkles clung to the stems of cordgrass, just out of reach of the tide. A fly buzzed around my head. Another month and the mosquitoes and greenheads would be out in force. I yawned and stood up to leave.

Before stepping down to the beach I leaned over the bank and picked a leaf from a cluster of plants, probably sea lettuce, that waved in the water below. A feathered red weed swayed nearby. I broke off a piece of that as well, sticking both in my shirt pocket for a closer look at home.

I did not remember the weeds until hours later, when I was sitting at the kitchen table with several books about the salt marsh. I pulled the thin strands of vegetation from my shirt, disappointed to find them wrinkled and limp. The green weed was almost certainly sea lettuce, but it looked far less attractive on my kitchen table than it had in the sound. The red weed was so badly wilted I had no hope of identifying it, at least not while it was dry. I filled a glass with tap water and put both plants in, stirring with a finger as I flipped through a book to find a drawing of sea lettuce. I looked back at the weeds for a second, then dropped the book and leaned close to the glass, astonished.

The water swarmed with life. Planktonic animals with antennae and many pairs of legs swam around the weeds, which fanned out and swayed slowly back and forth. The animals were mere specks, far too small to identify without magnification. They moved in a cloud from the top of the glass to its base, lurching against the sides.

I cornered one of the organisms with a spoon, scooped it up, and arranged it on a glass slide. My only microscope was a short copper tube with a small mirror, and through its lens I saw a fuzzy tangle of limbs. I adjusted the focus. The animal began to kick and swim, moving in and out of the range of the lens, but after several minutes I could make out two sets of antennae and at least four sets of legs. I thumbed eagerly through a field guide. Assuming they were all the same—and how would I ever tell?— the animals in the glass might be any of a hundred marine invertebrates. At least I could try to narrow the choices. The animal on the slide had large black eyes, and its clear, fragile body curled up like a shrimp. Could it be a bent mysid shrimp? Probably not, since they live in the ocean. Besides, its back legs looked too long to be a shrimp. Was it an amphipod? That seemed likely, but what kind? Not a four-eyed amphipod, since it had a single pair of eyes. Not a digger amphipod, since it did not have a pair of bulky front legs.

I looked at the glass. The animals had reached the bottom and were swarming back to the top. Several bumped against the water's surface, as if trying to catapult into the air. It occurred to me suddenly that they might be a form of swimming larvae. Would all these things turn into mosquitoes? I grabbed a lid and clamped it over the rim of the glass. Whatever the creatures were, they were not going to take wing and bite me in the middle of the night.

Mosquitoes, ticks, black flies, deer flies, snakes, snapping turtles. Of the different terrains along the coast, the salt marsh, with its roster of biting creatures, is widely considered the least hospitable. Even without the hazards of insects and reptiles, tidal marshes are full of sucking mud, slippery algae, foot-slicing oysters, and rotten, sulfurous smells. Little wonder, then, that until the 1950s they were considered useful only as sources of shellfish and convenient places to dump trash. This perception changed slowly as ecologists became aware of the role marshes play in adding nutrients to the marine food chain and nurturing young marine animals. Nevertheless, after thirty years of constant study no one is really sure how the saltmarsh ecosystem works.

Perhaps the most influential work on tidal marshes was published in 1962 by John Teal, a marine biologist at the celebrated laboratory at Sapelo Island, Georgia. Teal's study concluded that the leaves and stems of the dominant *Spartina* species are major sources of carbon, one of several nutrients critical in the development of plants and animals. He found not only that *Spartina* marshes are unusually productive but that about half the carbon they produce is "fixed" by bacteria—that is, transformed into organic carbon that can be digested by the fauna of the marsh. The carbon, which is either dissolved or contained in small particles of decaying matter, is flushed into adjoining sounds and bays. Eventually some of the nutrient even spills into the ocean and enables planktonic animals to grow and reproduce.

Teal's results suggested that there might be dire consequences to dredging and filling salt marshes, which were then being developed at an alarming rate. If his findings were true, the widespread destruction of marshes conceivably could affect life deep within the sea. The study added weight to the emerging sentiment for preserving wetlands in their natural states, even in areas of high population density.

The only problem with Teal's early carbon-export theory is that no one has ever been able to verify it. After twenty-five years and hundreds of studies, the only indisputable conclusion is that the food webs within marshes are far more complex than Teal ever dreamed. In addition to changes in salinity, the plants and animals must adapt to the muddiness or clearness of the water, the speed of the tide, and the flux of chemical compounds like hydrogen sulfide. Rather than carbon into surrounding waters, some tidal marshes may actually consume more of the nutrient than they produce. And biologists are still not sure how much *Spartina* is consumed by animals and algae and how much is left to decay.

When a plant produces new growth, the shoots either die or are eaten by insects and animals—the first link in what biologists call the grazing food chain. Dead plants are set upon by bacteria, which convert the stringy stems, leaves, and roots to detritus, a source of food for some invertebrates, including many of the animals that live among the seaweeds in a tidal marsh. A single particle of detritus might be eaten and digested several times, until the organic carbon in the plant dissolves and is dispersed with the tide. Teal's study concluded that, in a Georgia marsh, grazing organisms consumed only 10 percent of the annual *Spartina* growth. The remaining 90 percent simply died, providing a large amount of vegetation for the detrital food chain.

Scientists have since come to believe that a significant portion of plant matter is grazed upon by the algae of the marsh, which Teal did not consider in his study. Nevertheless, detritus feeders occupy a significant niche in the marsh ecosystem, voraciously consuming the remains of plants and each other. The animals I had brought home in my pocket seemed to be detritus eaters; I could see the largest ones stuffing limp, brown particles into their mouths. But my tap water was too fresh for them. Within twelve hours everything but the sea lettuce had died and sifted to the bottom of the jar like brown, soggy crumbs.

I returned to the marsh the next day, this time with a glass flour canister. It was again late afternoon, and the wind had shifted to the northeast, pushing the sound away from the marsh. No waves slapped against the mudberg; instead, the receding water left the marsh bank exposed almost to its base. A scant two inches of clear, calm water covered the sandy bed of the sound. Wading out from the narrow beach, I tipped the mouth of the canister beneath the surface, then picked several handfuls of sea lettuce and dropped them into the container. Once again the water inside began to swarm. I screwed on the lid and started for home. Whether the animals were larvae or adults, I would keep them alive as long as I could.

That day I ordered a hand magnifying lens from a biological supply company. A week later when the lens arrived, the animals in my canister had nearly doubled in size. To my relief none of them had taken wing or otherwise transformed. The stage in which I had collected them was apparently the final stage of their lives.

I unpacked the lens and pressed it against the side of the jar. One of the larger animals swam by sideways, its tiny legs kicking furiously. It landed on a leaf of sea lettuce and stopped. I could make out two sets of antennae and, after a long look, tiny, translucent claws on the two frontmost pairs of legs. I had to catch one of the animals and examine it on a slide before I could count five additional sets of legs. The animal's body was clear, with a dark intestinal track running through it. Turning it on its side, I counted seven body segments, each with a tiny spine on the back. I had preserved in alcohol one of the animals from my first trip to the marsh. The animals I had collected on the second trip seemed to be of the same species.

I devoted most of the next day to watching the animals in the canister, which occupied a prominent spot on my kitchen table. They swam energetically on their sides, clinging to leaves and scouring the bottom for food. They were undoubtedly a species of amphipod, with their soft claws and seven body segments, but I could not decide what kind. Another several days passed before it occurred to me that there is a type of amphipod, *Gammarus*, that is sometimes called "side swimmer" or, more commonly, "scud." Checking a field guide, I learned that the species of *Gammarus* found most often in brackish water has a series of tiny spines on its back; it lives in teeming colonies among rocks and seaweed. I had collected a jar full of scuds. What an ugly name for such an enticing creature.

The sea lettuce had begun to disintegrate by the time I had identified the animals that clung to its leaves. Now that I had discovered what they were, the scuds might be in danger of dying for lack of oxygen. Over the next week I watched in dismay as the sea lettuce crumbled into brown shreds and settled to the bottom of my makeshift aquarium. Yet the tiny animals gained weight and became even more active. After two weeks in captivity several were nearly an inch long—five times as long as when they were caught. The largest ones took to swimming around with smaller scuds cradled against their abdomens, two squirming, curling, shrimplike creatures bumped up against each other as tightly as they could fit.

My scud study was becoming part of a daily routine. Each afternoon I examined them as the late rays of sun slanted through the west kitchen window and illuminated the canister with a pure, white light. One day a large scud swam toward the surface of the water and began to curl and uncurl its body, writhing rhythmically, as if trying to wriggle out of its skin. After several minutes the animal uncurled a final time and released something, a series of dribbles, from the bottom of its abdomen. Immediately the dribbles split into tiny specks and began to swim. Baby scuds! But how had they been born? I had assumed the scuds would lay eggs if they ever reproduced. And I had certainly not expected them to reproduce in a canister where normally I keep whole wheat flour.

The following morning I drove to a library set up by naturalists at the national seashore office in Buxton. In a thick volume on invertebrate zoology I read that a male *Gammarus* will grab a female from behind and carry her beneath him for several days as part of their courtship. So. The scuds I had seen cradled together were preparing to mate. The couple separates briefly to allow the female to molt, then the sperm is swept into the ventral brood, a chamber in the female's belly, where the eggs are fertilized and where they hatch. A female *Gammarus* releases fifteen to fifty live young in dribbles, unfurling her body to expel them.

To this day the flour canister sits on my kitchen table, and the latest generation of scuds—the fourth, I think—spends its time feeding on the detritus that muddies the bottom, raking up particles with their antennae and continually stuffing their mouths. In the six months since I discovered the backyard marsh, I have added sound water to the flour canister three times to adjust for evaporation. Otherwise I have left the scuds to their own devices. In the absence of fish predators they reproduce at an accelerated rate and occasionally die in great numbers. Always a handful manage to survive and soon begin to prosper, swimming busily about on their sides, raking food into their mouths, munching and crunching on their brothers' remains. Scudville, I've come to call it.

Courtney Hackney pulled his pickup to the side of the road, turned off the engine, and reached for the thermos of coffee that never seemed to be far from his side. The road was a lightly trafficked two-lane highway that wound through piney woods, scattered marshes, and small housing developments. Hackney had parked at the edge of a bridge that spanned a marsh bisected by a murky, meandering creek. "Look at this—you can really tell it's tidal in here," he said. "This is one of the first places I bring my students to give them an idea of how quickly the vegetation can change when you get into an area that's flooded by brackish water."

An irregular band of vibrant cordgrass paralleled the creek, then gave way to *Juncus roemerianus*—the needle-tipped, blackish-gray rush of higher banks. In the distance stood scattered cypress trees, their branches kinked and twisted upward. The mosaic of plants was a classic example of the limitations imposed by the movement of tides. Where salt water flooded the marsh bank, nothing prospered except cordgrass; but just out of reach of the regular rise and fall of water, the rushes grew almost to the bank, tying up nutrients with which the cordgrass might expand its range. Under the gray mid-morning sky the marsh glistened with moisture and color. Even the normally dull rush stems were the rich tan of spring wheat, with scattered shoots of dark green and tips of black.

Hackney took a long sip of coffee and pointed upstream to where the creek narrowed and began a gentle arc. "See the line where that real tall stand of *Juncus* comes in?" he asked. "That area's under water occasionally, but probably only once or twice a month on the highest spring tides. Now we'll go look at some marsh that's completely tidal." He started the truck and pulled onto the road.

It was a day in early summer, and I was being treated to a tour of the salt marshes outside Wilmington, where the University of North Carolina has based a small but reputable marine biology department. Hackney, an estuarine ecologist at the university, had agreed to squire me into the expansive cordgrass marshes that back the barrier islands south of Cape Lookout. A wiry and talkative man, he manages to teach, attend conferences, take on consulting work, juggle numerous research projects, and grow prize-winning orchids in a greenhouse at his home.

As a scientist Hackney is insatiably curious, and he is more relaxed in a salt marsh than virtually anywhere else. Graduate students regard him as a notorious taskmaster, since each of his courses includes extensive field work and laboratory work. Halfway through the previous course, someone had taped a picture of a skeleton to a bookcase in a small office shared by several students. Underneath the picture the person had written, "This is the only survivor of Estuarine Ecology."

Hackney acknowledges that his courses are demanding, but he points out that estuaries and marshes are unusually complex systems, and he has difficulty understanding how biology students could fail to be intrigued by the life within them. "There's just so much we don't understand about shallow water communities," he said. "You can go out in the open ocean and in fifty miles you won't find as many organisms as you can collect in the mouth of one tidal creek." To him there are few panoramas more beautiful than an expanse of *Spartina alterniflora* broken only by creeks.

"One of the things about estuarine species is that they're adapted to being wiped out occasionally," he said. "You could literally kill every blue crab in North Carolina this year so none would spawn, and next year we'd have all the crabs we could catch. Their larvae are made to disperse, and they produce millions and millions of them. We can conceivably screw things up for ten years, and when we finally realize what we're doing wrong the organisms will all come back. But there is a limit.

"I grew up in Florida, in the lower Keys. When I was a kid we would go out and get as many spiny lobsters as we could eat. The same with green turtles. We'd go out on the beach at night during nesting season and just pick the one we wanted. With a limited number of people harvesting the resource, there was no way we could deplete it. But in a very short time the city of Key West expanded from a little settlement on part of the island to literally covering the entire island. I watched the fish and shellfish go from being abundant to being hard to find—you had to know where to look. There were just too many people vying for the same things. And they completely destroyed the resource.

"That's exactly what's happening in eastern North Carolina now. Five years ago when I first got to Wilmington, I could get a five-gallon bucket of clams in an hour and a half. Easily. And I could find them close to my house. I can go out now and search everywhere, even the most inaccessible places, and have a very difficult time filling a five-gallon container. There haven't been natural disasters that could account for that big of a change; it's just pressure from the increase in people. It's frightening. Eventually things are going to change, and change drastically."

We had reached a marina where the university had moored several small boats. Hackney parked near a shallow fiberglass skiff and pulled a salinometer, a seine net, and a paddle from the bed of the truck. "We'll probably never use this stuff, but we may as well take it along just in case we stumble on something interesting," he said.

We got into the skiff, and a few minutes later we were planing across the calm, turquoise waters of the Intracoastal Waterway toward Figure Eight Island. On Cape Hatteras the frequency with which salt marshes flood depends as much on the direction of the wind as the rise and fall of the tides, and saltmeadow hay and needle rush crowd almost to the banks of Pamlico Sound; but the coast south of Cape Lookout is exposed to a higher tidal range—the vertical distance by which the sea rises and falls—and twice a day water floods a great area on the west side of barrier islands. Instead of the wiry blades of saltmeadow hay, the marshes we now passed were filled almost entirely by cordgrass as dense and verdant as if it were being farmed. Away from the banks the cordgrass grew as tall as five feet, its stems thick and inflexible, like green bamboo. Another six hours and all but the leafy blades would be submerged. For the moment, though, only about an inch of water stood in the marsh.

Hackney drove slowly and gestured to a thin strip of grass on the east side of the channel. "That marsh was much wider thirty years ago," he said. "By building up so many spoil islands, the corps of engineers really changed the system, because they changed the flow of water over the marshes. After the Intracoastal Waterway was built, a lot of the water that had flooded the marshes either bumped against spoil islands or was redirected into the channel. Instead of a smooth flow of water that lets sand and silt settle out, you now have water being funneled quickly into certain areas. But the waterway was built in a time when there was plenty of marsh and no transportation.

"We're finding evidence that because so many channels are being dredged and so many inlets are stabilized by jetties, the marshes are actually being robbed of sediment that would normally build up their soil. They no longer get a constant replenishment of sand and silt. Every time humans dredge a channel or somehow change the estuary, it has an effect on the marsh. It's conceivable that as sea level rises, the marshes are going to drown for lack of sediment."

He turned toward Mason Inlet, where breakers blocked a narrow passage to the ocean. In the middle of the channel he slowed the skiff to an idle. The small boat bucked uncomfortably in the chop. "This is the kind of beating that the mainland would have to withstand if not for the islands," he said. "The islands are literally barriers that disperse the wave energy so these calm bays and marshes can form.

"One of the things I find interesting about inlets is they're so turbulent that no organisms are able to establish themselves on the bottom. You get fish moving in and out to the ocean, but that's about it." He tapped the throttle and retreated to the calmer waterway, turning north toward a marsh where he had inserted some instruments into the mud to measure water tables at low tide.

The smooth, protected channels were a deep bluish-green, like tropical lagoons. The tide had dropped to its lowest ebb, and Hackney had to maneuver carefully to make his way up a shallow creek. Minnows scattered before the boat, riffling the surface.

I pulled on an old pair of sneakers and struck out across the mud after Hackney, stepping on cordgrass stems to keep from sinking to my calves. A rich organic smell, sharp but not unpleasant, filled the air. Several metal tubes had been stuck lengthwise into the mud to measure the flow of water on and off the bank, but Hackney did not seem interested in them. Instead, he halted thirty yards into the marsh and bent down, sniffing in an exaggerated manner. "Do you smell sulfur?" he asked as I approached. Indeed the smell of the marsh had changed to one of rotten eggs.

"That's what I thought, but I would expect to see a lot of oysters and other animals growing around here, and I don't. I'm trying to work up a project now on marsh energetics and how they're affected by the presence of hydrogen sulfide." He pointed to a patch of silvery black mud. "See this dark area? That's where hydrogen sulfide gas is released from the marsh sediment into the air. We call them vents. In the past couple of years oceanographers have been finding thermal vents in the ocean floor off California, and the amount of life around them is amazing. Giant worms, big species of fish, and other things, all in water so deep and dark it shouldn't support those kinds of organisms.

"The key seems to be the presence of hydrogen sulfide and a certain bacteria that uses the sulfide as an energy source. What I've come to suspect is that the same thing happens in the marsh—where you have sulfide vents and the right bacteria, you have a rich area for organisms. Look over here." He made his way to where large oysters were scattered through a patch of darkly mottled, black and silver mud. Sulfur fumes permeated the air.

"You see this kind of thing all the time," he said, "and there's got to be a reason for it. The problem is that once the sulfide reaches the surface, it oxidizes and becomes a different compound. A way to measure it is to take out plugs of soil, but then you only get a one-time reading. We want to take continuous readings over time, but we need to figure out how to take underground measurements without exposing the soil to any oxygen at all. I think we've come up with a way to do it using electrodes."

He walked onto a sandy flat near the creek bank, where twenty male fiddler crabs were sunning themselves and waving their large claws to attract mates. Frothy water had begun to trickle onto the flat, and swirls of thick white bubbles nudged against the grass. "Looks like soap suds, doesn't it?" Hackney said. "I've gotten calls from people complaining that someone had dumped a bunch of detergent in the marsh. It's really just dissolved organic compounds that are forced out of the sediment by the tide."

A movement on the far side of the creek caught my eye, and I started toward the bank. Three American oystercatchers had landed on a sand bar and were piping to each other in a late-season courtship, pumping their necks and pointing their orange bills straight down. I called back to Hackney, who approached me slowly, thumbing among the cordgrass stems in a search for snails.

"Oh yeah," he said with mild disinterest when I pointed to the birds. "You see those a lot out here."

"Let me tell you one other thing about this system before we head back," he said after we had climbed into the skiff. "See this creek bank?" I glanced toward the dark sediment, rising vertically from the creek like a natural dam. "There's probably all sorts of junk in there that's accumulated over time. Estuaries and marshes—especially marshes near freshwater outlets like river mouths—are garbage burial grounds. A lot of pollutants come flowing downstream from the rivers, and as soon as they hit salt water, they settle out. Marshes by their very nature are catching sediment all the time. So the stuff that would otherwise pollute the oceans is all getting buried. "It's a natural trap. Humans could not have designed a more beautiful system."

Mid-August in the backyard marsh. A dead calm settled in, a short-lived lull as the wind shifted from southeast to southwest. I had been sitting on the rock at the edge of the mudberg for most of the morning, taking note of the quiet fauna around me. In two hours I had counted more than a thousand animals and fish. Before I even reached the rock I had seen seventy-odd fiddler crabs scurrying through the grasses, their shells clicking against each other in their haste to get out of my way. Thirty or forty small amphipods flitted across a puddle in the middle of the marshy point, and a colony of mud crabs sunned themselves on a finger of peat that sloped precariously toward the water.

Near my rock several dozen marsh periwinkles clung to cordgrass stems, and the dark shapes of minnows—anchovies maybe?—moved in the water, shaded by the rise of the bank. Occasionally the black head of a diamondback terrapin poked up from the silvered surface and dropped out of sight. A half-hour after my arrival a snowy egret landed on the next point to the south and began to hunt, crouching among the cordgrass and crooking its ivory neck like a snake. Behind the bird, shaggy green grasses stretched into the distance, pushing and receding against the blueness of Pamlico Sound.

It was nearly autumn, a season of death and fading light, yet around me were signs of life bursting at the seams. I had settled onto the rock and watched the water spill over the bank, thinking of the tiny organisms—short strands of algae, larval forms of fish, and fully grown crustaceans too small to see—that might be present in the waves. A yard from the bank was a row of widgeon grass interspersed with hydroids, the delicate flower-shaped animals that frequently have skeleton shrimp clinging to their stems. Even farther out were the bottom dwellers of sounds and bays, the bryozoans and boring sponges that look like fossilized rocks. The petrified monsters of the sound.

Scientists estimate that hundreds, perhaps thousands, of unnamed plants and animals live in this country's tidal marshes and bays. Some can be seen easily by the naked eye, but many more would require dissection under a microscope for positive identification. A few are European species transported to the United States in the holds of ships during the eighteenth and nineteenth centuries. Even if we could identify every organism, it would be another matter entirely to study their life cycles and sort out the relationships that bind them together or drive them apart. It is believed, for instance, that some amphipods always carry certain species of bacteria within pockets of their bodies, the way a baseball pitcher keeps a wad of chewing tobacco in his cheek. On moonless nights the bodies of these invertebrates glow with phosphorescence. It seems likely that both the animals and the bacteria derive some benefit from this arrangement, but what this might be remains unknown.

Animals studied in detail have been shown to have remarkably intricate physiological cycles that enable them to survive the stresses of living in salty, receding waters. In my backyard marsh the smooth, reddish-brown shell of *Melampus bidentatus*, the saltmarsh snail, is not nearly as abundant as the grooved, bluish-gray marsh periwinkle, but small numbers of *Melampus* can be found beneath swirls of saltmeadow hay. The saltmarsh snail has a small lung and cannot live under water. Twenty years ago John Teal and his wife, Mildred, wrote that the snail has the ability to anticipate changes in the tide, and that it will climb *Spartina* stems well before the water rises. "The snail has a built-in cycle, a kind of inner alarm clock, that goes off after a little more than twelve hours passes," the Teals wrote. "This corresponds to the time between successive tides. How the clock gets set is not known."

Subsequent research has cast doubt on the Tealses' assertion, but the studies have shown that the saltmarsh snail responds to another persuasive biological clock. Because its larvae can survive only in water, the snail's reproductive cycle coincides with spring and neap tides, the extreme high and low tides that occur, alternately, about every two weeks. During neap tides, when only the edges of the marshes flood, the saltmarsh snail lays more than eight hundred eggs on dry mud, usually under a layer of grass stems or other debris. The eggs hatch in about thirteen days—just as spring tides flood the entire marsh—and the free-swimming larvae are carried into nearby creeks. In another two weeks the next spring tide deposits the larvae back in the middle of the marsh, where they metamorphose into their adult, air-breathing forms.

All this happens silently and invisibly. As the *Melampus* spawn and grow, the *Spartina* grasses take up brackish water and filter out salt with special membranes on their roots and glands on their leaves. Oysters and ribbed mussels close their shells tightly at low tide to protect their moist flesh; plankton and algae reproduce prolifically as the tide ebbs and begins again to rise. Every animal and plant that lives in the marsh adapts in one way or another to the absence of oxygen, the periodic intrusion of water and salt, the drying power of sun and wind. My backyard marsh is a pleasant place most days, but in a moment it can become too cold, too hot, too wet, or too windy for easy survival. In mid-October, when I accepted Courtney Hackney's invitation to spend twenty-four hours with a group of students sampling inlets and tidal creeks, I would discover just how uncomfortable the salt marsh could be.

It began with a deluge at 1 p.m., only an hour after the students had pitched tents for their supplies and set their instruments in place. The morning sky had been blue, though hazy, and we had all thought—we had all hoped fervently—the day would be dry. At 8:00 that morning Hackney and ten students had gathered at a marina and loaded an assortment of instruments into three boats, cramming backpacks and piles of clothes in among seine nets, tidal gauges, salinometers, and empty milk jugs. Our first stop was Coke Island, a sparsely developed barrier north of Wrightsville Beach that would serve as a base. Behind the island, fields of leafy cordgrass rose from slow jade creeks. I could think of nothing more pleasant than spending a sunny fall day watching the world in a tidal lagoon.

The storm clouds appeared first as a distant smudge, then as a quickly advancing blot. When the rain started, I was in Hackney's skiff just off Coke Island.

"Well, here we go," he said cheerily. He had spent hundreds of nights taking biological samples in the marsh; as a veteran, he knew how to prepare for virtually any weather. I had thought my raincoat was waterproof, but as the creek turned white beneath the pelting drops I felt moisture seeping through my shirt.

"This is what the animals of the marsh have to go through every single day," Hackney said. "Humans never really think about the kind of stress that's involved in being outside in every kind of weather. This is nothing but a little rainstorm, not a hurricane or a prolonged northeaster. I won't be surprised, though, if there are some uncomfortable people out here by about four a.m."

Neither would I. Two hundred yards upstream, four students

huddled in a skiff at the mouth of a narrow tidal creek. Nearby, a rod marked with centimeters had been driven into the bank to measure the range of the tide during the long night ahead. The students had already sounded the bottom of the creek to draw a contour of its bed, which they would use later to calculate the volume of water flowing through. For now they had settled into the tedium of collecting data, a task that would not end until noon the next day. Every fifteen minutes they were to check water temperature and salinity, dissolved oxygen levels, and the speed and height of the tide.

A short distance away another group of students had been fitted with chest waders and put ashore in the marsh with a seine net, a pair of binoculars, and instructions to keep records of the animals and fish they encountered. A third team had anchored in the inlet between Coke Island and Figure Eight Island, where they were to monitor the temperature, salinity, and dissolved oxygen content of the surf. Every few hours the students would switch stations.

Hackney had designed the trip to make his students aware of the tremendous physical changes that occur with the rise and fall of the tides. "A lot of people have spent an hour or two out in the marsh," he said, "but few people have actually watched the tide rise and fall for a night and a day. Until you do that, it's difficult to have an appreciation for how the different components of the estuarine system work."

I had looked forward to Hackney's annual overnight expedition, despite a premonition that the weather would be cool and damp. It was mid-October and nighttime temperatures had begun to dip into the fifties, low enough for hypothermic conditions. Now the early afternoon rain was quickly sapping my enthusiasm. Hackney wore a calm, rather oblivious expression as he steered upstream toward the skiff in the creek. The students sat hunched down in the boat, their backs to the rain.

"Kind of bad luck to start out with," Hackney said as he pulled alongside them. "It's tough to get soaked right away, but at least it's early enough that we can still dry out if it clears up."

A blond student looked at him with pursed lips and a resigned expression. "Might as well look on the bright side," he said.

I was to stay in the skiff with three students for the next several hours. I climbed out of Hackney's boat and slid onto a wet metal seat next to a young woman, who introduced herself as Karen. Hackney waved and retreated. Jeff, the blond man, looked after him and sighed.

The rain had let up a bit. Karen pushed back the hood of her rain slicker and picked up a metal notebook. "Time," she said. It was just past 1:00, and although the tide at the inlet had been dead low at 12:30, muddy green water still flowed slowly out of the marsh. She tossed an empty two-liter Coke bottle into the creek and watched it drift downstream for a half-minute, until a string attached to its neck pulled taut. "This is our fancy current meter," she said. "When the tide is this slack, a mechanical meter can't measure the flow accurately enough, so we have to improvise."

Jeff opened a black case that held the salinometer, an instrument that measures water salinity and temperature. He lowered an electrode into the murky creek and turned a dial as a needle slid across the rectangular face of the meter and bounced to a stop. "Okay," he said to Sam, a dark-haired man who held a notebook with soggy, curling sheets. "Temperature, twenty-one." This was in degrees Centigrade: 70 degrees Fahrenheit. Jeff turned another dial and measured the salinity at thirty-one parts per thousand, four parts lower than the average salinity of sea water. A second meter showed the level of dissolved oxygen to be four parts per million on the surface, slightly less than that two feet below. With the tide almost slack, the oxygen had probably dropped close to its lowest level. Much of it had been used by the small animals and fish of the marsh.

Theoretically the amount of oxygen in the creek would start to rise as the marsh flooded with ocean water. Oxygen is unusually precious in the marsh, with its dense, airless soils and teeming fauna. But in the open ocean, as waves glide and slosh and collapse against shore, the surface waters become rich in dissolved gas. The incoming tide should bring enough oxygen to sustain the marsh animals through the night and into the following morning, when plants would start producing oxygen through photosynthesis. Theoretically the salinity in the creek would also rise with the tide, and the water, now turbid and warm from the sun, would clear and slowly cool. The students knew what should happen. It was up to them to see if it would.

"Time," Karen said.

"Already?" Jeff had just put the salinometer away.

It was 1:15, slack tide. When Karen tossed out the Coke bottle, it simply bobbed by the side of the boat. Sam held a plastic milk jug under water and watched it fill. Karen reached into a box for a bottle of formalin solution and added a few drops to the water sample to preserve the plant and animal matter within. She capped the jug and marked the time on its side. The sample would be examined in the laboratory for detritus and carbon, and its contents would be compared with others taken throughout the day. At low tide, with little water flow, the suspended particles were probably as thickly concentrated as they would get.

The water samples would give the students one more lens through which to study the effects of the tides. "If detritus really drives the energy flow of the marsh," Hackney had told me, "then we need to know when the most detritus is present in the creeks and at what point the concentration begins to change." As I sat in the crowded skiff, I wished I had a microscope so I could look at the plants and animals within the jug. Field work would be easier if one could make immediate conclusions, I thought. The sun came out briefly, showering us with molecules of haze. I took off my raincoat and steamy chamois shirt, laying them across a seat with the hope they would dry. Beside the boat stood a forest of cordgrass, each blade a greenish yellow rimmed with a line the color of blood. Funny that I had never noticed the red before.

"Time," Karen said.

By 2 p.m. the tide had risen seven centimeters—a little more than two and a half inches—and the dissolved oxygen had increased to five parts per million. The temperature and salinity had not changed. At 2:30 the roar of Hackney's boat roused me from a tangle of daydreams. The students, silent for nearly an hour, perked up.

It was time for some of us to switch stations. Hackney suggested that I ride with him, Karen, and Sam to where another team had been placed to count animals in the marsh. He maneuvered slowly up a creek, turning the skiff so it bumped against the bank gently and grounded.

Sam got out, and Hackney, Karen, and I turned toward the waters of the inlet, where prisms of blue danced across emerald-colored crests. Despite the lingering clouds, the day had turned steamy. Fishing skiffs and ski boats zipped past the students' Privateer, which was anchored near the edge of the channel. The team reported that the salinity and temperature of the inlet had changed little in two hours. Since that morning, however, the surf had calmed from a frothing chop to a gentle roll. "Do you know why?" Hackney asked me.

I shook my head.

"When the tide's flowing out heavily and there's a strong east wind like this, a lot of water gets pushed through the inlet against the tide. So for an hour or so there's a lot of wave action. Wait till tonight. I bet we'll see some rough water out here."

Karen climbed aboard the rocking Privateer, and we returned to camp, where Hackney's wife, Rose Ganucheau, was heating a cauldron of seafood gumbo over an open fire. A native of southern Louisiana, she had made the stew with shrimp, crabs, squid, anchovies, and croaker caught the previous month, when the class had spent the day on a trawler.

I pressed close to the fire, and steam began to rise from the legs of my jeans. Ganucheau, a fair-skinned woman with round glasses and a bubbly laugh, looked at me and chuckled. "You volunteered to go through this? The students must think you're nuts."

"They do," I said. "A couple of them don't seem very happy to be here."

Hackney snorted. "If they want to be scientists, they'd better get used to it."

"Maybe this will change their minds," Ganucheau said.

"Sometimes I think it's going to change my mind," Hackney said. He poured some coffee from a thermos and passed it to me. "This is pretty much all there is to the annual overnight, though you'll see some interesting stuff after dark. There's nothing really eye-opening about this trip, but it's amazing what you can see if you sit still and look. It's funny to me that scientists spend so much time tinkering with things in their labs and so little time outside looking around. Fishermen often know a lot more about an area than scientists who have studied it for years, because they see it every day. To me the outside work is the fun part, but you've got to know how to prepare for it."

Just before dark Hackney and I climbed into the skiff and turned toward the boat in the tidal creek, where I had chosen to spend most of the night. It was again time for the students to change stations, and the three men with whom I settled in seemed jovial, despite the work that lay ahead. As the roar of Hackney's motor faded in the distance, the steely darkness seeped farther into the marsh, and the lonely, rattling cry of a clapper rail split the air. The cresting tide had risen 120 centimeters—four feet—but had not cooled. The boat bumped against cordgrass stems that jutted from the water like spears. A hundred yards away, two figures pulled a seine net through water that lapped against their chests.

The air seemed warmer, and I propped my feet on the side of the boat. The men with me were unusually efficient, and though I volunteered to record readings in one of the notebooks, I spent most of my time quietly looking around. An hour passed, then another. The speed of the outgoing tide quickened, until the students set aside the Coke bottle float for a propeller-driven tidal gauge. Shining a flashlight into the water, I could see the elliptical shapes of fish rising to the beam. I dipped my hand into dark water, and phosphorescent plankton splashed against my fingers in silvery beads.

If you want to know what goes on in the world, Hackney had said, you have to watch. A simple and obvious philosophy, but one that can be difficult to carry out. During my months on Hatteras I had learned to see minute forms of life and slight variations in landscape, water, and light. How difficult would it be to observe the same subtle changes in a city, with its closed spaces and perpetually moving traffic and crowds? Sitting in a skiff in a flooded marsh, I decided I probably couldn't do it. The clarity of sight I had developed on Hatteras would cloud over when exposed to a constant barrage of color and artificial light. Even now my vision was far from perfect. During the past months I had studied plants and animals more closely than I had ever studied anything, yet I had never noticed the blood-red outline on autumn cordgrass leaves. Before this trip I had sat in cordgrass for whole afternoons. I straightened my back, trying to stay alert, struggling to subdue a fog of drowsy, reflective thoughts.

The night passed. As the tide ebbed, Hackney returned with Karen and Jeff, who had just finished their turn at the station in the marsh. "Climb aboard," Hackney said to me. "I've got something over here to show you."

Small, dark shapes covered the mudflat where he beached the boat. Leaning close to the ground, I saw hundreds of mud crabs frozen in the beam of my light. "I can't believe how these things crowd up," Hackney said, "and there doesn't seem to be any clear reason for it. I've seen places where you find thousands of them in a square meter."

He leaned over and pulled a cylindrical mesh of mud and sticks from the ground: a tube worm. "I'm sure you've seen these," he said, "and over here is a penaeid shrimp." He pointed to a crustacean several inches long with glowing orange eyes. "But here's what I really wanted to show you." He got back in the skiff, pushing it off the bank so that its bow slid into a stand of cordgrass.

A foot of water still covered the marsh. When Hackney shined his light into it, a host of small worms rose to the surface and boiled around the beam, like a shower of meteorites across a winter sky. Light brown and less than a half-inch long, they swam in frantic patterns, staying roughly within the range of the light. There must have been thousands of them, but they moved much too quickly to count. "They're annelids of some sort," Hackney said. "We noticed them a little while ago back in the marsh. They think the flashlight is the moon, and they're coming out to spawn."

As I looked down into the lighted water, the number of worms swimming around the beam increased, until they began to knock into each other like bits of barley in a bubbling stew. I clicked on my own light and shined it into the water on the other side of the boat. For a few seconds there was only darkness, but then a dozen worms appeared, and then a hundred, and more. We watched them for only a few minutes, until Hackney turned off his light and started the motor. It was just past midnight.

The annelids had occupied only a fraction of my time that evening, yet the sight of them, and the knowledge of their sheer numbers, proved more enduring than anything else. I resumed my vigil in the skiff at the creek, dozing and shaking myself awake, joking with Karen and Jeff, jotting down readings with stiffened hands. Below the boat were animals I would never see, more animals than I could fathom. The air grew chilly, then piercingly cold just before dawn, when silence and haze thickened over the marsh. And well past sunrise, into midmorning, all through the last sets of measurements and the packing up, annelids danced before my eyes. As I drove north under warm, sunny skies, past stands of cordgrass, needle rush, and deep cedar swamps, the image of the worms stayed with me, like the afterglow of a sudden flash of light. Tiny brown blimps flew across a pale beam, turned, and raced back, over and over, in a simple, unstoppable cycle of life.

7
$\mathscr{L}$OGGERHEAD RITES

ONE JULY EVENING just before dusk I stood on a narrow, gently sloping beach two hundred miles south of Cape Hatteras with the hope of catching a glimpse of prehistoric times. A southeasterly wind tousled the sea oats, and a calm surf with thin coils of foam rolled across a mosaic of footprints in the sand. Next to me Cindy Meekins yawned, touched her toes, and did a spurt of jumping jacks in an effort to wake up. Behind us were two pale blue, woodframe houses with porches rimmed by short white railings, the kind of fusty, weatherbeaten retreats that tourist guides describe as charming.

The exclusive resort where I had settled in for the night could not have been farther removed from Hatteras and its gritty souls. An hour before, the yacht that serves as the ferry from Southport

130

had taken me from a private parking lot to a private dock, where two suntanned porters in docksiders and tennis shirts relieved me of my baggage and escorted me up a gangway to a waiting tram. After four months without dependable water and lights, arriving on Bald Head Island was like being thrust into a foreign world where niceties can be taken for granted. But by the time I stood on the beach in the thickening darkness, I had forgotten the island's opulence and turned my thoughts to the activities of the night. At 9:30 I was to mount a three-wheeled, all-terrain cycle and embark on a search for loggerhead turtles, a species of giant sea turtle that once nested abundantly in the middle Atlantic and is now threatened throughout its range.

The sky was covered solidly with clouds, and occasional flickers of lightning appeared on the western horizon. Meekins, the island naturalist, yawned again, glanced at the sky, and frowned. "You may not have picked the best night to come," she said. "We generally run the patrol in any weather except thunderstorms, but if it gets rough it's less likely that the turtles will come in. You're almost guaranteed to see something this time of year, barring terrible weather. Let's hope this storm stays to the south."

Her words were disheartening. I had driven to Bald Head, the island that forms the tip of Cape Fear, in hopes of watching a loggerhead female dig a nest in the sand and lay a clutch of eggs. During the previous month I had helped the Pea Island National Wildlife Refuge run a daily patrol to check for loggerhead tracks on a thirteen-mile stretch of beach where only about a dozen sea turtles nest each summer. On several mornings I had found the tractorlike marks where a turtle had dragged herself across the sand. But I had yet to locate a nest. I knew I stood little chance of seeing a turtle on Pea Island, so I had decided to travel south to the most frequently used nesting ground in the state. Each year more than a hundred loggerheads lay their eggs on the beach at Bald Head between late May and late August. In mid-July it is not uncommon for ten or more two- to three-hundred-pound reptiles to lumber ashore in a single night. I had timed my trip to Bald Head for what Meekins predicted to be the busiest week of the season, and now a storm threatened to steal the show.

I dug my toe in the sand and tried to ward off a feeling of gloom. As the director of the island's turtle program, Meekins had given me permission to stay at her headquarters that night; I was not sure her schedule would allow me to stay longer. And if a front settled in, most of the turtles would probably remain in the surf until it passed.

Oh well, I told myself, I still might get lucky. If not, at least I had gotten to sample some new terrain. From the ferry an electric tram had taken me down a winding, washboard road past two pillar-trunked cabbage palmettoes and through a tunnel of live oak, laurel oak, and grape. The dwarfed, knotted trees pressed tightly against each other, clamping a hedge over the road. The forests of Bald Head are about six hundred years old—very old in terms of Atlantic maritime forests—and riding through them gave me the sensation of being deep within a maze. My brief passage into the culture of the wealthy began to fade; I imagined the tram winding me back to a not-so-distant past when Bald Head was unclaimed and undeveloped and giant sea turtles were more common on the beach than human beings.

Fossil records show that as early as 175 million years ago, the middle of the age of reptiles, a few species of giant tortoise developed the ability to survive in the seas. Some paleontologists believe marine turtle fossils from 90 million years ago, the time of the largest dinosaurs, may have been early species of *Caretta*, the genus to which the loggerhead belongs. Other scientists argue that the fossils do not show enough anatomical detail to be certain. But it is clear that sea turtles evolved long before mammals, and perhaps as long as 160 million years before man.

The loggerhead and five other species of turtle—the hawksbill, leatherback, Kemp's ridley, olive ridley, and green turtle—bred prolifically in the Atlantic before humans began harvesting their eggs and relishing their meat. Loggerheads, the most abundant North American species, once nested on sandy beaches from

Virginia to the Caribbean. They were especially prolific along the Florida Atlantic coast, which still is believed to be the largest rookery in the world.

The nesting ritual of the loggerhead is utterly common but difficult to observe. Sea turtles normally come ashore well after dark and reenter the water before dawn. When a female turtle emerges from the surf, she crawls to the dunes, inspects the sand, and—if satisfied with the location—thrusts her front into a dune and uses her rear flippers to dig a round nest about two feet deep. A person who happens on her before she begins to deposit her eggs will almost certainly spook her back into the surf. Once she begins to lay, however, she goes into a trance; virtually nothing will disturb her until she has produced about 130 small, round eggs. She corks the nest with a lid of sand, rests for a few minutes, and returns to the surf.

Between sixty and seventy-five days later, the eggs begin to hatch. Bit by bit each turtle scratches out of its shell with a small spine on the tip of its nose. Not until all the eggs have hatched will the turtles begin to dig out of the nest, and then they will come in a burst. In the cool of night the sand erupts with life, and a company of reddish-brown hatchlings two to three inches long scampers across the beach. A substantial percentage are snatched up and devoured by ghost crabs and raccoons. Those that survive crawl to the water and duck under the breakers, where they can still be eaten by fish.

What happens next is a matter of some debate. Most biologists believe loggerhead hatchlings swim frantically for the Sargasso Sea, the warm, salty gyre that lies just east of the Gulf Stream and reaches more than halfway across the Atlantic. The gyre's northern edge is roughly on the same latitude as the mouth of the Chesapeake Bay, and it is bounded on the south by equatorial currents. To reach it the turtles must swim at least fifty miles and cross the Gulf Stream. It is widely thought they achieve this without food or rest, although some biologists argue that the energy provided by the yolk of their eggs cannot sustain the hatchlings for the entire trip.

Once they have crossed the Gulf Stream, the loggerheads spend their early years floating on huge mats of *Sargassum*, the bushy brown seaweed common in the open Atlantic. Often the mats are carried by currents to the east Atlantic, where biologists have found loggerheads that weigh between twenty and thirty pounds near the mouth of the Mediterranean. When the turtles have matured to a weight of about forty pounds, they ride equatorial currents back to the western Atlantic. Or so many scientists believe. The issue is debatable, because biologists have been unable to observe large populations of loggerheads less than three or four years old. Once the hatchlings plunge into the sea, they simply drop from sight.

Neither is it known for certain when loggerheads reach sexual maturity, although it is believed they mate for the first time between the ages of ten and thirty years. Thereafter, females become fertile every two or three years. In a fertile season a loggerhead female will lay four or five nests, and each time she must drag herself onto the beach. Scientists estimate that only one in every hundred hatchlings will live long enough to reproduce.

The reproduction rates were probably much higher before the widespread development of the southeast coast of the United States. Marine turtle meat was considered a delicacy by early American settlers, and turtle eggs, which have whites that do not harden when cooked, were used to make unusually moist pound cakes and breads. Hides were tanned for shoes and handbags, and the beautiful plates on the shell of the hawksbill were fashioned into tortoise-shell jewelry. However, it was not until the Florida coast was thickly settled in the 1940s and 1950s that the population of sea turtles began a precipitous decline. Turtle steaks and soups, always a specialty of the region, became increasingly popular in the 1950s, and bakeries began to market specialty products made with loggerhead eggs. At the same time, a wave of oceanside development severely decreased the areas where loggerheads could safely nest.

Despite an aversion to bright lights and developed beaches, turtles occasionally nest in the most populous areas, usually with disastrous results. When a loggerhead nest hatches, the young turtles instinctively make for the brightest horizon, which on dark, empty beaches is the starlight and moonlight reflecting off the surf. Before the establishment of turtle hatchery programs, beaches and streets in resort cities sometimes began to swarm with loggerhead hatchlings on still September nights. The hatchlings clambered toward the lights of restaurants and motels with resolute determination—even when turned around and placed in the surf. If they survived an onslaught by ghost crabs, the next day they were eaten by fish crows or they dehydrated and died.

Each year the number of nesting loggerheads on the Atlantic coast steadily decreased. Although no one is sure how many loggerheads live in the Atlantic, nesting surveys indicate that the number of turtles coming ashore to nest fell by as much as 75 percent in the thirty years after World War II. By the late 1960s southeastern states began to ban the killing of loggerheads and the harvesting of their eggs. Marine scientists began recommending that fishing trawlers, which accidentally catch and kill thousands of loggerheads each year, use nets with special doors that enable sea turtles to escape. And in 1978 the loggerhead was listed by the federal government as a threatened species.

Since the early 1970s wildlife biologists have started programs to monitor loggerhead nesting on federal and state preserves in North Carolina, South Carolina, Georgia, and Florida. Most of the projects are operated on slim budgets and staffed by students or volunteers who search for loggerhead nests and, when necessary, excavate the eggs and rebury them in areas safe from predators, encroaching roots, and high tides. Frequently the programs move the nests to fenced hatcheries.

The protection programs were heralded as a major step toward correcting the pressures of overfishing. Yet the earliest efforts unwittingly may have caused more harm than good. For several years some programs dug up nests and stored the eggs in styrofoam boxes that protected them from fungi and kept their temperatures from fluctuating. Wildlife experts believed keeping the eggs at a constant temperature of about 82 degrees

Fahrenheit would increase the proportion that hatched. However, in the early 1970s a French biologist discovered that the sex of a marine turtle is determined not by the embryo's chromosomes but by the temperature at which the egg incubates. Biologists in the United States began checking the sexes of loggerheads hatched from eggs stored in styrofoam and found a disproportionate number to be male. They increased the incubation temperature of another group to about 90 degrees. All the hatchlings that emerged were female. The eggs kept above ground had been exposed to consistently lower temperatures than they would have been in sand—and the hatchery programs had produced nest after nest of males. If the practice of incubating eggs in styrofoam had continued, the species' reproduction rate might have dipped to an all-time low.

Ever since, the techniques for managing loggerhead stocks have been the subject of vigorous debate. Among North Carolina wildlife experts, Cindy Meekins is known for her adamant opinions on how loggerhead protection projects should be run. As I neared the headquarters of the Bald Head Conservancy program, I had the feeling I was in for a remarkable evening, turtles or no.

The wood-frame houses that headquarter the conservancy's turtle program are perched side by side on a dune far from the bustle of Bald Head's only marina and inn. To their west was a tract that would be developed soon, but for now the forests there were dark and quiet. On the island's eastern end, the largest trees stood leafless and brown, burned the previous fall by the salty rain of Hurricane Diana.

Meekins had been waiting at one of the houses. Round-faced and blue-eyed with short blond hair, she is thin and feminine, but with a solidness that comes from years of strenuous outdoor work. Frequently she slips into the precise, formal manner of speaking common among scientists. On Bald Head she is known as the turtle lady, a nickname that seems too flippant, given the force of her personality.

In 1982, while completing a master's degree in coastal biology at the University of North Carolina at Wilmington, Meekins took a seasonal job with the Nature Conservancy to establish a loggerhead protection program on the Bald Head beach. To accomplish the task she was given a three-wheeled Honda cycle with wide, studded tires, a stack of data sheets, and a drafty, cramped trailer for quarters. From the beginning of nesting season in late May until the end of hatching in late September, she rode the beach alone all night, every night. In the next three years she built the largest and best-funded of the seven loggerhead programs in the state.

Since 1984 Meekins's year-round salary has been paid by the nonprofit Bald Head Conservancy, and each summer she hires three college interns to conduct the nightly patrols she once ran alone. The students live dormitory-style in one of the blue houses. Meekins works seventy-plus hours a week on public relations, administrative chores, and escorting Bald Head residents on nightly hikes to look for nesting turtles. In the winter she compiles nest data, attends conferences, and prepares for the coming season.

I had dropped my pack next to the guest bed in Meekins's room and wandered to the living room to find her reclined in a deep chair. "It's hard to get a full night's sleep this time of the year," she sighed, "but it's also a very exciting time. Strangely enough, we've had a high proportion of false crawls the past couple of days, and no one is sure exactly why." In a false crawl the turtle returns to the surf without depositing her eggs.

"Does it have anything to do with the phase of the moon?" I asked. I had heard that turtles nest in greater numbers when the moon is full. Only a sliver would rise that night.

"That's an old wives' tale. There's absolutely no validity to it," Meekins replied. "There are lots of misconceptions like that about turtles. But at least people are interested in them now, and that's a great improvement from my first year here. The cottage owners were completely in the dark; so were the developers. By and large the people we've dealt with since then have been tremendous. But it's taken some work to get things to a manageable point."

Almost all the nests are moved, she added, because erosion has drastically narrowed the beach. If left alone the nest cavities would almost certainly flood in high tides. The interns patrol twelve miles of coastline. Nests found within the five-mile stretch that lies inside a state park are moved to nearby dunes, but nests laid on private beaches are taken to a hatchery surrounded by a wood-and-chicken-wire frame.

The interns work as speedily as possible to reduce the mortality rate. Just after an egg is laid, the embryo floats to the top and attaches itself to the shell with a thin filament. If the egg is turned over, the embryo will be crushed. "It's thought that the embryos are free-floating only for the first six hours. That's spelled out in the handbook we use," Meekins said.

I asked whether moving most of the eggs to the hatchery might produce a disproportionate number of females or males.

"You have to remember that eggs laid early in the season are going to incubate at different temperatures than the ones laid in late July," Meekins replied. "As far as we can determine, we are getting enough temperature flux to ensure some variation in sex typing. Of course, ninety percent of our turtles may be male. That's the pattern up here at the northern end of their range. In Florida many more of the hatchlings are female."

She stood up suddenly and stretched her hands toward the ceiling in a gesture that emphasized her strength. "I've got to wake up," she said. "Want to see the beach before it gets pitch dark?"

The temperature was dropping. As I looked east across the water, the breeze grew stronger and the night began to smell of rain. Meekins finished her jumping jacks and slapped her arms against her sides. "I hope I don't have any smart alecks on the turtle walk tonight," she said. "One reason we have to be so strict with regulations is that this beach is going to be used with increasing frequency as the island is developed. We've already had some problems this year with people scaring turtles back into the water before they've nested. There are a few people every year who refuse to go by the rules. But we're just not going to tolerate it.

"Records show turtles used to nest in Virginia, which means their range has already decreased by an entire state. We think the decrease was caused mostly by development and a decline in the turtle population. That's why the Bald Head Conservancy is so determined that development here be managed. The bottom line is that we are going to preserve the beach for turtles. If that means we have to pass an ordinance restricting people from coming on the beach at night, we'll do that. And whatever other measures it takes."

I was to ride that evening with Jennifer Bender, a twenty-two-year-old intern from Norlina, North Carolina, who had graduated from Wake Forest in June with a bachelor's degree in biology. Bender was large-boned and strong, with a manner of speaking that was light and full of humor. She had also worked with the program the previous summer. At 9:25 we donned raincoats and long pants, then sprayed our wrists and necks with insect repellent. Two other interns, Kim Vanness and George Kosko, were to take a second three-wheeler.

We pulled out onto a narrow paved road, my back against the wooden box that contained stakes, wire, and a wooden rod used to probe the sand for air pockets surrounding the eggs. The Honda's red headlight barely illuminated the road. Loggerhead eyes do not detect red light, so the interns had covered the lamp with a filter. From my position in back of Bender it seemed that the darkness had softened and shrunk in dimension. The butterflies in my stomach were inexplicable.

In front of us the scarlet beam from the other cycle bounced off the dunes. We passed the boxlike enclosure of wood and wire mesh that formed the hatchery and rode onto the beach.

"You're bound to see something tonight, even if it's only a false crawl," Bender said over her shoulder as she turned the cycle south toward the tip of Cape Fear. "I'll be surprised, though, if those two turtles that came in last night don't come up and nest immediately. You know they're out there, just waiting for the conditions to be right." I glanced toward the surf, which was calm and lit with pale blue-green phosphorescence. Without warning, Bender released the throttle and let the cycle glide to a stop. Before us was a set of deep slashes in the sand that led straight toward the dunes but doubled back in a meandering path. "I'd have stopped earlier if I'd only seen one set of tracks," Bender said, "but there she goes." A dark, oblong lump moved across the sand near the tide. We got off the cycle and silently approached from behind. The cumbersome animal paused, aware of our presence but presumably too tired to lunge into the waves. In the red flashlight beam her shell appeared black and lusterless. I stood close behind her, afraid to move lest I should scare her more.

"Go ahead and touch her," Bender said. I leaned over and placed my hand gingerly on her smooth, cool shell. She slid forward a few feet, then stopped. Bender followed her and wiped her hand across the crest of the shell, creating a swath of phosphorescent sparks. "These aren't particularly bright," she said. "Sometimes you can write your name in them." The turtle shoved herself forward with her flippers and disappeared into the surf.

"Off to a good start, even though it was just a false crawl," Bender said, remounting the bike. "Some people ride almost all night and don't see that much." I realized I had been holding my breath. Having convinced myself I would not see a turtle, the encounter had rendered me speechless. Bender turned the bike up the beach toward the dunes and traced the tracks. "That's so we know we've already checked it out. It gets confusing if we don't run over the tracks as soon as we find them."

"Was that one of the same turtles that came in last night?"

"There's no way to know, but probably. She's got to be ready to nest."

We rounded the island's southeast point and drove west toward the Bald Head Inn and the Cape Fear River. The beach rose and dipped in red ridges before us. Peering into the soft night,

I barely had time to brace myself for jars and bumps. Lightning continued to flicker on the south horizon, and the air grew moist. We had ridden for more than an hour when we came upon the other cycle parked next to a single set of tracks. Vanness and Kosko stood near a thicket of brush beside a large loggerhead that had thrust itself into the brambles. "Hey, Jen, look at this big mamma," Kosko called.

We scrambled off the bike and up the beach. "Good Lord, that's the biggest I've seen in a while," Bender said. And indeed the turtle looked much larger than I had expected. Vanness had measured her shell length at forty-five inches. Patches of a thick, mosslike algae coated portions of her back, and flesh protruded in great pink folds from the bottom of her shell. Her flippers and neck were scaly, rough, and darkly blotched. A liquid the consistency of honey dripped from her eyes. "Those are the tears they use to keep sand out of their eyes and to excrete salt," Kosko said. "She's really crying." The turtle emitted a low groan. "Did she nest?" I asked.

"Yep. She's all through. See that depression?" I turned to see a shallow hollow about five feet by five feet. "The eggs are in there somewhere. Luckily we saw her just as she was finishing up, so we have a pretty good idea of where they are." The turtle groaned again and began moving toward the surf. At the back of her shell I could see a wide, fleshy stump of a tail. She moved her flippers alternately but quickly so that it looked like she was wriggling—if an animal with a carapace can wriggle.

Vanness and Kosko had already begun scooping out a hole in the shallow depression. Gnats swarmed in my eyes and nose, and I pulled up the hood of my jacket. Within minutes Kosko had located the eggs. He pulled two of them out and plopped them into my hand. Round and white, they were no greater than three inches in diameter, the size of Ping-Pong balls. One dented under the pressure from my thumb. "Don't worry," Bender said, seeing my sheepish look. "A lot of them give like that. It doesn't hurt the embryo's development."

It was time to continue our patrol. I positioned myself on the cycle and readied myself for a long ride. I had begun to fear that my chances of seeing a turtle at her nest were growing slimmer with each passing hour. I began scanning the waves. The phosphorescence in the foam had intensified. With the blue of the lightning to the west, the glowing waves to the east, and the wide beam of our diffused red light, the night was cast in two muted, jarring hues. We crested a ridge and Bender stopped.

"Aha," she said. "I see tracks going up, but there's none coming back."

Halfway up the dune I could see a dark shape. I got off the bike with the intention of walking toward it, but Bender cautioned me back. "Right now's a real critical time, because if you approach her before she starts laying she's likely to go back into the surf."

We leaned against the cycle, and I slapped a mosquito that had landed on my cheek. "Buggy tonight," Bender said. Overhead the lightning grew brighter, but no thunder sounded. I eyed the lump in the sand. It appeared to be moving to the north, parallel with the dune. Finally it stopped and I stood up, restless.

"Let's do it," Bender said.

She grabbed her flashlight and walked slowly toward the dark shape, but veered south well before she reached it. "Look at this," she groaned over her shoulder, "look at this. We've been watching a bush." To her left a turtle was positioned over the hole that formed her nest. To her right and farther up the dune was the shape we had been watching—a clump of myrtle.

"But it moved," I said.

"We just thought it moved. This red light can do funny things to your eyes."

We crouched in back of the turtle. Pure white barnacles that glistened with phosphorescence were strung down her shell like uneven strands of pearls. Through a gap between the animal's belly and the opening to the nest, we could look inside at the wet, round eggs. The turtle sighed a hard, raspy breath, curled up her back flippers, heaved her shell, and produced three eggs. She flattened her flippers, curled them again, and pushed out two more. The gap was about five inches wide, plenty wide enough for a person to reach inside. I remembered reading that raccoons had been known to steal turtle eggs as they were being laid. I watched closely as more eggs squeezed out. This was a sight from the archives of evolution, a sight too precious to be lightly forgotten. The sides of the nest were round and damp, and I could see scrapings where the turtle had pushed away the sand. Eggs fell from her in pairs and landed with a plop, forming a neat stack in the cavity's middle.

I put my hand on the turtle's shell. Unlike the larger animal we had seen earlier, her shell was clean of algae and sand. "She's an old girl," Bender said softly. "See how her shell is more dome-shaped than the others? That's usually a sign of age."

I walked around to the turtle's side and trained the red light on her eye, which stared straight ahead, unblinking and dull. She had thrust herself half into a dune, which had crumbled around her. Her front flippers and large, flat head rested on a shelf of sand. Her mouth was a jagged, tightly closed line. Loggerheads feed on crabs, jellyfish, and seaweeds, and their powerful jaws can crack a horseshoe-crab shell in a single bite. To me, the mouth looked no more oversized than the rest of the beast. She let out a hard, grating breath. Her eye moved; her left back flipper scooped a lump of sand into the hole. "She's done," Bender said.

I walked back for a last look at the heap of eggs. Bender moved into the dunes to search for a spot to relocate the nest. Carefully, laboriously, the loggerhead shoved sand into the cavity with her back flippers, shifting her body from side to side with each swipe. She dug her front flippers deeper into the sand, presumably to keep from sliding down the dune. The motions were tediously slow; for me, knowing we would dig up her work within minutes of her return to the surf, the process was painful to watch. I flipped off my flashlight and sat down. The turtle heaved with another deep sigh and began breathing loudly, but with a more regular rhythm. The sound was harsh and resonant, like the sound of breath through a snorkel tube. Pulses of lightning outlined her shell. The irregular flashes tinted the seeds of the grasses, the ridges in the sand, the ghostly foam of the surf. We were miles from civilization, miles from anything resembling modern time. Without warning, she moved her front flippers, smearing sand over the area to camouflage the location of her eggs. Finished, she rested and sighed.

I followed three yards behind when she finally turned and began crawling back toward the water. Bender, strolling by with the tools she would use to move the nest, pulled a tape measure from her pocket and strung it across the turtle's carapace from front to back, then from side to side. "Thirty-seven by thirty-two," she said. "What you have here is a Joe-typical turtle." The turtle resumed her laborious crawl, stopping every ten feet. The resonant breathing continued. She moved faster as she neared the water, pausing a final time as the first wave hit her, raising her head and remaining motionless for thirty seconds, maybe longer. I could still see her when the second wave broke over her shell, but by the third wave she was gone.

Bender had begun to dig with her hands when I climbed back up the beach to the nest. "This sand is full of oyster shells, which really makes it hard to feel for the eggs," she said. "Geez, if we hadn't seen this turtle laying, we might have been here looking for the eggs all night." She dug with her hands for several more minutes, until she uncovered the small, moist balls. Before extracting them she lined the bottom of a plastic ice cooler with sand from the nest. "Whenever we relocate eggs we always include a little of the sand from the original nest," she explained. "I don't think anyone knows for sure if it makes a difference, but it's something we like to do."

The eggs were closely packed, and Bender could bring out three and four at a time. I put my hand into the nest cavity and cautiously pulled out two eggs. They were covered with sand and a transparent liquid. "You need to handle them carefully," Bender said, "but remember that she dropped them down two feet into the nest. They're not as brittle as chicken eggs." Together we extracted seventy-eight eggs, an unusually small number. After

Bender measured the nest's dimensions, I felt the rounded walls of the cavity with my hands and was surprised to find the air inside moist and warm, as if it had been heated by someone's breath.

We carried the cooler up a small dune to a flat area that seemed well out of reach of the tide. "This is the part that makes me nervous," Bender said, "because I feel a tremendous responsibility to make sure the eggs are in a safe spot." She began scooping out sand to form a pear-shaped cavity twenty-three and a half inches deep and twelve inches in diameter—the exact size of the original nest. She arranged the eggs inside, packed sand over the top, and covered the sand with a wire netting with openings large enough to allow hatchlings to crawl through but small enough to keep out foxes and raccoons. I marked a stake with the numerals 167, the number of the crawl, and inserted it into the dune.

The lightning had intensified by the time we had loaded the gear back on the cycle and resumed our patrol. "Time for a midnight break," Bender said, flagging down Vanness and Kosko. We drove to the beach in front of the blue houses and went inside for snacks.

The kitchen's fluorescent light irritated my eyes. Squinting and sniffling from the breeze, Vanness tore open a package of Lorna Doones, a delicacy someone had brought back from town. We had just consumed our first cookies when the wind gusted with a ferocity that sent us scrambling to close windows and doors. Shutters banged against the side of the house, and within minutes the sky began to throb with blue light that leaped and spread like the flickering of fire. Thunder cracked nearby, and we heard the approaching roar of rain. It hit the house in a burst, pouring over the gutters in thick streams and seeping through the windows on the southern wall. The atmosphere pulsed with light; it seemed that there was more electricity than darkness in the sky. Any thoughts of continuing the patrol had been banished. All we could do was hope instinct and fright would keep the turtles off the beach.

I could not help thinking of the fury of that night two months later as I boarded the ferry for a second trip to Bald Head. The thinly overcast dome seemed a pallid version of the lightning-filled sky that had driven us from the beach. The air was damp and limp.

The hatching season was at its peak, but the interns had gone back to school. Instead of riding the beach all night to watch for loggerheads erupting from the sand, I would join Meekins on her nightly check of the hatchery at 9:30. If none of the nests in the enclosure happened to be ready to hatch I was out of luck. And even if some of the clutches had broken out of their eggs, the turtles would not catapult through the sand covering the nest. As we waited for dusk, Meekins explained that for some reason most of the nests in the hatchery had developed pockets of air at the top of the cavities. When the hatchlings were ready to dig out, they could not reach the sand overhead. To compensate for the problem, she had started opening nests by hand after the eggs had incubated for seventy days.

"Usually if I just stick my hand down four or five inches—not enough to disturb the eggs, if they haven't hatched—I can see a head or two," Meekins said. "Then they all come pouring out. It looks like we may have built the hatchery on an overwash fan. The sand is very coarse, and that may have affected the way the nests held their shape. The nests in the state park are hatching out with no problems."

I had half-hoped to be able to see the hatchlings from the eggs laid by 167, the number assigned to the turtle that had nested as I watched. But barely sixty days had passed since that visit, and a nest laid by turtle 127 had hatched only the night before. "We're almost halfway through," Meekins said. "Every time a turtle makes a crawl, we give her a number. We had more than two hundred crawls and a hundred and thirty-three nests, a few more than last year. We thought we had a hundred and thirty-one, but the interns missed two nests that were laid near the inn."

Since Meekins and the interns hadn't known about the nests,

they were surprised when someone called to tell them baby loggerheads were crawling in the roads, the yards, and the marshes near the inn. "They were everywhere, even back in some of the freshwater ponds. People helped us collect them as fast as they could. I have no idea how many there were. That's what it would be like all the time if we didn't run this program. Absolute chaos."

It was time to go. A quarter-mile off the beach a trawler rocked with its outriggers extended in a wide V. "There's the enemy," Meekins said. She was not joking. Most of the fishermen I knew scoffed at the notion that the species needs federal protection, because loggerheads are still common sights in southeastern waters; the turtles chew up crab pots and rip holes in fishing nets, and many fishermen would welcome a decrease in their numbers. As I mounted the Honda behind Meekins, I was surprised to see the headlight shining white against the trees. "I just ripped the red cover off one day," she said. "We don't need it anymore. We even use a white flashlight to lure the turtles down to the water."

There were no sightseers at the hatchery to witness the night's release of baby turtles. As Meekins opened the pen door, she shined her flashlight around the edges in a search for hatchlings and tracks. The short wooden stakes that marked the nests gave the pen the look of a cemetery. A hundred yards to the east I could see that the phosphorescent waves were even brighter than on my previous trip. "Any activity in here?" Meekins asked, stepping into the pen. "Aha. I see some tracks. There he is. . . ." A dull brown turtle three inches in length crawled toward the beam of her light. She scooped up the animal and handed it to me. Cool and smooth, it wriggled in my hand. Its flippers moved alternately as it tried to skitter across my palm, but when I held it aloft by the shell its movement changed to the rhythmic butterfly stroke it would use in the surf. At Meekins's direction I placed it inside a wooden frame that surrounded nest 149.

"None of these are sinking in, so I guess we'll have to check the ones that are farthest along by hand." She bent over and began gently scooping out sand. About eight inches down she uncovered a turtle head. "Okay, these are ready to go." She pulled out the lead turtle and two others, then shined her light into the small cavity for me to inspect.

The sand below was writhing with life. Tiny flippers appeared from all directions and sank beneath tumbling grains of sand, rising and squirming in a wild attempt to break through to the top. Heads gaped and stretched toward me as rivulets of sand poured down. I reached in and brought out four of the animals. Four or five more immediately filled in the gaps. "They've been patient for so long," Meekins said. "Now every ounce of energy is geared toward getting out." Hurrying to free the leaders so those at the bottom would not be injured, I pulled dozens of turtles to the surface. Sand clung to their moist limbs and shells. Until hatching they had maintained a fetal position, and their shells, although stiff, were slightly curled. Each had a small yellowish nodule on its belly, the last of the yolk. I lowered my cupped palm into the warm sand and let it fill with turtles. Gently I pulled the hatchlings out and again curled my hand into the nest. I could feel turtles squeezing in between my fingers, like water seeping through cracks. Scraping at the edges of the hollow, I uncovered six hatchlings that seemed to be having difficulty digging out of packed sand.

At length they stopped breaking the surface, and I could feel no more wriggling limbs. In less than five minutes I had extracted seventy-five turtles. They bumped against each other in the frame, following the flashlight beam like a school of minnows rising to the surface for food. A few that had turned over on their backs pressed their tiny rear flippers together in a gesture of self-defense. They looked like miniature versions of Winnie the Pooh's friend Piglet. I had difficulty imagining them as three-hundred-pound adults.

We put the hatchlings in four buckets and started toward the beach. It is Meekins's custom to release hatchlings at a different point every night in hopes of reducing predation by fish, and we walked north to a wide stretch of beach. "Someone asked me the other night if I didn't feel horrible releasing these poor baby turtles into the surf to fend for themselves," Meekins said. "I said, 'listen, if I can get them this far I feel like I've done them a big service'."

The sand near the water lit with sparks beneath our steps. Fifty yards north of the hatchery Meekins stopped and set down the buckets. "I'll get in the water with the light to make sure the turtles head in the right direction. Try and release as many of them at once as you can." She kicked off her shoes and strode ankle deep into the surf, leaving me to dump four buckets of turtles simultaneously.

I gathered the buckets around me and watched her dark silhouette. The flashlight beam turned toward me. "Ready?" she called.

I lifted two buckets and tipped out their contents gingerly, spreading turtles across the sand. The ones that landed upright fanned out immediately, and not all toward the surf. I emptied the last two buckets and began righting turtles that lay on their backs and turning others toward the surf. Their frenzied movements never stopped, even when I picked them up, as if the purpose of their lives was to get somewhere, anywhere. I reached for a turtle to my right, lost my balance, and stuck out my foot to save myself from a fall. "Watch where you step," Meekins called sharply. I couldn't blame her; I could have easily killed six or seven hatchlings, maybe more.

The majority of the turtles were toddling toward the surf. Dark shapes dotted the sand as Meekins played the beam of light across the beach in a search for stragglers. I moved carefully up and down a five-yard area, collecting wayward hatchlings as quickly as possible. Within minutes the final turtles had scampered to the water's edge. The surf was rising and strong, and the spent waves swept sharply to the south, carrying the turtles in a wide arc. I took off my shoes and waded out beside Meekins; pricks of light dotted the foam that surrounded my feet. Despite the coolness of the night, the ocean was as warm as it had been in midsummer. A small hatchling ventured down toward the water, only to be caught by a wave and deposited neatly back on the beach.

Again it crawled down, and again it was knocked back. Meekins and I chuckled. The turtle's struggle had all the comic appearances of a small child trying to tackle a giant. "If they can get out a little ways and then stay low, the waves will break right over them," Meekins said. The straggler caught a wave on the ebb and rode past us stroking furiously, a baby on a water slide. Another wave broke over it, but it did not reappear.

I watched the phosphorescent breakers silently for several minutes. "That was some sort of show," I said.

"No it wasn't. It's not a show. We have people coming out here all the time who think it's a show, and they're the ones who can do the most harm because they don't take it seriously. A natural wonder, an awesome sight—you can call it anything like that. But please don't describe it as a show."

That was the last of my dealings with turtles this year, or so I believed as I rode the ferry back to the mainland. But ten days later I learned that the Pea Island refuge crew had encircled two loggerhead nests with a wire mesh to corral the hatchlings as they emerged. The turtles were to be taken to the state Marine Resources Center in Manteo and kept for a year to gain strength before being released. They were due to hatch any day. One night just past 12 o'clock I went out to the beach to see if the sand over the nests had started to sag in, a sign that the turtles were preparing to break through.

The evening was still and clear and moonless. The Milky Way stretched across the sky in two wide swaths. I picked my way slowly through myrtle and knots of saltmeadow hay, stumbling occasionally as grasses grabbed at my feet. The nests were on the south edge of the tern and skimmer colony, but no birds scolded me as I sneaked over the dunes. All of them had gone, leaving a peace that struck me as thick and unnatural. Anywhere else on the beach the silence would have seemed soothing. Here it only heralded the end of the year's richest season and the coming of cold.

I found the turtle nests with no difficulty. They lay only a yard apart, with cylinders of wire mesh around them. With a flashlight I could see that the sand over them was still packed firm. A ghost crab burrow had been excavated next to one of the cavities, but the crab had been unable to dig deep enough to invade the mesh. It skittered a few feet from the beam of my light, too timid to come close but too intent on the possibility of a meal to be driven away.

The sand showed no sign of collapsing, and the weather was too cool for me to stay on the beach without a sleeping bag. I turned out the light and walked toward the surf with my head back to gaze at the stars. Familiar constellations hugged the horizon—the sprung W of Cassiopeia and the pinched triangle of the Pleiades. Spread between them were specks of light that receded and floated toward me in deep, layered darkness. A hole in the sand caught me unawares, and I flung my arms wide to keep from falling. I turned on the light to see what I had stepped in. When I did, eight ghost crabs scrambled to the edges of the beam.

I shined the light north, then south. Hundreds upon hundreds of ghost crabs froze momentarily and danced away, as closely packed as a living, moving mat. Their numbers extended as far as I could see in both directions. In the diffused beam their shells appeared very white, like chips of plaster. It was an army of crabs afoot in search of food. I thought of the turtles below the sand, pipping through shells, unfurling their bodies as grains of sand trickled around them. The wire mesh surrounding their nests was the only reason to think they would live longer than two minutes.

Whatever turtles were still beneath the sands of Pea Island would have to evade a mob of crabs to reach the surf. The odds of breaking through those lines seemed remote, maybe worse than a hundred to one. And ghost crabs were only one of a dozen threats to the remaining clutches. The survival of any loggerhead still buried in the North Carolina sands would be jeopardized seriously by the events of the coming week.

8

ℋURRICANE

In late september, a tropical depression in the Caribbean attracted the alarmed attention of meteorologists at the Cape Hatteras weather station in Buxton. The system had formed off the coast of northern Africa, and it gathered strength at an unusual rate as it moved east toward the Lesser Antilles. Its spinning, counterclockwise winds accelerated, then slowed, then doubled in force, skimming salty moisture from the ocean and tossing it into the clouds. At the center of the storm warm air plunged downward, causing drastic shifts in pressure. Like the iris in an eye, the core widened and narrowed. By September 23 the storm had become Gloria, the largest hurricane ever to develop in the Atlantic Ocean.

On Hatteras, news of Gloria's northward movement was

greeted at first with little interest. The summer rentals had begun to empty for the season, and the pace of life had slackened. The ponds at the Pea Island refuge had filled with widgeons, teals, and a smattering of migrant shorebirds. The slant of sunlight had changed in a matter of days from the direct glare of summer to the more diffused sheen of autumn, staining the sand orange and streaking the sky with vermilion and mauve. The waxy tassels of sea oats had dried a crisp brown. As the wind shifted from southwest to northeast and back, the ocean color changed from celadon to a cold, broody blue and then to jade. During the third week of the month, the surf spread up the beach with unusual force as the moon slid directly between the earth and the sun to create the year's greatest tidal pull. At night, black waves crept almost to the dunes, wetting my feet with a velvety hiss.

Early evenings I relaxed on my back porch and counted the lime-colored tree frogs that hopped among the pieces of wood and piles of shells I had collected during the summer. Brittle, cone-shaped cocoons constructed by bagworm moths hung like ornaments from the cedar outside the kitchen window. The air, fresh and slightly damp, was full of the melancholy that signals that the hottest days of summer have passed. It was far too pleasant to dwell on the possibility of a major storm. Besides, Gloria was the third hurricane of the season that forecasters had said might swing our way. The others had not come close.

By Tuesday, September 24, Gloria had become enough of a threat to the Atlantic seaboard to merit comment among my neighbors. The next morning I wandered over to the Island Convenience, a small store owned by Mac and Marilyn Midgett. A sprawling complex by Rodanthe standards, it includes a quick-stop grocery, gas station, garage, crane hoisting service, storage yard for broken-down cars, and a real estate office. It is also the place neighborhood residents cash checks and catch up on gossip. The newspaper I picked up had a small story about Gloria on page one. I glanced at it as I pushed my quarter across the counter toward Mac's sister, Mildred Midgett, a solid island woman who is perpetually calm and pleasant.

"How are you, Mildred?" I asked absently, leafing to the paper's back sections.

"I'm fine, but I'm already tired of people talking about this storm. Seems like that's all anyone can think about this morning."

"Really?" I turned to the front page for a closer look. At press time Gloria had been eight hundred miles south of Cape Hatteras.

"One man already came in and said he was evacuating. He said it wasn't worth waiting until the last minute. I guess we'll have some sort of big storm tomorrow, whether it's a hurricane or not."

"Huh. I didn't realize it was that much of a threat. You think you'd leave if it started coming this way?"

"I haven't left for a storm yet."

"I don't know. If the forecasters said it was going to hit us dead on, I think I'd leave. I don't trust my house to stand up in a-hundred-and-thirty-mile-an-hour winds."

Mildred, one of the kindest souls I had met on Hatteras, looked at me askance. "That house has stood through more storms than you have," she said.

Outside, Randy Hall and Debbie Bell, my next-door neighbors, were talking to a car full of surfers, all of whom wore sunglasses with white frames. Hall had been leaning into the car, absorbed in conversation, but he extracted his hand and waved when he saw me. "It's coming. There's no doubt about it," he hollered. "There's a high-pressure system that's going to suck it right up the coast."

The day was cloudy and warm, but the air felt dry. I dropped the paper on the kitchen table and made a pot of coffee. I had no television, no reliable radio, no way to monitor Gloria's progress. Neither could I force myself to concentrate on the work I had scheduled for the day. If Gloria did drift toward Hatteras, I would have only a few hours to decide which of my possessions I most cherished and pack them up. But I was letting myself get rattled; I needed to get down to work. I would feel better if I got down to work.

After an hour of staring out the kitchen window at five gulls that circled and swooped above the myrtle, I walked across the street to see Mike Halminski, a wildlife photographer. He emerged from his darkroom with a marine radio and set it on the back porch.

The announcer reported that Gloria was 680 miles south of Cape Hatteras and moving north at fifteen miles an hour. If the storm followed the predicted course, it would make landfall on the cape sometime Thursday night. "Hurricane Gloria is a dangerous hurricane with winds gusting to a hundred and fifty miles an hour. Residents of the Outer Banks should be aware of its progress. . . . Windows should be boarded or taped, and objects outside that could serve as missles in hurricane-force winds should be secured. . . . The biggest loss of life in hurricanes results not from high winds but from drowning. . . . Heavy surf already threatens to overwash portions of Highway Twelve at Pea Island, the S curves north of Rodanthe, portions of Hatteras Island north of Buxton. . . ."

"Pretty scary," Halminski said.

The clouds had grown thicker, and the air was now heavy and damp. "Maybe I'm imagining it," I said, "but there's a really strange feeling in the air."

Halminski looked south toward the Chicamacomico station. "Maybe I should park my truck on that little hill and go on up into the station. It's stood through a lot of storms."

"If it starts to look bad I'm leaving. It's not worth taking the chance."

Robin Gerald, a local jack-of-all-trades, appeared in the doorway. "Anyone want to buy some pictures to remember this place?"

"Or some oceanfront property?" Halminski asked.

The two friends had moved to Hatteras more than a decade before, when they were in their early twenties and the island was only beginning to be developed. Both loved the violence of the Hatteras weather, but neither had ever experienced a major hurricane.

"She blows through here, my house is gone," Gerald said

loudly. "That property over there's one of the lowest points on the island. Your house might be okay, might not." He was enjoying himself.

"It would be something to see a storm like that blow in if you knew for sure you were in a safe place," Halminski said.

"I don't have anywhere to go even if I did evacuate," Gerald said. "Nowhere's safe from them things, nowhere that I can go. Better to stay here and go down thrashing."

My stomach churned as I walked back to the house. There was nothing to be concerned about, not yet. Gerald had a knack for embellishment, and I was letting it overpower my common sense. The previous year Hurricane Diana had stalled south of Hatteras for two days, and park service rangers had cleared the beaches of tourists under fair skies, even as Diana lost much of her power and turned inland two hundred miles south of Ocracoke. Something similar could happen with Gloria. Above all I wanted to avoid being an alarmist. I got the keys to my pickup and pulled into the line that had started to form at the Island Convenience's gas pumps. Inside Mildred and Marilyn were ringing up purchases with studied efficiency, as if nothing unusual was going on. A balding man I had seen but couldn't place walked in behind me. "I'm getting ready to evacuate," he announced.

"You are?" Mildred asked. She seemed surprised.

"Yes. If it was just me I could take care of myself, but I have to think of mother, you know."

At home I called Wally DeMaurice, the meteorologist I had talked with about hurricanes and northeasters the previous spring. Gloria had been declared a Category Five storm, the worst on the scale, with winds of 150 miles an hour or greater. "Looks like your predictions of doom may come true," I said when DeMaurice reached the phone. "But really—is this storm any different from Diana?"

"Oh, very much so. It has the potential to be a real killer. There's no reason to expect it to lose strength, and it will be approaching our area at about twenty-five miles an hour. That's

five times faster than Diana. And one of the complicating factors is that we're in a period of astronomically high tides. We're
already running about three feet above normal, which with heavy
northeast winds is enough to cause overwashes in several sections of the island. I'm going to send my wife and son off the
island tomorrow if things keep looking like they look now. I've
got to stay. Get back in touch with me after the storm, if I'm
still around." He chuckled grimly.

I hung up with a shaky hand. For the first time I looked hard
at the photographs of my family, the porcelain jewelry box on
my dresser, the jeans and sweaters in my overflowing closet.
Which of these could not be replaced? I had far too many things
to take, but how would I whittle down my list of valuables to a
manageable size? To calm myself I began gathering notebooks,
sorting papers, making mental lists. The framed pictures would
have to come off the walls in case the house started shaking—
which seemed more than likely in hurricane-force winds. The
stereo could be moved to a cabinet in the dining room.

Did I have enough water in jugs for after the storm? I took
down a kerosene lantern, filled it, and checked the wick. The
electricity could go off at any moment, hurricane or no. Outside,
I unlashed the bird feeders I had hung on the clothesline supports, and I piled cinder blocks on top of two doors I had stored
on the back porch. Could a hurricane hurl a cinder block through
a wall? Maybe, but if the wind reached that strength the house
would probably break up.

Nearby I could hear the whirr of saws and the hammering of
nails as a cottage owner boarded his windows. I had no plywood,
but most of my windows contained small mullions that might
withstand the wind. It was barely afternoon, anyway, and I would
probably not leave until the next morning, if at all. For something to do I wandered down to the beach. The steel-gray water
swelled fully but broke with little force. In recent weeks the beach
had steepened. Now it dropped to the water in three steps: a six-
inch ledge at the high-tide mark, a thirty-degree incline at the
low-tide line, and a final scarp ten yards below that caused

incoming waves to break a second time. Beyond that, the bottom had built and flattened as the weaker summer surf carried sand inland from nearby shoals. Nothing appeared the least unusual.

A wave glided toward me, and the sand began to bubble with mole crabs. In the past month they had doubled in length and weight. They would probably survive if a hurricane hit full force, but what would happen to the houses on the beach? It occurred to me that in a mere six months I had grown inordinately fond of the two miles of beach to the north, where I had climbed dunes, watched ghost crabs, and puzzled over the spread of shells across the sand. In a matter of hours a hurricane conceivably could render it unrecognizable. I went home and turned my dilapidated radio to an AM channel, which was blurred with static.

Gloria had moved fifty miles closer and was expected to pick up speed. The Dare County Commissioners advised Hatteras Island residents to prepare for evacuation before sunset. A mandatory evacuation had already been ordered for Ocracoke Island, since rough water was expected to suspend ferry operations by midnight, and it was not unlikely that Highway 12 would be flooded by dawn. If the storm continued on its predicted course, the Outer Banks might receive ocean surges of up to eighteen feet. The ground beneath my house was only four feet above sea level. An eighteen-foot tide would put the first floor under water.

I had no choice but to leave. Hurrying to the kitchen, I pulled from the cabinets a hand-painted platter that had been a gift from a friend and a pair of delph candlesticks my father had brought me from Holland. In my office I moved a clock, a vase, and an antique microscope away from the windows and stuffed my most important files into boxes to be put in the truck. I considered carrying a few things upstairs to protect them from flooding, but remembered that the roof could possibly come off.

I lowered the storm windows, moved furniture away from outside walls, stuffed a suitcase with clothes, packed a single box of mementos. The rest could be replaced. I had heard that a few windows should be left cracked to relieve sudden, drastic pressure changes as the eye of the hurricane passed over, so I raised two of the storms. The telephone rang with calls from anxious friends: I was leaving, wasn't I? I opened the door to the freezer and looked at my stockpile of food. All of it would be lost if the power went out for days. But if that were all I lost, I would feel exceedingly lucky.

I paused on the front porch long enough to wave to Halminski, who was loading boxes into his truck. "I'm going tonight," he called. "No sense hanging around and taking a chance on the roads." He was not alone. A steady flow of cars, campers, and trucks with trailered boats had begun moving north.

Near 8 o'clock, an hour after dark, I surveyed the rooms a final time to check for items that needed to be secured. The sounds of sawing and hammering had grown louder; probably they would continue well into the night. I glanced briefly at two posters tacked to the kitchen wall and a ceramic pitcher on top of the hutch—they really could be replaced—before breezing through the living room and bedroom. On my dresser I spied a roll of film I had taken the previous week. Dropping it into my purse, I turned out the lights and locked the front door. As I drove away a feeling of nausea and fear settled firmly in my gut.

I drove only as far as Nags Head that night, bedding down on a friend's floor and making plans to turn inland the next day. By 11 p.m. the pace of the storm had slowed, and it was still five hundred miles south of the cape. I went to sleep feeling calmer and slightly foolish for fleeing so soon.

At daybreak the air was motionless, the sky cast with a textureless layer of cloud. The morning felt ominously empty, like the sudden, heavy silence that precedes an explosion of temper. Every television channel was filled with news about Gloria's move to within four hundred miles of the cape. I called the National Park Service and learned that Highway 12 had not flooded; as I had feared, I had been spooked into leaving too soon. I wondered about the condition of Pamlico Sound and the height of the surf. It seemed ridiculous to leave when the storm was not due for twelve hours or more. At the very least I had time for a trip back across the Oregon Inlet bridge.

I could see the tide washing high on the beach as I crossed the first leg of the bridge and began to climb to its crest. Below, the sound glistened, glassy and flat. The breakers at the inlet appeared small and less frenzied than usual. Great egrets crooked their necks to spear fish in the marsh beneath the bridge, and a tri-colored heron dashed across a mud flat on skinny legs, as if trying to chase down a crab. Above the north shore of Hatteras, a kingfisher perched on a wire with its bill pointed west. The scene was so calm and normal as to be spooky. I pulled into the parking lot at the bridge's southern edge and turned my truck back to the north.

At the time I began my drive inland, Halminski and Gerald sat on the porch of Mac and Marilyn's store and debated whether to leave. Despite his intention to evacuate the evening before, Halminski had worked until 1 o'clock moving his camera equipment to higher ground. Now he and Gerald—neither of whom had evacuated during the long threat of Hurricane Diana—quietly watched as Coast Guard vans and the last trickle of tourists and residents headed north. Neither wanted to go, but each was hesitant to stay alone. Debbie Bell, Randy Hall, and the rest of the immediate neighbors had already left. Finally Mac Midgett wandered out of the garage. A burly man with thick, curly sideburns that creep to his chin, Mac is known on Hatteras for his physical strength and fearlessness. "Looks like the whole island's gone," he said.

"Fleeing like a pack o' rats," Gerald said.

"I guess I'll load up and go."

"You're leaving?"

In the end only about four hundred people would stay on Hatteras, most of them in Buxton. More than two thousand residents, including the most weatherworn Hatterasmen, fled by dusk. As I drove west, past motels with "No Vacancy" signs in Columbia and Plymouth, past crowded emergency shelters in Williamston, Gloria neared shore and began to threaten

Morehead City, fifty miles southwest of Ocracoke. As I arrived at a friend's house in Kinston and unloaded my gear, the hurricane turned north, directly toward Hatteras. The wind rose. The heavy rains expected all day began just after dark. I sagged into bed at 10:30 with Gloria ninety miles off the cape and moving north at twenty-five miles an hour.

If the storm traveled up Pamlico Sound, Hatteras Island would be to its east. The greatest winds and most dangerous storm surges occur in the northeast quadrant of a hurricane, where the forward motion of the storm boosts the power of the gusts. If the wind speed alone was 120 miles an hour and the storm moved north at 25 miles an hour, the combined winds would be 145—strong enough to destroy most buildings. Even if it passed east of the island, the damage could be significant. Maybe, I thought, maybe it will still stall and go out to sea. The branches of two red maples scraped the roof as I fell asleep.

At 2:30 I woke up, startled by the quietness. The wind had quit, and my head felt stuffed with cotton. I crept downstairs to the living room and turned on the television. A weatherman was pointing to a map of the United States that had giant snowflakes pasted on top of Utah and Colorado. I kept the volume down until a map of eastern North Carolina flashed on the screen. "And as we reported an hour ago, Gloria did make landfall at Buxton on Hatteras Island about one-fifteen and is making her way up the coast," the weatherman said. "Reconnaissance flights show that she has already passed through the town of Avon, and the eye is about ten miles north of there at this time. It appears that the serious damage from the storm will be limited to the Outer Banks. So most of us in eastern North Carolina have a lot to be thankful for this evening."

Ten miles north of Avon! Five miles south of Rodanthe! Right now the winds would be blowing hard out of the east, three times as hard as during the northeaster that had kept me awake all night in April. The house would be shaking; dishes might be crashing out of cabinets. Gloria had been downgraded to a low Category Four hurricane, which meant gusts of only 130. A difference of twenty miles an hour did not strike me, just then, as significant. At least the storm had hit near low tide; the strong lunar pull meant that tides would be unusually low as well as unusually high. Low tide at Hatteras Inlet had occurred a few minutes after 1:00. Still, the ocean would be splashing over the dunes at the S curves and flowing down Highway 12, which would become a riverbed. Water would be lapping at my front door, my back door, maybe trickling into cracks. As the eye passed over, the air would grow still for perhaps twenty minutes. Then a hard west wind would slam the house, bringing a flood from the sound. I should have boarded the windows. I should have boxed up the ceramic pitcher.

I am standing in the kitchen. The wind has ripped my favorite posters off the wall. A spray of rain is blowing through a shattered window, and the water in the house is already six inches deep. Two plastic cups bob next to the hutch, which is lying on its side. An avalanche of broken glass spills from its open door. The flood is rising fast, but it hasn't reached the paintings I piled on top of the pub table in the dining room. Maybe it won't. The table's no great loss; it needed to be refinished, anyway. . . . I am in my bedroom shaking my head at the twisted frame of my iron bed. A minute ago the dresser fell over and bent the footboard so badly it can never be straightened. The house is still vibrating, and it looks like the two northeast windows will be broken out by waves any time. Upstairs the roof is leaking; water has begun to drip down the stairs.

The light the next day was a splendid yellow glaze that ricocheted from puddles and stabbed at my chafed, swollen eyes. The sky was cloudless, the weather unseasonably warm. By the time I reached Nags Head, the day had attained a peacefulness that only heightened the numb sensation produced by my lack of sleep. The waves that had swamped the causeway between Manteo and Nags Head drained off before noon. By 1 o'clock a line had formed at Whalebone Junction, the crossroads in south Nags Head where Highway 12 forks to the south. Some Hatteras residents had been able to return home by boat, but the rest of us were told we would have to wait until the highway was reopened at 6:00.

The information available about conditions on the island was sketchy, and certain details only heightened my worry. Most of Hatteras had flooded; there was talk, in fact, that a new inlet had been cut through. Rumors circulated that three houses had burned in electrical fires. Other rumors reported that damages were surprisingly light. Telephone calls to the Buxton weather station and the Dare County sheriff's office in Buxton brought news that the wind speed had reached only eighty-seven miles an hour on the island and that no one had been killed. Nevertheless, the force of the winds that preceded the storm had pushed most of the water in Pamlico Sound northward into the mainland's rivers and creeks. The harbors at Hatteras and Avon had been sucked dry; then, after the eye of the storm passed, the water had gushed back in a twelve-foot wave. Many homes had been badly flooded; a few had collapsed. A radio station in Kinston reported that two houses in Rodanthe had exploded. My heart lodged firmly in my throat.

By midafternoon tempers had begun to boil among the people who waited at Whalebone Junction. Many telephones were working on Hatteras, and calls to people who had ridden out the storm produced reports that Highway 12 was easily passable by four-wheel-drive truck. Still, the county commissioners had ordered that the highway remain closed until 6:00 to give workers time to scrape away sand and debris. Not even firemen would be allowed through. It was a dictum several Rodanthe men did not look upon kindly.

Shortly before 2 o'clock, a state highway trooper stationed at the turn-off to Hatteras Island looked up to see a line of pickups and jeeps speeding toward two patrol cars being used to barricade the highway. The shoulders of the road, although soggy, were clear on either side. The trucks whipped around the cars in a spray of water and continued south. The tactic signaled that Hatteras residents were determined to protect their property from fire and thieves—and that lawmen had best not stand in their way. Within the hour county officials had a change of heart; by

3 o'clock firemen and emergency service workers were granted permission to return to their homes.

The rest of us sat in our cars, grudgingly, as the sun began to set. Just before 6:00—forty-five minutes before dark—the barricades were moved aside and a mile-long string of traffic unleashed. Cars and trucks crowded behind recreational vehicles that slowed for four-inch-deep puddles. I drove three miles, then stopped dead behind an airstream trailer. Five minutes later, the line of traffic moved on.

Muddy water washed beneath my truck and sloshed to its bumper. On dry sections of highway, streaks of sand showed where dunes had eroded, and pockets of myrtle leaned to the east as if punched in by a fist. Otherwise, little damage was visible north of Oregon Inlet. But as I began the descent from the bridge I could see water lapping into the ridge of shrubs along the sound. The six-yard-wide beach in front of the shrubs was submerged. Farther south a line of telephone poles keeled badly to the east, and wire tangled on the ground. Thick swirls of eelgrass and rushes marked where the sound had crashed across the road and into the fields, almost to the primary dunes. Patches of mud, rippled in a pattern left by waves, covered the pavement. To my surprise, the tall, stately dunes on Pea Island appeared unscathed.

The sun had become a leaking red globe. Shadows stretched across the land as the sky turned to rose. I passed North Pond, only glancing at the squat profiles of two black-crowned night herons against the north dike. Normally they stuck to more secluded areas of the pond; normally I would have hit the brakes at the sight of them. Water from the pond brimmed close to the highway, as close as I had ever seen it. Birds appeared everywhere—hawks and herons, kingfishers and kestrels—but for once I did not care. Cars began to pass me at more than seventy miles an hour.

Bulldozers had scraped sand off the road at the S curves and piled it into six-foot mounds, next to chunks of wood and piles of rush stems. I braked briefly for the turns and accelerated in a burst. The roof of my house was still there and still shingled. I pulled carefully into the driveway—numb, anxious, afraid to go inside.

Flounder, pike, and croaker carcasses were strewn among the reeds, and the standing water smelled of marsh and mud. A wave had deposited a line of eelgrass on the top step, but the front porch was dry. Still aware of the traffic streaking by, I unlocked the door in the diminishing light, sucked in my breath, kicked off my sandals, and stepped into the living room. The rug was dry. I shined my flashlight on the windows, across the sofa to the stairs, and back into the kitchen. Except for a small puddle in the kitchen that had blown under the back door, the entire downstairs was dry. The second story was also undamaged. This cannot be, I thought, letting my gaze float around the rooms, to the paintings on the pub table, the posters in the kitchen, the ceramic pitcher. I lit the kerosene lamp and sat down, slowly, in the kitchen. The last light of evening I had come to love so well seeped through salt-sprayed windows.

On the beach that night, a waxing moon tickled the waves with bright ribbons of white. Where two days before the beach had been scarped and steep, it now sloped gradually to the surf. The breeze was light and from the southwest, the water as tepid as tea. Pulses of lightning turned the few clouds that remained on the horizon a fleeting, burning orange.

"We should have stayed. Man, think of the waves we could have had yesterday morning."

"One of my cottage owners, a window of his blew in and he had glass literally embedded in his carpet."

"Nobody wants to go look in the graveyards. In this much water them bodies are likely to come floating up. They'll have to figure out who's who and rebury 'em."

"There was so much salt in the air you felt like you were standing on the deck of a ship in the middle of the blowing ocean."

"We were damn lucky, that's all I've got to say."

The next morning, when finally I pulled myself out of bed,

the grass in my yard was an ashen gray from salt and mud. Traffic cruised slowly past the house as the first groups of sightseers trickled into town. Most declared Rodanthe a disappointment—nothing to see except residents drying out clothes and carpets—but in Avon the damage was more sensational. At least two houses lay in shreds. Eelgrass festooned the tops of beacons in the sound and the tips of six-foot shrubs on the east side of the road. In places, planks of fine-grade lumber had been carried by water from construction sites and strewn along the road.

The towns of the cape began to buzz with the camaraderie and good will that accompany disasters. Normally taciturn neighbors toured each other's houses, inspecting the damage and trading tales. People whose homes had not been flooded made up spare beds for the less fortunate, then pooled their foodstuffs and cleaning supplies. My house had been one of the few ground-level structures to escape flooding as Gloria pushed four feet of water through town. A fish house on the creek near my backyard marsh had exploded, its walls apparently pushed out by changes in pressure. Beyond it lay a swath of reed stems and trash thrown to the northeast—directly toward my house—by the surge from the sound. In the old village of Avon, two hundred houses had flooded, some by as much as seven feet, and the reported damages would exceed one million dollars. But the towns of Hatteras had stood, had even suffered remarkably little damage. Like several of my neighbors, I began to wish I had stayed through the storm.

I went to see Wally DeMaurice at the weather station, where he and two of his staff had worked through the night of the storm in a reinforced concrete-block building. During the twenty-six minutes that Gloria's eye passed over Buxton, DeMaurice had taken time away from his instruments only to dash outside and release a weather balloon. He pulled a paper from a file and slapped it on the table where I sat. It was a chart of barometric pressure during Gloria's approach. By 6 p.m. the pressure had begun a nearly vertical decline. At midnight it dropped completely off the chart.

"Never in twenty-six years of weather watching have I seen the barometer drop so fast," he said. "I know some people are wondering what all the commotion was. But keep in mind that we were extremely lucky. There were about six factors that worked in our favor. If any one of them had been different, the damage would have been much, much worse. That storm traveled from the west coast of Africa. If it had passed twenty miles to the west of us, up the sound, we would have been in the maximum energy field. It would have raped the Outer Banks. If it had hit at high tide, we would have had twelve feet more water than the predicted tide for that date. As it was, we only got about three to four feet more over most of the island, maybe five to eight feet in Avon.

"Remember, at one point this was the biggest storm ever to develop in the open Atlantic. Now, it lost a lot of its strength, but it still had the power to push all the water in Pamlico Sound to the north. When you think how much that amount of water weighs, you know the force behind it was staggering."

Whatever thrills I may have missed, I had been wise to leave. And for the next several days the residents of Hatteras would be granted a reprieve from work, since life would not return to normal as long as the electricity remained off. Why not relax and enjoy the commotion?

Meals became unusually festive as freezers defrosted and stocks of food thawed. Saturday night Halminski boiled ten pounds of shrimp, and Debbie Bell grilled eight pounds of steak raised at her father's farm on the mainland. In the absence of normal life, people organized their days around meals. Only minimal clean-up work could be done without electricity to pump water, and even when the power was restored, many wells would be salty from the tide and polluted from overflowing septic tanks.

Stories began circulating of people who had stayed through the storm, what they had witnessed, and how they had reacted. In Avon, where wind gauges had recorded gusts of more than a hundred miles an hour, residents retreated to the second stories of their houses as water poured into their living rooms and dens.

Many of the oldest houses in town had been bolted to their foundations after the hurricanes of 1933 and 1944 had floated them to the beach. As Gloria pushed water from the sound through the village, a few residents cracked open their doors to allow it to flow through their houses rather than splinter the frames.

Rachel Austin pried loose two floorboards in her living room to prevent the flood from pushing up her entire first floor. As the sound tide swept through their front yard and toward the swaybacked house where the Austins had lived for forty years, the seventy-two-year-old woman and her husband, Willie, began piling up their furniture and appliances. Within ten minutes after water began gushing through the floor it had crested the window sills, turning Rachel's flowered wallpaper and yellow curtains a muddy gray. The refrigerator toppled over, and the stove twisted from its pipe. A mantel fell out from the wall. But the house was one of the oldest residences on the Outer Banks. Assuming it would stand through one more storm, they retired for the evening in their second-story bedroom after securing as many of their possessions as they could. All night they could hear water slopping against their furniture. They slept fitfully, but were content to be dry and warm. The next morning they went downstairs to find the kitchen blown off the house.

Again and again I heard people relate tales of stepping out into the eye of the storm and seeing stars, of walking to a neighbor's house in the worst of the wind, of drifting off to sleep and waking disappointed to find Gloria past. A few admitted twinges of anxiety after the sound flooded the island. Only once did I hear a resident express unbridled fright.

Brad Nash has yellow-white hair and a face so tan his blue eyes seem to shine through it like those in a jack-o'-lantern. A crabber and furniture builder who lives with his parents in Avon, he has resided on Hatteras full-time for seven years. As Gloria moved up the coast, he dismissed his parents' pleas to evacuate and settled into the third floor of his house, with his dog and two cats. The fourteen-year-old wood structure sits on three-foot pilings on a canal near the sound.

Nash had tracked Gloria as it moved up the coast and had noticed it was losing strength. As dusk approached and the winds rose, he tuned his maritime radio to the Cape Hatteras station and positioned himself in the living area at the southeast corner of the house. Nearby he had a wind gauge, a telephone, a life preserver, and an open notebook.

"At some point I decided I needed to keep a journal, if only to keep myself sane. I'm not sure when it became clear to me that the storm was actually going to hit. But by seven-thirty or eight I knew I was on Hatteras for good, that there was no getting off."

Nash's notes began at 8 p.m.

Winds NE, steady 50 to 65. Gusts to 85. I feel very much alone. House shaking, pets okay.

8:07—Winds 60 to 75.

"It occurred to me about this time that the buildings around me might pose a big threat. I wasn't worried about this house blowing apart on its own. It's too solid. But there's a house next door on stilts, and I began thinking that its windows might blow out and it might fall over, like a sprung umbrella."

9:00—Gloria 140 miles south of Hatteras. Gusts to 90.

As the hurricane appproached, Nash began to receive phone calls from his anxious parents and from a friend who was driving east from Chicago to Maryland. The conversations eased his tension; as long as the phones continued to work, things couldn't be too bad. Periodically he ventured outside, where he used a large floodlight to watch the water level drop in the sound. By 11:00 the canal beside his house was empty. He remembered that his neighbor had moored a forty-five-foot fishing boat on the far side of the canal. The thought suddenly made his stomach flip. If the boat broke from its mooring after Gloria's eye passed, it would probably ram his house.

The winds increased until Nash could no longer open the eastfacing door to a third-story deck.

11:30—Winds 80 to 90, gusts way past 100. House rumbling and shaking bad.

11:50—Something crashed and broke downstairs. Winds steady at 100+. Much wind noise—whistling and shrieking.

"At one point I jammed tissues in my ears because I couldn't stand the noise. It was very shrill. About this time too, an ash tray jumped across a desk and fell on the floor. That's how bad the house was vibrating. It would move considerably; it was like being on board a ship."

12:30—Barometer down to 29.

1:12—Ears starting to pop. Must yawn to help.

1:35—Eye here, with winds at 10 mph. Seems dead calm. Barometer at 27.8.

1:55—Eye gone. Winds west at 40. Very west. Still bone dry outside.

2:24—100+ west winds.

2:56—Strongest winds so far. House moving badly.

3:22—Phone dead. House being blasted.

Nash's journal did not make note of what time the sound tide rushed back in from the north. By then, however, he had opened the east-facing door to relieve changes in pressure and had gone outside to survey his immediate surroundings with the floodlight. He watched as a twelve- to fourteen-foot wave approached, lifting debris to its crest and slinging it forward.

"Everything started bobbing and dancing. There was debris all over the place, and the water was just sloshing violently. I had some piles of juniper six inches wide and sixteen feet long; they were flying around like Fritos. Waves started hitting the upstairs window.

"The thing that worried me the most was the big boat across the canal. It was straining at its ropes; I thought it had gotten loose. It would pull toward me during a lull, and then a gust would get it and flip it back away from me, like a slingshot. It danced around like crazy, like the tail on a kite. Sometimes I could barely see it, it was moving so fast. And then it would whip toward me again.

"It was about this time that I put on the life preserver."

Around 3:40 Nash crawled out the eastern door, digging his

fingers in between the planks on the deck. He could hear bangs and thumps coming from the sound side of the house, but without his floodlight he could not tell if the structure was being damaged. He wore a pair of goggles to protect his eyes. Slowly he slid his head and shoulders around the corner of the house to the west, bracing himself for the impact of Gloria's gusts. The wind caught him in the chest and threw him against the deck railing. He crawled back to safety, but not before he had seen that waves were tossing the fishing boat very close to the house.

3:44—*Big boat hitting house. Wind won't die. Can hear lumber cracking and breaking. House might go down.*

4:15—*Helpless. Wind won't stop. House can't stand the damage. I'll have a Dr. Pepper and a cigarette.*

4:39—*Wind down some. It'll be daybreak and nice weather soon.*

4:40—*It will subside.*

Before dawn he realized the fishing boat had rammed into a pile of lumber and lodged several yards from the house. By 5 o'clock the wind had dropped to between seventy and eighty, and the sound had begun to recede. Three feet of water still churned through his yard. Two lower-story windows had blown out, and water had washed into his shop on the first floor. But the building was intact.

"At that point," Nash said, "I kissed my pets, I went downstairs, I got on my very wet mattress, and I went to sleep."

9

_A_ FEVER FOR DRUM

AT THE END of a narrow, eastwest road in Rodanthe, the Hatteras Island fishing pier marches into the ocean on wide-set, creosoted legs. From the boardwalk fifteen feet up, the late fall surf seems not so much to curl as to heave. What appears from the beach to be a regular and predictable rhythm looks from above to be a ceaseless and violent thrashing. Long coils of water lunge toward shore, trailing veils of spray. Peaks of water pulse, hit the pilings, split, and fade. At night the sallow beams of pier floodlights cut through spray-soaked air and fall flat against the creamy water in a strange scene of perpetual motion and shadow. Just before 12:00 on an early November night I walked four hundred yards over angry breakers to the big-game area, a platform at the end of the pier where anglers crowd to fish for red drum.

Shortly before, an inch of rain had fallen in less than an hour, and a northeast wind had set whitecaps dancing on the sea. It was a moderate blow by Hatteras standards, but big enough to bring the forty and fifty-pound red drum closer to the beach. On the far end of the pier I could see a line of hunched yellow figures. No tourists were angling for bluefish and flounder now; everyone out in the midnight drizzle had one purpose, one pursuit. I stepped carefully on boards streaked with slime and blood. A knot of fishing line bounced in the wind. The pier shook with the weight of the breakers, which hissed by and crumbled, leaving a dead, hollow sound in their wake.

At the end of the pier, a row of ten-foot-long fishing rods had been propped side by side as close as the rails in a picket fence. Thirty-five fishermen in green and yellow slickers crowded in small groups and talked in fragments, conserving their energy against the damp air. In the spray-soaked light, the hooded figures were hazy, faceless, painted with shadow. No women had come out. Two teenage boys dozed on a bench in wet, rumpled sleeping bags.

I leaned against the rail and began counting the seconds between breakers, my way of passing time during what had become a nightly vigil. A fisherman beside me pushed his hood back, scratched a globe of curly hair with both hands, and shook his head. Another in a red-plaid hunting jacket pulled his hands from his pockets, reeled in a line, and backed away to cast. Two men to his right ducked as the sinker shot close by their heads. The caster returned the rod to the rail. "Might as well do something to keep myself awake," he muttered.

We were all waiting for a sound, for the high-pitched whizz of line stripping off a reel. On an autumn night in rough surf, only drum and shark are likely to seize a piece of bait and run. All talk halts when a reel begins to whirl. Anglers bolt for their rods, since drum commonly strike two or three hooks at once. Once a drum takes a piece of bait, it swims straight toward the beach or straight to sea. To land it, an angler must set the hook firmly and quickly take in slack line.

All week the big drum had been striking between midnight and 2:00, usually on a falling tide. I had yet to see one caught, although I had visited the pier several nights. That evening, an hour before I ventured out in the rain, a fifty-pound drum had been caught and two others lost. The one fish lay on the boardwalk near the entrance to the game-fishing platform. "You want to catch drum, you come out when the weather's worst," a ruddy-faced, barrel-shaped man told me, finishing the sentence with a quick nod of his head as if to say, "Damn straight."

The drizzle showed no sign of letting up. Every two minutes or so a large breaker rattled the pier, first to the north, then to the south. I took a seat on a bench next to the sleeping boys. The wind picked up momentarily; a chasm of sky split the clouds, then closed. The men debated whether to give up or fish another hour, whether to sleep at home or in the truck so they could start fishing again at dawn. A little before 1:00, when a line finally began to drag out, I had reached the numbed state that makes everything seem as if it is happening on the other side of a thick pane of glass.

Shoulders thumped together as ten fishermen rushed toward the southeast corner of the pier. A lanky blond man in camouflage pants picked up a rod that bent in a tight arc and, bracing himself, brought it back sharply. "Let him run, let him run," the ruddy-faced man shouted. Line spun off the reel for nearly a minute before the angler began taking it in. He jerked the rod clumsily and reeled furiously as the men around him hollered advice. I threaded my way to the side of the pier in time to see a dark shape break the surface and roll on its side. The lanky fisherman edged to the side of the platform, near where I stood. "It's a drum all right," someone shouted.

"Big one too. Sixty pounds."

"Thar she blows. Grab that net."

A dozen hands reached for the pier net and lowered it to the surf. But just when it seemed the current was about to push the fish into the silver rim, the line went slack.

"Damn," the lanky man said. "That's the third one I lost this week."

"What happened?" I asked.

"Shark got him and bit him clean off the line."

Someone directly behind me coughed roughly, as if trying to stifle a laugh. I turned around to see a dark-haired, broad-faced man in a green slicker. He backed away from the crowd and walked to the opposite edge of the pier, where he picked up a rod and began reeling in. I waited a minute before I crossed and looked over the rail, pretending to study the surf. The man finished reeling and caught his line, deftly flicking a soggy square of mullet from his hook and baiting it with a fresh chunk. "People seem to lose a lot of fish out here," I said.

"They lose more than they catch, that's for sure," the man said.

"Did a shark bite off that fish?"

"Nah, he just got flipped over and got off the hook. The line was too slack."

This was Tommy Gray, one of a half-dozen local, long-time drum fishermen who could be counted on to catch a couple of big drum from the pier every fall. At the height of that evening's downpour he had landed the fifty-pound fish that lay on the boardwalk.

I asked if he had played the fish for very long.

"Fifteen minutes. You don't have to play them long off the pier, not like off the beach." I had talked to anglers who had told of hourlong fights to land big drum on the beach.

The wind had calmed and men were beginning to leave. Gray reeled in two rods and said something about having had enough. He shouldered his rods and looked down at the drum, which lay gasping on its side. The air was damp and cool enough to keep it alive. "Guess I'll come back for that," Gray said, stepping around a group of men.

The lanky man in camouflage pants glanced down at the drum and glared at Gray's receding figure. "He should have thrown that fish back," he said. "There aren't enough of those big fellows left for everyone to keep what they catch." I turned away, startled by the scorn in his voice.

In a few minutes Gray returned, slipped his right hand under the drum's gills, and hoisted the fish in the air. He carried it only a few yards, then dropped it and picked it up with his left hand. A third of the way to the pier house he lowered his catch to the boardwalk and, flexing his hands, went off to search for a dolly or a gaff. The fish was directly under a light. Its pectoral fin flapped up and down, the edges curled by the wind. Moving closer, I watched its blood-red gills pumping like bellows and its mouth, rimmed by white cartilage, gaping open and closed. The copper had already faded from its sides. The drum was suffocating, slowly gulping in air. A decade or more of fighting the surf—hunting in sloughs, feasting on crabs, and dodging sharks—all to end up as Saturday night stew. The ruddy-faced man, passing by, paused to admire Gray's prize. "You're looking at fifty pounds of good eating, right there," he said.

Drum. The name derives from a sound, a dull thump-thump the fish makes by vibrating muscles around its swim bladders. Some people refer to the species as redfish because of its coppery color; others call it channel bass because of its habit of feeding in deep holes. At weights of between forty and ninety pounds, drum is the cape's trophy, the blue marlin of the beach. Of the fish landed on the cape each year, full grown drum comprise but a small percentage. Yet business owners estimate that for every one caught in the fall, Hatteras restaurants, shops, and motels take in a thousand dollars.

All night in October and November, as schools of drum move south along Hatteras Island, pickups and jeeps rumble over the plank ramps that bridge the dunes. On weekends as many as a hundred poles line the rail of the Rodanthe fishing pier, which extends far enough to enable casters to reach drum that feed on the east side of the outermost bar. Drum fishing is generally a male sport, since few women have the strength and technique to land a forty-pound fish. As such, it is a kind of fraternity in which members suffer gladly through long, cold nights of wind and rain. Family men with full-time jobs sacrifice meals and sleep to keep lines in the surf until dawn. And because the trickiest part of catching drum is simply finding them, theories on where and when the fish feed tend to be especially complex. Some anglers fish only on rising tides, some only on falling tides. Others, arguing that a stiff breeze will push crabs and small bait inland, fish only with the wind in their face. Still others believe drum feel most comfortable feeding near shore during the highest monthly tides, when more water fills the channels off the beach.

The rituals of drum fishing frequently exceed the bounds of reason. Normally unsuperstitious men use only their luckiest rods and rely on hunches to decide where and when to fish. If a fisherman catches a trophy-size drum at low tide, on that date a year later he may return to the same spot at precisely the same tide. And drum have given anglers some reason to resort to such charms and incantations. On November 7, 1973, a local schoolteacher landed the world-record red drum—ninety pounds—from the Hatteras Island fishing pier in Rodanthe. Eleven years later to the day, a Washington, D.C., biologist broke the record by catching a ninety-four-pound fish on a beach north of Avon.

Anglers divide red drum into three categories, depending on size. The smallest of the species is known in the local lexicon as puppy drum. Once a drum reaches a weight of about fifteen pounds it is called a yearling, although it is probably about four years old. Puppy drum and yearlings have firm and flavorful meat that is sold commercially in North Carolina in small quantities. The same species is harvested prolifically in the Gulf of Mexico, where it is known as redfish, a popular item in Louisiana cuisine. Once a fish reaches a weight of thirty pounds, its meat becomes tougher and brindled with blood. Scientists have not devised a precise aging method for red drum, but they believe the species needs about ten years to grow to a weight of thirty-five pounds and about twenty-five years to reach eighty pounds.

When anglers find drum they usually find them in profusion.

After spending the winter in a less active state offshore, as many as a thousand of the biggest and oldest drum move toward the coast in tight schools. Yearlings and puppy drum drift along the beaches in more loosely packed groups. As the water temperature nears 60 degrees, the schools travel north along barrier beaches in a search for a route to the sound. Columns of fish begin to peel off at Drum Inlet, Ocracoke Inlet, and, in April, Hatteras Inlet. A week or so later the fish reach Oregon Inlet. Some schools move north to Virginia and the Chesapeake Bay, and a few wander as far as New Jersey. Biological studies suggest that drum remain in the same groups and return to the same inlets each year.

As a school reaches an inlet, it scatters and mills through the deepest channels and sloughs, moving sporadically up and down the beaches. For six weeks it will stay near the inlet's rough waters; then it moves into quieter estuarine waters to feed. In late summer and fall drum wander back toward inlets to spawn. By the time the fish return to the ocean in October and November they are fat and at their fullest strength.

The species' habit of forming tight packs and passing through inlets in bursts makes it an easy mark for commercial fishing boats, which can deplete an entire school in a matter of days. During the 1950s marine biologists noticed that schools of drum in Virginia and North Carolina had diminished in size. In 1956 conservationists became concerned about the number of drum caught by accident by commercial fishermen, especially by crews fishing along beaches with haul seines. After sportsfishing clubs pushed for protective measures, the red drum became the first fish in North Carolina to be regulated by length limits and daily catch limits. Puppy drum must be at least fourteen inches long, and recreational and commercial anglers alike may keep only two drum a day longer than thirty-two inches. Even restaurants and fish packers may not possess more than two large drum at any time.

In spite of the restrictions, the species faces a new threat from anglers who fish for sport. In the past five years tackle shops have doubled and tripled their annual sales of the heavy rod and reel sets used to fish for drum. The sudden popularity of the sport is mitigated somewhat by the rate of success. Most anglers spend two to three years pursuing drum before landing a forty-pound fish. But so little is known about the habits and sizes of red drum schools that state biologists have no way to gauge whether the population has stabilized or continued to decline. Debate over how to manage existing stocks is vehement.

To most sportsmen the value of drum lies simply in the prestige of having caught a trophy-class fish. Many anglers who do not eat drum argue that every fish over thirty-two inches should be released. To Hatteras residents, however, the meat of even the largest drum is considered a delicacy to be divided among relatives and friends. Most frequently it is boiled with potatoes, onions, and salt pork. Because drum stew has always been a staple on the cape—one of only three or four truly local dishes— Hatteras natives do not take kindly to suggestions that they participate in conservation efforts by returning big fish to the surf.

The length and catch limits have stood virtually unaltered for twenty-five years. But on Hatteras certain laws have always been a matter of local option. Only one state game warden patrols seventy miles of beach, marsh, and water between Oregon and Ocracoke inlets. In the spring and fall, local fishermen commonly anchor near inlets as drum begin to move into Pamlico Sound. When the boats return to harbor, fifteen or twenty large drum are quietly unloaded and quickly disbursed to neighbors and friends. Hatteras residents blame mainland and out-of-state anglers for depleting stocks of their favorite fish. To provide for the natives is considered a local custom and privilege.

Where drum fishing is now a sport of fashion, ten years ago it was the sport almost exclusively of Hatteras residents and a smattering of avid saltwater anglers. On the Sunday night in 1973 when Elvin Hooper caught his ninety-pound, record-winning fish, only three other men, all Hatteras natives, were on the Rodanthe pier with their rods baited for drum.

Hooper had left home with a hunch. "I even told my wife,

don't expect me home too early, but when I come I'll have the world record drum. I figured I was about due for a fish, and I just had a feeling it was going to be a big one." A resident of Salvo with a moustache and dark, curly hair, he has fished for drum his entire life. He and three friends arrived at the pier about 1 a.m. as the tide began to rise. From his years of drum fishing, Hooper had come to believe that it is the water temperature, not the motion of tides, that makes drum most active and brings the biggest fish close to shore. "They feed when they get good and ready. That's all that counts. They're scavengers; they'll eat whatever the tide churns up, which is why they like rough water."

The air had a slight nip, and there was a moderate northeast wind. Hooper had brought two rods—a nine-and-a-half-foot rod with twenty-five-pound test line, and an eight-foot rod with fifteen-pound test line. He baited the hooks with cut mullet and settled back. Nothing happened right away, but that was to be expected. He checked his bait and waited.

About 2 a.m. the heavier test line began to drag out, but Hooper could tell by the play of the rod that he had hooked something small. He reeled in, watching the ocean until a skate broke the surface, flapping its squarish sides. A skate was nothing but a bother. By then, though, his other line had begun to play. He reset the drag on the reel and let the skate drop to the bottom.

Something large had struck the other line, too large by its feel to be a drum. If it was a shark it would probably break free, but it was worth playing for a few minutes. He began to reel, only to have the rod go slack. The shark had frayed the line and cut itself loose.

A skate and a shark. So far no luck. Hooper picked up the rod that had hooked the skate. To his surprise, the reel was stuck. "It wouldn't move. Wouldn't budge. So I yanked the rod hard." A second later the line began to whizz out with the force and speed that signaled drum.

Without knowing it he had driven the hook hard into the mouth of his record-breaking fish. He held the rod as the fish ran straight out from shore, then began to reel when he felt it pause. It did not seem to be a particularly powerful fish. Five minutes later when the drum rose to the surface sixty yards off the pier, Hooper and his companions were shocked by its size. "We knew it was a drum because it was acting like a drum. But it looked just like a barrel."

For ten minutes the fish remained on the surface, rolling frequently on its side in its struggle to break free. As Hooper brought it close to the pilings, the other men lowered the net and positioned it so the waves would push the fish, tail first, into the net. All four men helped haul it up to the pier. With a girth of nearly thirty-nine inches, it was the fattest fish Hooper had ever seen. "It was just a fat female that had grown so big she could swallow anything."

The flat tail of the skate still protruded from her mouth.

"It's been a strange year for fishing," Frank Merillat was saying. "A dry spring and the shrimpers make a killing, and now this; no drum, no mackerel, nothing but rain and big blows, one right after the other. The hurricane didn't help things either, it left the ground so soggy. Can't even get out to the point because of the water."

We were driving north from Buxton shortly past 11:00 on a still, moonless night. I had dressed in long underwear, my heaviest sweatshirt, a wool sweater, a rainslicker, wool pants, and rubber boots. It's been a strange year, period, I thought. The previous week a tropical storm had dropped nearly eight inches of rain in six hours, and a tornado had ripped the roof off a building at the Hatteras ferry dock. With a northeast wind at fifty miles an hour, a handful of men had remained on the Rodanthe pier, casting for drum even as the structure lurched from side to side and water lashed the wooden walkway. For their trouble the fishermen had landed two fifty-pound drum.

Much of Hatteras Island was still under water. Pools three feet deep filled the wide swale at Cape Point where the park service runs a campground, and the runnels in Buxton Woods were soggy with mud and decaying grass. The weather had curtailed what should have been the best fishing of the year. Highway 12 buzzed with trucks and jeeps carrying heavyweight rods on front racks, but few people were catching drum from the beach. Two mornings before, the annual blitz had begun from the Rodanthe pier. Between midnight and 7:00, anglers had landed eighteen trophy-class drum. The same night only five big drum were caught from the beaches to the south, where in a normal year thirty fish might be landed during the height of the fall run.

But the poor catches would not keep the most dedicated drum fishermen, including Frank Merillat, from trying. At this point in his life, Merillat is more avidly a surf caster than he is anything else. Thirty-seven years old, he spent much of his teens and early twenties mating on charter boats that fished offshore from San Diego. He had worked for several years as a drug and alcohol counselor in the mountains of Virginia, but a year and a half earlier he had brought his wife, Dhanyo, and son, Canaan, to Hatteras Island with the hope of settling down for good. To make money he paints houses, or sells tackle in a Buxton store, or packs fish on the Hatteras docks. Whenever possible he goes fishing, but only for certain fish. "I don't take pot luck, if you know what I mean," he once told me. "If I go out fishing for speckled trout, I don't want to come home with a bluefish." Recently he had started working as a guide for anglers who wanted to catch drum from the beach, and we were riding in a 1976 banana-yellow Wagoneer he had purchased for guiding trips. Merillat had a habit of stringing spare leaders from the sun visors. The thin filaments looped down into my line of vision like strands of spider webs.

During the previous two weeks Merillat had spent seven nights on the beach, usually setting up rods for three or four customers and standing by with pointers when they hooked drum. On this particular evening he had decided to go fishing for fun and had invited me along, although I had neither the skill to cast a ten-foot-long rod nor the strength to reel in a trophy-class fish. So far this season he had done well. Early in the month, when few other surf casters had been hooking drum, he had landed a fifty-pound fish north of Avon. He had caught several other drum, but the fifty-pound fish was his biggest of the year.

We peered at the highway through a line of fishing poles propped in plastic pipes on the bumper. The effect was of looking through the bars of a cage. A metal platform to which Merillat had strapped a cooler stocked with bait protruded from the front of the truck. This is standard equipment on Hatteras Island; on weekend afternoons large, lumbering pickups fill the beach at Cape Point, bearing rods and coolers like offerings before them. Merillat slowed and turned toward the beach, stopping to shift into four-wheel drive. In front of us a wooden ramp rose over the dunes from two deep, sandy ruts. He flicked off the headlights to keep from spooking the fish and drove on.

The beach was as dark as I had ever seen it. Strips of clouds lined the horizon, and the breakers foamed dim and gray, with none of the phosphorescent plankton of summer. The jeep lurched and bumped across the sand. "I can't see a damn thing," Merillat said, stopping to get out and survey his surroundings. To our right the sand dropped steeply to the water, a soft ridge that would collapse under the jeep. Fifty yards ahead were several trucks clustered near rods propped in the sand. "They pulled four fish out of that hole night before last," Merillat said. "They've been crowded thick around it ever since. I've got another spot we're going to try." He leaned far out the window to watch for a large X he had made that morning at the base of a dune.

When drum swim close to the beach, they pass through breaks in sandbars and enter deep, turbulent sloughs, where they feed on crabs and small fish that cannot swim well in strong currents. Anglers find these channels by looking for spots where the surf does not break. As we parked, baited our lines with cut mullet, and pushed three rod holders a foot into the sand, I could see waves splitting again and again around the same swath. The break seemed obvious to me, but there were no other trucks nearby. Merillat waded knee-deep into the surf and cast. I knew from watching him in daylight that the rig would travel seventy yards before dropping into the surf. Now all I could see was the rod catapulting forward in his hands.

With three lines out, we pulled beach chairs from the jeep and sat down. A weak beam from the Hatteras lighthouse swept rhythmically across the sea and onto the beach. I was already cold. There would be no quitting before Merillat was ready to quit, and I doubted he would be ready much before dawn. The rods leaned above us, their tips bending with the tugs and jolts of the surf. In the darkness I could barely see the lines sweeping down to the water. Unlike pier fishing, beach fishing is a lonely sport; it would be easy to fall asleep and wake up to find a rod dragged out of its holder by a shark or a drum. For diversion we had brought beer and coffee to drink, sandwiches and donuts to eat.

Merillat sat down uneasily, as if anxious for a strike. A compact man with a dark, gray-streaked beard, lopsided glasses, and wiry, untamed hair, he seemed full of energy considering the lateness of the hour. "Do you know what to do when you get a drum on?" he asked suddenly.

I shook my head.

"The first thing you need to learn is that drum like to run. The way you fish 'em, when a line goes off you need to just let it go. The other night a kid in one of my parties hooked a big drum. I set the hook for him, so I'm pretty sure the fish was on there good. If he had kept his head he would have gotten it to the beach. But the fish kept running and running, and this guy started to panic. He decided the drag was set too loose, so he started messing with the tension. And boom, the fish was gone. Broke the line right off.

"Letting 'em run is the way to tire them. You run a hundred yards and see if you're not tired. Then when he sees he's not going to get away by running out to sea, he'll turn and let you ride him in a good way before he really starts to fight. He might try to rub the hook off on the bottom. Imagine how you'd feel if you had this irritating little thing pulling at the side of your mouth." Merillat grabbed a section of his cheek and pinched it.

"So he tries to rub it off and it's still there. He tries something else. He starts to run again, but this time back toward shore. That's when you take in your line. Keep tension on the line; back up on the beach if you have to. You don't ever want it to go slack."

As the drum is pulled into shallow water, it will swirl its tail from side to side, moving its body in the shape of an S. "That's one of the prettiest sights you'll ever see—a red, red drum coming out of blue water."

We rebaited the lines and then sat in silence after the rigs were cast. Merillet rose frequently to check the tension on the lines. Since he had begun working as a guide, fishing seemed to have become more of a chore; every time he took someone out, even a friend, he felt under pressure to hook a big drum. "All you can do is read the water and go from past experience. If the drum come to the beach, they come. Lots of nights they don't," he said simply. Yet he constantly had to choose between taking his parties to crowded locations where drum were known to feed, or trying more remote, chancier spots. Some nights his gambles paid off, some nights his parties simply sat, as we were sitting now.

Near 2 o'clock the moon, red-orange and streaked by clouds, appeared on the horizon. Its top quarter was obscured, as if a segment had been cut away to make a bowl. Directly above us a swath of clouds split into bumpy ribs. Occasionally a pocket of cold air, a sudden arctic breath, moved across the beach. The night was refreshing and surprisingly calm. Not good drum weather, some fishermen would say. It occurred to me that I had no idea why Merillet had chosen to come out that particular night, or why he fished for drum at all. "Why do you spend so much time chasing one kind of fish?" I asked.

"I just like it, that's all I can tell you. I just like the way it fights, the way it looks when it comes across the swash, especially in the day. It's a thrill to catch one of those big guys."

"How do you pick the nights you want to fish?"

"I go when I like the tide, and when I feel like I might catch something. I tend to fish low water, because I've done better then."

"You mean you play hunches?"

"Yeah, it's just intuition. Sometimes Dhanyo gets hunches. She tried to get me to go to the point the other day about two in the afternoon, but I wanted to go get some mullet for bait. I should have listened to her. They had a big run of drum about two-fifteen."

He paused.

"Sometimes, I see the fish I'm going to catch. I see it under water, or I see something else. The night I caught that last big drum I had come home from work tired and not really in a mood to fish. But I couldn't get settled down. I was watching the World Series, and all of a sudden I saw one of my black rods go off hard, almost out of the holder. Real clear. So I tried to stir up some interest in going fishing, but Dhanyo didn't want to go.

"I really didn't feel like going by myself. I went to bed and just lay there for a little while. About twelve-thirty I said, 'I'm going.' Dhanyo said she still didn't want to. So I got up and started getting gear together, and then Dhanyo got up. And then Canaan got up. The whole family went."

An hour and a half later Merillat had stood in the swash with a drum on his line. For forty-five minutes the fish struggled as he walked it a quarter-mile down the beach, a group of fishermen cheering him on. When it was at last on the sand, Merillat guessed it to be about fifty inches in length and thirty inches in girth. He picked it up, admired it, estimated its weight at better than fifty pounds, and—since a neighbor had just given him a mess of drum to eat—returned it to the surf. "It was one of the best fights I've ever had, and I almost didn't go fishing that night."

He leaned back and tapped his fingers on the edge of his chair. By catching that drum he had justified every hour spent on the beach, before and since. Pretty soon he would get another; although he didn't say so, he seemed convinced. Every good drum fisherman believes it is just a matter of putting in time.

The moon had worked its way across a quarter of the sky.

"What do you feel like we'll catch tonight?" I asked.

Merillat popped open a beer, his first, and laughed. "Maybe a cold," he said.

At 4 o'clock several mornings later, eight fishermen huddled on the end of the Hatteras Island fishing pier. Although it was the middle of the week, for days the drum had been feeding within fifty yards of the pier just before sunrise, and the parking lot had been filled with cars bearing license plates from Virginia, West Virginia, and Washington, D.C. Most of the fishermen were asleep in their trucks. In an hour and a half the platform would be full; the early risers knew no matter how vigorously they tried to defend their positions, the latecomers would crowd their rods along the rail.

The previous weekend, anglers had stood shoulder-to-shoulder on the end of the pier in a fifteen-mile-an-hour northeasterly breeze. A low-pressure system several hundred miles offshore had caused the ocean to swell against the beach, and the waves had peaked and crumbled with unusual force during light wind. Anglers had weighted their rigs with ten-ounce sinkers to keep them from rolling and tangling in the surf. Early Sunday morning a bystander had been struck in the head when a sinker had snapped off a line as an inexperienced fisherman tried to cast.

Nobody seemed happy about the crowds, least of all the men who had fished from the Rodanthe pier for more than ten years. But with the increased interest in drum fishing had come a shift from polite country protocol to jaw-clenched competition. In years past when a line had begun to drag out, other rigs were immediately taken in so the angler would have room to play the fish. Now the whizz of a stripping reel only induced fishermen to crowd close to the rail.

Since 3:30 I had dozed on a bench next to a fisherman's girlfriend, one of two women I had seen on the platform in a week. Just past 4:00 the pier's business started to pick up. Every ten minutes or so another two or three fishermen arrived, rods and bait boxes in hand. At 5:10 a young Virginia Beach man caught the first drum of the morning, and the first of his life. Ten minutes later nearly forty men had cast and were watching eagerly for strikes.

Daylight was only a half-hour away; a royal-blue glaze had spread across the sea and was being rolled back from its eastern edge. A soft southwest wind began to hum through the lines that dangled from the rail. As it puffed and lulled, the eerie whistle rose and fell in pitch as if someone were strumming a harp. Snicky Arches, the eighteen-year-old who had caught the day's first drum, plopped down next to me and shoved his hands into his jacket pockets, grinning widely. He had come to Hatteras with Pat and Arch Bracher, twin brothers who between them had caught thirty big drum in the past two months. Snicky had come to Rodanthe to learn the twins' technique. He had not disappointed his friends.

The Brachers strive to catch as many drum as they can, as quickly as they can. In October and November it is not unusual for them to spend five nights a week on the pier. Each drum they land is tagged for a migration study. The more they catch, the more they can tag—and the greater their chances of breaking the world record.

The previous summer the twins had graduated from Old Dominion University with undergraduate degrees in business management, but both worked as mates on sportsfishing charter boats. Pat, a thin man in a green slicker, chuckled as he told me about his degree. Wisps of dark, curly hair strayed from beneath a cap. "Don't we look like big-biz types?" he asked. His brother, a sandy blond, grinned and wiped his hands on his blood-streaked rain pants.

In two days Arch would leave for Venezuela, where he would spend the winter fishing offshore for marlin. Although looking forward to the trip, he was sorry to leave Hatteras before the conclusion of the fall run of drum. "I'd much rather be drum fishing than fishing offshore, especially off the United States," he said. "It would be different if there were anything out there to catch. Five years ago you'd go out and see ten white marlin in a day. That was fun. Now you're lucky to see five in a week."

"So you like drum because you can catch a lot of them?" I asked.

"They're unique," Pat said simply. "It's the best fishing we do. You can't catch anything bigger from shore, and besides, they're pretty." He reached into a bag and extracted a thick strand of fishing line three inches long. One end had a steel dart attached to it; the opposite end was coated with yellow vinyl tubing printed with a number and instructions to contact the state fisheries department for a reward. "This is the tag we put on a fish when we release it. You slip the dart under a scale and force it into a back muscle."

"Do you think the fish lives after you throw it back?" I had heard some fishermen claim that a trophy-class drum can quickly ingest enough air to kill itself.

"There's a hundred percent chance that the fish lives. Believe me, you can't kill these big guys without really trying," Arch said.

I was inclined to question his logic, but Pat, anticipating my questions, opened a log book that listed twenty-seven fish tagged by anglers and released during a blitz on the pier a few days before. "At least some of these fish will be recaptured in the next couple of weeks," he said. "You'd think they'd learn, but it's not unusual to catch the same fish again within a couple of months. To me that shows there's a good survival rate." I started to ask how many fish they had tagged since September, but stopped in mid-sentence. A line on the southeast corner of the pier had begun to whizz out.

Fishermen scrambled for their rods, then scurried out of the way as Arch danced diagonally across the platform with a black rod bent almost in a U. He raised and lowered it three times, his actions quick, fluid, and almost mechanical. There was no emotion in his face. It was a dance he had repeated hundreds of times. "He's got him," Snicky said. As Arch moved to the rail and began to reel, no one doubted those words.

The drum broke the surface only twenty yards off the south side of the pier and began to drift closer. Arch stopped reeling and cooly maneuvered his catch into the net. In all, he had taken less than five minutes to play the fish, and it looked as though it weighed at least fifty pounds. When the drum was raised to the pier, shimmering copper and gold in the sun's first rays, Arch's detached facade exploded in a burst of energy. He threw down his rod, grabbed a tag from his brother, and ran to the fish's side. Pulling up a scale below the pectoral fin, he slipped the tag's barb beneath it. Beside him Pat used a tape measure to check the animal's length and girth. In less than two minutes Arch pulled out his hook, slipped his hand into a gill, and stood with the drum dangling at his side as Snicky positioned himself with a camera. The shutter barely clicked twice before Arch heaved the fish over the railing.

Waves instantly dispersed the ripples where the drum had plunged into the surf. Below the pier was nothing but a sloshing, sunstreaked sea and a web of fishing lines that hummed in the breeze.

10

ᏈREAD -AND- BUTTER FISHING

IN THE HARSHEST months of winter most of Hatteras Island slumps deep into solitude, insulating itself from a crippling northwest wind. At dawn a weak sun rises in a cloudless sky. A cold, blue current pushes south past Rodanthe, flat and foamless like a giant glacial lake. The cottages are empty, the windows boarded, the water pumps drained. By early January the traffic on Highway 12 has thinned to a trickle.

People hide indoors, but waterfowl appear in abundance, bobbing on ocean swells and gliding across sapphire ponds at the Pea Island refuge. Scoters and cormorants fly low in messy lines. Red-throated loons appear in the surf and vanish without a ripple. Snow geese, their feathers gold in the slanted sun, pull grasses from pond muck that coats their heads and necks with a reddish paste. Whistling swans pipe in low, dissonant tones, like the flat notes of a wooden flute—a primitive, repetitive song that never completely ceases, daylight or dark.

Offshore, gray trout bunch together, hanging in the waters near Avon until the full onset of cold forces them south to the lee of Cape Point. A migratory species, they spend their summers as far north as Cape Cod, but by Thanksgiving they have begun to reach Hatteras, one of their primary wintering grounds in the East. Millions of fish swim near the bottom in water as deep as a hundred feet. They press closely together in schools that may be as narrow as a small house or as broad as a football field. Sometimes they startle at the sound of a boat overhead and split into smaller schools, darting only a few yards before settling down. And the past two winters, the roar of workboats has become increasingly common in the waters within twelve miles of shore.

For the fishing fleet of Hatteras village, winter is a reversal of the norm, a season of long days and short nights. By dawn, up to eighty boats have passed through the narrow channel at Hatteras Inlet. The captains and mates who fish them will not return home until the day's catch has been packed, which is frequently not until midnight or later. On the deepest nights of the year, gill-net boats bump against the docks of Hatteras village, and conveyors carry trout and bluefish to packinghouse tables to be culled into sizes, weighed, packed in ice, and shipped to market. Winter, with its cutting winds and feeble light, is the season of aching muscles, shivering limbs, and swelling hands—of bread-and-butter fishing.

By 9 p.m. eight boats had unloaded their catches at Risky Business Seafood, and three more waited at the dock. From a small room off the main packing area came the constant clickety-clickety-clickety of a staple gun. The woman using the gun could not be seen behind the tiers of waxed cartons she had assembled and marked with the letters MGT—medium gray trout. In the center of the fish house, a metal conveyor belt dropped stiff, gaping trout onto a second belt to be sorted into bins according to size.

For nearly six hours Steve Bailey, the owner of the fish house, had stood at the second belt culling fish. His hands darted quickly across the table, flipping trout into bins and other species into wire baskets. The room was wide with a low ceiling, and a dank smell rose from a drainage hole in the cold cement floor. On each side of the conveyor, a scale with a large dial hung from a rusty chain. Bailey, the two men shoveling ice behind him, and a woman working at a scale all wore oilskins—bright-orange waterproof overalls—and yellow slip-on sleeves, plus several layers of clothing to protect them from the damp, salty air. Above the squeak of the conveyors and the scrape of shovel against ice, a radio blared the whine of country fiddle and pedal steel.

The flow of trout trickled and then stopped. Bailey glanced up, annoyed. "C'mon, c'mon," he hollered in a husky voice, "let's have some fish."

Out by the dock a tall, muscular man dipped a shovel into a mass of trout that lined the deck of a forty-foot boat, a typical workboat in the Hatteras fleet. There was no flying bridge, just a square-topped cabin with one seat. Toward the stern a reel four feet in diameter held a coil of monofilament gill net—the drop net, as it is called in these parts. It would take the man close to an hour to empty the boat. He shrugged once as if trying to loosen his shoulders, then resumed a mechanical shoveling. The conveyor carried trout up a steep incline, through a washer, and dropped them by ones and twos onto the belt where Bailey waited. "Let's get some more cartons," he yelled, looking around him. "Need more ice. Let's go, let's go, keep it up."

Earlier that evening I had stopped in the fish house to watch a boat being packed. I was handed a pair of oilskins and told to get to work; a crew member had failed to show up. It was a night in early March, but it could have been any evening from Thanksgiving to Easter, the typical beginning and end of drop-net season. I pulled on the clammy, oversized oilskins, cinched them with a belt, and began shoveling ice, first into a large plastic wagon and then into boxes packed with fish. A short time later

I was sent to the small room to make cartons. For the next two hours, until the regular crew member arrived, I surrounded myself with pillars of cardboard.

Making cartons is the easiest job in the fish house, the task generally assigned to newcomers, especially women. To spend an evening packing fish requires strength, stamina, and at least a modicum of speed. To pack fish night after night all winter requires more than fortitude—it requires a willingness to ignore pain and exhaustion for five or six dollars an hour. When fishing is slow, the packers work for only three or four hours at a stretch. But more frequently crews begin about 3 p.m. and work past midnight, until every boat has been emptied.

The most taxing jobs are bailing fish from the boat and stacking cartons, but any of the chores become excruciating after twelve straight hours. In addition to aching back muscles and arms, the packers may suffer from fish poison, an inflammation of the joints that comes from being stuck by the spiny fins of certain species, including trout and bluefish. Although they wear nylon gloves to protect their hands, many fish packers cannot close their fists for most of the winter.

Fifty pounds of fish are put in every carton. As a bin on the rim of the culling table fills, a worker lets up a small gate so that the fish slide into the metal scoop of a scale. The scale needle pushes past forty pounds, then to forty-five, forty-eight. A large fish is added or a small one taken out, until the needle is as close as possible to fifty pounds. The worker tips the load into a carton to be surrounded with ice, and the carton is stacked on a pallet. All the while the captains and mates stand by, drinking beers, not talking much, keeping an occasional eye on the scales.

On the dock a balding captain I knew only as Steve was chopping meat from the tail of a monk fish he had caught with the trout. His face and hands were deeply tanned, a striking contrast to the pasty complexions of the workers inside. The thick lips of the monk fish protruded from pink, blubbery folds. "Cute, isn't he?" Steve asked.

"You guys do good today?" A man who worked in a nearby fish house sauntered up.

"Pretty fair. Fifty boxes. Do better if the price weren't so low." Fifty boxes equaled a hundred cartons, or five thousand pounds. That day the boats would receive fifteen cents for each pound of medium trout. The mate and the captain would each get a fourth of the take, after expenses.

"You guys didn't catch so many fish, price wouldn't be so low."

"Them guys from up north didn't run their mouths on the radio, price wouldn't be so low. The whole damn world knows when we set a net on a school of fish. Including the dealers." Steve slung the head and spine of the monk fish over the edge into dark, oily water.

Somewhere in the darkness two other boats waited, one with its mate and captain catnapping on board. Steve's boat was nearly empty, a half-hour sooner than I had expected. I watched as the last trout traveled up the conveyor. Steve stepped inside, where three pallets of dripping cartons awaited his inspection. The woman at the scales was counting the cartons. She had sturdy shoulders and a round, handsome face. A diamond pendant hung in the hollow of her neck. "All right, I got fifty-two boxes," she said. "You want to count them?"

"Nah, I trust you guys."

Bailey appeared in the doorway of his office and handed Steve the fisherman a pink ticket. The fisherman looked at it, nodded once, and said, "Thanks much." There was nothing, neither satisfaction nor disappointment, in his voice. There is not much room for shows of emotion in the business of fishing. Strength, machismo, and sometimes anger, but seldom joy or sadness. It is almost as though, by denying themselves the luxury of feeling, the fishermen cushion themselves against the exhaustion that is a daily part of their trade.

The mate started hosing down the decks. Bailey was already gearing up for the next load, wiping off the scales and calling for more ice and cartons. A man pushing a whirring forklift deftly transferred the three pallets to a loading platform outside to be put in a refrigerated truck. Another boat, and then another, and then four or five hours' sleep before the Pamlico Sound crabbers would start coming in about 9 a.m., and it would all begin again.

In the morning when the first drop-net boats cross the bar at Hatteras Inlet, the sun is still two hours from rising. On the marine radio channels, captains pass information about the condition of the inlet, the roughest water they will encounter all day. Even the most seasoned fishermen occasionally entertain thoughts of losing their boats in Hatteras Inlet. The radio throbs with static and chatter.

"How's she looking out there?"

"There's a breaker right in the middle of the inlet, but if you ride it fast through the middle shouldn't be no problem t'all."

"Looks like it's smooth outside. Pretty fishing."

"Pretty cold, I'll tell you that."

"Okey-doke, I'm going on through."

Once past the inlet they chart a course for Diamond Shoals, the treacherous shoals off Cape Point. If the trout have moved to the south side of the point, the boats will run only two to three miles offshore and ten or twelve miles north. But early in the winter, when the schools congregate off Avon, the boats must travel as far as twenty miles north. For the slowest of the Hatteras fleet, the trip can take as long as three hours, one way.

All the while, the captain monitors a small screen that shows readings from a sonic depth-finder, watching for marks that appear when the boat passes over a school of fish. At the captain's signal the mate tosses out a round float, the reel begins to grind, and a web of net feeds out with the force of water behind the boat. The mate stands by, controlling the speed of the reel with his shoulder or hand. One side of the net sinks under the weight of lead pellets. The other side, tethered to a series of floats, pulls toward the surface to form a free-floating underwater fence. As fish swim into it, their heads poke through the weave; their gills push through, but their bodies will not fit. They can swim neither forward nor back.

Some boats "soak" their nets for a half-hour or an hour, hoping to trap a school on the move. Others retrieve them after only a matter of minutes. As the reel grinds in, the captain and mate pull on nylon or rubber gloves and pluck the fish from the net as fast as they can. Many fishermen use an L-shaped metal pick to stretch the mesh open, but some work the fish free with their hands. The quicker they pick the nets, the sooner they can reset them or return to harbor. The boat rolls with the swells, the breeze blusters and calms. On cold days spray freezes on the upper deck.

It is an independent means of making a living, fraught with physical danger and financial risk. And it is one of the few ways small commercial operators can make enough to survive.

"Hello-o-o to the Bette G. What'cha readin' there, Rudy?"

"Nothin' but a bunch of bait. Not a fish in the sea today."

"Marked a school awhile back, but damned if I can set on 'em."

"Hello-o, Mamacita. You got anything goin' there, Big Bill?"

On and on all day, with captains switching channels to withhold information from certain boats and share it with their friends. On and on, as lines of fish appear on the screen, splitting into small groups at the sound of the boat, swirling like leaves caught in a current, vanishing just as fast.

Sixty years ago the first drop-net boats on the cape used no sonic "fish finders" and no reels to pull in their nets. The tricks for gill-netting were the same, but the fishermen of the 1920s, 1930s, and 1940s watched the birds and the surface of the water to locate the great wintering schools of trout. They raised and lowered their nets by hand.

Captain Ernal Foster began fishing with his father in the 1920s. The boat he still owns, the Albatross, was built in 1937 and is a low-slung, forty-three-foot boat with a fluted white hull and a narrow stern, as graceful in the water as a thin slice of the moon. It is the jewel of Hatteras Harbor. From its decks Foster caught the first blue marlin, the first white marlin, and the first sailfish ever taken on a charter boat from the cape. A replica, the Albatross II, was constructed in 1948 and has been piloted for many years by Foster's brother Bill. The *Albatross III* was added to the family fleet in 1952. All three boats regularly cross the bar at Hatteras, although Foster himself has been grounded by a weak heart. White-haired and tanned, with black-frame glasses, he spends many of his days whittling on the dock where he moors his boats.

One rainy afternoon Foster ushered me into a storage garage behind his house. On tables and benches were piles of nets from years past—cotton and linen nets, Dacron nets, monofilament nets. Stuffed above the rafters were several old feather mattresses. Weatherworn plastic floats hung from nails, and on a cluttered, dusty shelf was a wire screen Foster's father had used to sieve caviar from sturgeon roe. "I'm a keeper," Foster said. "I keep everything. They keep telling me I need to come in here and clean all this out. But look," he fingered a net of thin cotton twine, "you can't buy 'em like this anymore. You can't get 'em like this anymore."

In the 1920s and 1930s the gill-net fishermen of Hatteras and their women tied their own nets from five-pound balls of cotton twine. They looped the strands around blocks of wood to keep the mesh sizes even, and they floated the finished nets with cork. "Some of them women—my mother was one—they could tie net awful fast," Foster said. "A woman could always tie net faster than a man. But even if you were fast, you didn't tie very much net in a day. You might tie five or six yards."

Hand-tied nets were generally a hundred yards long and sixty meshes deep, with different mesh sizes for catching trout and bluefish. Between trips the nets were soaked in a solution of lime and water to break down the slimy residue from the fish which, if left on the net, would eventually eat through the cotton strands. Although the nets in Foster's garage were thirty years old and had been used heavily, they were still white and strong.

"We'd take four men with us, and two would pull the net, and two would pick the fish," Foster said. "You'd start in the fall, the last of November. The first two weeks would be a little rough. Your legs and arms would get tired, but you'd be in good shape.

Oh, you'd be in good shape. We never fished Sunday. If Saturday came along and the weather was bad, you'd be happy because you'd get two days off.

"We'd watch the water, the currents and all, or we might set out part of a net to see if we'd catch some. Sometimes the birds will lead you to 'em. Sometimes you'd find 'em by instinct. Or you didn't find 'em at all. Today you got push buttons—everything's push-button. Nothing to it. Fish finders and reels to pull in your nets. These boats go right past fish and don't even look around to see they're there."

The gill-net boats continued to set in the ocean into the 1940s. Trawlers were also appearing offshore, many of them from as far away as Virginia. In warm months the trawlers fished in Pamlico Sound for flounder and shrimp, but around Thanksgiving they moved into the ocean and began dragging for croaker and trout. Their numbers increased by the hundreds at the close of World War II. "There were twelve hundred trawlers licensed to work out of Pamlico Sound, from Beaufort, Morehead City, Englehart—the towns over there," Foster said, waving vaguely toward the west. "You'd try to go across the sound, and it was like a big city out there. Lights all around you. You had to weave your way through."

Early in the winter of 1948–49 between three hundred and four hundred trawlers moved into the ocean and began fishing within sight of shore. The trout had arrived early, and in great quantities. Trawlers and gill-net boats alike began bringing in dozens of boxes a day. Even though the price dropped to three and four cents a pound, the heavy fishing continued; with so much trout, everyone could make plenty of money in time for Christmas.

December passed, and then New Year's with its promise of biting, lingering cold. But the fishermen of Hatteras would not spend day after chilling day on the sea, not that year, for in early January the trout disappeared.

"You couldn't find 'em anywhere. They were just gone," Foster said. "I knew a fellow, he had a wife and a couple of children, and I told him to go get a job, that there wasn't going to be any more fishing. And there wasn't."

"What happened?" I asked.

"They were just gone."

"Did they get fished out?"

"Some people'll tell you that, but I don't think so. I think fishing just goes in cycles. There've been cycles as long as I've been here. They're catching the trout now, but one day they'll all be gone again."

With offshore gill-netting no longer profitable, the fishermen of Hatteras had no choice but to find alternative incomes. Some, like Ernal Foster, concentrated on building a charter fishing business, trolling offshore for billfish, tuna, wahoo, and dolphin. Other men joined the Coast Guard or trawled for shrimp in Pamlico Sound during the summer. For a few weeks in spring and fall they also set haul seines in the surf to catch migrating schools of fish. The gray trout had dwindled, but the striped bass, bluefish, and puppy drum remained plentiful, passing close to shore in schools large enough to set the surface churning and bait fish skipping through the waves like bright silver lures.

Beach haul-seining is among the hardest forms of fishing, one that requires patience and taxing physical labor. For days the haul-seiners watch the breakers, waiting for the churning water or oily slicks that signal the arrival of the fish. Working in a crew of four to six, the seiners ride past the breakers in a dory, laying out net as they go. The net can be set in a number of ways—in a semicircle to surround a school, for example, or in a diagonal line from shore, like the hypotenuse of a triangle that can be swung in toward the beach. When the net is hauled in, thousands of pounds of squirming flesh may come with it. The crew members stand in the swash, picking up fish and tossing them into waiting trucks. In the process the beach might be smeared with slime and blood.

Beach fishing is a tradition on the Outer Banks, a mainstay of commercial fishing on Hatteras Island at least since 1842, but it is messy work. In the 1970s the number of local haul-seine crews increased, and crews from New York came to Cape Point with twenty-five-foot dories that dwarfed the Hatteras boats and mechanical winches that could pull in twenty thousand pounds of fish—enough to form a layer four feet deep across the beach. Such large catches were more the exception than the rule, but they furthered the cape's reputation as a rich fishing ground. By 1973 nearly twenty haul-seine crews were setting nets off Cape Point. Once a crew had pulled in its nets, it could not set them again until all other crews had taken turns. And since it was easiest to land the fish just after high tide in a calm sea, only two or three crews might set their nets in a day.

Even mammoth catches of striped bass provided only a portion of the year's income, and haul-seining was no more than a part-time occupation. Through the mid-1970s commercial fishing was considered too chancy to be a viable year-round trade on Hatteras Island. Men who would have preferred to fish full-time were working in the Coast Guard or running stores or motels. In 1970, when Big Bill Foster moved to the island from Raleigh, North Carolina, haul-seining and crabbing were the only types of fishing pursued by more than a handful of men.

Foster was a graduate student at North Carolina State University, and he came to Hatteras to conduct research for a doctoral dissertation on the biology of the red drum. (He is no relation to Ernal and Bill Foster of the *Albatross* fleet.) A heavyset man with an easy smile and a straightforward manner, he liked the relaxed pace of Hatteras village—so much, in fact, that he eventually quit school to become a full-time commercial fisherman. He began by fishing for croaker and spot with long haul nets in the sound and seining from the beach for striped bass. In the fall of 1973 he heard that Ernal and Bill Foster planned to experiment offshore with a new piece of equipment, a hydraulic reel that could hold hundreds of yards of monofilament gill net.

The previous year Sumner Midgett, an extension agent for a state agency called Sea Grant, had attended a fishing exposition in Seattle. Midgett had long been interested in the hydraulic winches that were used extensively in West Coast fisheries to pull crab pots and fish nets but that were generally unknown in the East. The large, spool-shaped reel had caught his eye at the show, and he purchased one for about $700. When he returned to North Carolina he learned that the Fosters had ordered a heavy monofilament net to fish for striped bass offshore. As in the old days, they planned to pull the nets in by hand.

Midgett contacted the Fosters and asked if they would try using the hydraulic reel on the *Albatross* at the state's expense. The brothers agreed. Big Bill Foster volunteered to help install the reel, rig the net, and pick the fish, if indeed any fish were caught. "The first couple of days all we caught were dog sharks," Big Bill recalled. "We started out looking for striped bass—rock fish—but we ended up making a lot of money that first year in big bluefish. We had a hundred and thirty yards of nylon net. We'd fish till we had caught fifty or sixty boxes of blues, and then we'd have to stop and spend a couple of days mending the net."

Three more years passed before drop-net reels appeared on other boats, and even then the fishermen of Hatteras were skeptical about their chances of gill-netting offshore with consistent success. Nevertheless, alternatives to haul-seining seemed more attractive every season. An ugly competition had developed between commercial fishermen and surf casters, who were frequently asked to bring in their lines so haul-seine crews could set their nets. Sportsfishing groups complained that so many commercial crews were fishing from national seashore property that the striped bass had started to disappear. In 1975, after a coalition of sports anglers from New Jersey asked federal officials to limit haul-seining, the national seashore closed Cape Point to commercial beach fishermen on weekends during the winter. If schools of fish happened to show up at the point on Friday night, Saturday, or Sunday, the commercial fishermen could do little more than sit and watch them go by.

In March of 1976, a Hatteras Island fisherman named Buddy Hooper decided to try experimenting with a monofilament gill net in the ocean. The stocks of striped bass had dwindled, and most of the area's fishermen were concentrating their efforts on the sound, where schools of croaker had suddenly become common. For several seasons, though, trawlers had caught impressive numbers of gray trout in the ocean, and now haul-seiners were snaring trout in the nets they set from the beach. It seemed reasonable to think that a crew could gill-net in the ocean from a moderate-size boat. Hooper had set some crab pots in the sound; after emptying them in the morning, he still had time to fish in the afternoon. Why not take a ride toward Diamond Shoals to see what he could catch?

Hooper did not have a hydraulic reel to pull the net on the twenty-three-foot boat he took through Hatteras Inlet one chilly week in March, but he had enlisted the help of several friends. The crew settled offshore and began to fish. Nothing much happened the first try, or the second. But by the third set the men managed to bring in about thirty boxes of large gray trout. It was worth trying another couple of days, Hooper figured, maybe another couple of weeks. The beach fishermen were having some luck too; instead of striped bass, their seines had started to yield pile upon pile of delicate gray fish speckled with black. Some of the fish were larger than the old-timers had ever seen.

The cycles of fishing had changed once again, had turned completely around. The giant schools of trout had come back, perhaps years before anyone really noticed. And in the next five years the fishermen of Hatteras, once considered a dying breed, would also multiply by leaps and bounds.

"Them trout were there all the time. Nobody tried to catch 'em, s'all."

"Ernal's right. It's cyclical, fishing is."

"The old-timers are still saying you can't make a good living fishing. Maybe that's right, but I'm sure as hell going to try."

Within two years of Buddy Hooper's first hauls of gray trout, a half-dozen Hatteras fishermen had mounted hydraulic reels on their boats, and another dozen were watching their success with interest. The gill-net fishermen discovered that sonic depth-finders could greatly simplify the search for tightly bunched schools of trout, and the instruments soon became standard equipment on Hatteras boats. Offshore fishing was still considered chancy, especially in the winter when storms and high winds could keep the boats in port for a week or more. To make up for lost days, the two-man crews had to bring in good catches—forty boxes or more—and they had to fish virtually every day they could, even when a period of fair weather lasted for ten straight days. But fuel cost less than a dollar a gallon, and the price of trout seldom fell below twenty cents a pound. By 1980 at least thirty Hatteras boats were making more than half their yearly income during the four months of drop-net season. And news of their luck was spreading.

Over the next four winters the size of the Hatteras drop-net fleet swelled, with boats coming to the village for the winter from as far as Morehead City and Stumpy Point, until the local captains and mates grumbled about the stiff competition. No one knew whether the great schools of trout could be depleted by overfishing; but year after year they returned. The winter of 1984–85 proved to be one of the richest seasons to date. By December 1, 1985, ninety-nine of the boats in Hatteras Harbor were rigged with hydraulic reels and gill nets. With so many fishing crews, any cooperative spirit disappeared. Offshore, the boats kept each other in sight, watching and waiting until a captain ran across a school of fish. As soon as one boat began to feed out a net, four or five others crowded around, sometimes setting their rigs so close that the currents would sweep them together and a single trout would be caught in two nets.

Early one rainy morning Big Bill Foster and I sat drinking coffee in Sonny's Waterfront Restaurant, the most likely place in Hatteras village to find fishermen between trips. Foster drummed his large fingers on the table and nodded every few minutes to men who appeared dripping wet in the restaurant's doorway. He had told me already of his early years of drop-net fishing on the *Albatross*, and now he echoed complaints I had heard from other captains and mates who had fished gill nets for trout since the 1970s. "When you have maybe two dozen drop-net boats, you have an ideal number," he said, "because you can rely on each other to find fish and help keep an eye out for problems, but you can spread out enough to keep from tripping over each other. When you get eighty boats at a time out there, though, it's too many for anybody to be real productive. You get guys running their mouths on the radio so much that the price drops before any fish ever get to the market."

Since 1982 Foster has fished from the *Mamacita*, a commercial boat constructed by a Hatteras boatbuilder. The *Mamacita* is one of the slowest of the fleet—about eight knots at top speed—but it is designed to take heavy seas, and Foster trusts it. To reach the hook at Cape Point by 7 a.m., he must leave the dock at 5:00. "I knew it wouldn't be fast, but it can take a good swell as well loaded as it does empty. If I hit bottom I don't have to worry too much about her breaking up." Most of the year he fishes with hooks and lines for grouper, snapper, tile fish, and sea bass, all species that live along the fringe of the Gulf Stream in water as deep as seven hundred feet. He has made good his intention to earn a living as a commercial fisherman. But to enjoy it he must be versatile and quick to change tactics.

"I like any kind of fishing as long as there's not too many people involved," he said. "The problem now is that you don't have any turn-around time. Used to be that if you got into the bottom fish real good in the early spring, say, it would take a while before any other boats could gear up for bottom fishing. You'd have a couple of weeks of good fishing to yourself. Now it's just a matter of days."

"Do you get people out there who just wait around for other boats to find fish so they can set in the same school?" I asked.

"There's some of that, but everybody's always looking, always watching the screen. Some days you find 'em, some days somebody near you finds 'em."

"Are people flat-out rude?"

"You get some irritable folks. I try and stay out of it. The faster boats do have the advantage at drop-netting, because if they mark a small school of fish they can keep going for a while, and if they don't find anything else they can come back. But fast boats cost money, more money than most of us have. You hear a lot of people complaining about nothing. The people who say everyone else is catching 'their' fish aren't looking hard enough for fish. There are millions of pounds of fish out there. We don't catch a fraction of a percent of 'em. Sometimes you get lucky, but if you work at it you find 'em. That's all needs to be said about that."

Three blocks away Carol Teague also was enjoying a day off from fishing. Tall and muscular, with blond hair that swings not quite to the small of her back, she is the only woman on Hatteras Island who fishes commercially full-time. After leaving Foster, I went to Teague's house, a small, cozy dwelling fronted by oaks and bordered in back by a lush cordgrass marsh. The money she used to buy her property has come from fishing, much of it from crabbing in late winter, going out alone in Pamlico Sound each morning to check pots set three miles from shore. In the fall of 1985 she decided to try mating on a drop-net boat for the first time.

I found her fixing coffee in the kitchen. Although she had been fishing nearly every day, she was smooth-skinned and evenly tanned. She has broken into an intimate, all-male circle and built a reputation as a reliable, hard-working mate; yet that day she showed no signs of physical wear. Perhaps more than anything in the world, she loves to fish. "So what do you think of drop-netting?" I asked.

"It's a challenge, boy, I'll tell you," she said, flopping into a rocking chair. "You have to be on your toes. Some of the schools aren't that big, so if you don't get the net out fast enough, you run right by 'em. Some days you'll be going along, and the captain will mark fish, and he'll start yelling, 'There's fish, get it out, get it out.' So I bust my butt getting the net out, and he says, 'Damn, we missed 'em.'"

One day the boat accidentally backed over a net, tangling the mesh in the propeller. Although the water temperature was 45 degrees, Teague had no choice but to cut the net off the prop.

She jumped overboard with a knife and dove below the boat, slicing blindly through murk. "I had to go down three times, but it didn't take me long," she chuckled. "You work fast in water that cold.

"You definitely have to be aggressive to make it drop-netting with so many boats. Some days it's absolutely wild. You get boats out there all in one area just watching each other. When a mate goes to the stern and gets ready to throw out a ball, you can just watch forty other boats turn and head in that direction. There have been days when I've just stood at the stern and laughed my butt off at the whole scene."

"Is it worth the hassle?"

"Yeah, if you go out and really fish. The only way to make money drop-netting is to go out every day you can and fish hard, unless the market's flooded. A few days we'd get out there, set the nets, and then the fish house would call and tell us not to bring any in, that the market was busted. That was a pain. We'd have to pick fish out of the net for nothing."

"Do you think there will be as many boats next year?"

"You know, I bet things even out. A couple of years ago there were a whole lot of people who set crab pots in the spring. We were tripping over each other, and we were all thinking, God, it's not going to be worth doing this if it gets any worse. But then the next year hardly anybody set out their pots. I really think the same thing might happen with the drop-netters next year."

I left Teague's house between rainshowers, refreshed by her optimism. Good fishing or bad, she would try to enjoy herself, even as the men she worked with groused about the weather, the price of trout, the number of drop-net boats. Fishermen are by nature pessimistic and suspicious of each other, although quick to help each other out in any real trouble. And indeed Teague's words were the only notes of optimism I heard about drop-netting in 1986.

"It's a damn highway out there."

"There're times I'd like to be invisible, keep everybody off my school of fish."

"I don't know's I can keep this up."

"Know what you need to drop-net this year? A fast boat, a radio, and a real bad attitude."

"I've seen some bad fishing weather, some cold fishing weather," Steve Bailey said, "but I can't remember a winter's stayed this warm this long. The mackerel never even got this far south."

We were sitting in the living room of Bailey's house, huddled indoors during an early January storm. The house, a 1920s single-story residence with high ceilings and a broad front porch, was a cozy haven in a strengthening breeze. In the corner of the living room a television flashed clips of a basketball game, and in the refrigerator a six-pack of Bud cooled next to a bowl of gritty oysters. Everything was as it should have been on a blustery winter afternoon. Everything except the direction of the wind, which for three days had blown hard and warm from the southwest. Because of the angle of the channel, a southwest wind makes Hatteras Inlet so rough that few boats dare to cross the bar. Temperatures were in the 50s, but the ocean hovered near 60, uncharacteristically warm for midwinter.

Autumn's strange fishing had continued past the first of the year. For nearly three weeks in November and December the commercial fleet of Hatteras had trolled without luck for king mackerel, even as the boats based at Oregon Inlet each brought in ten boxes a day—$800 at the prevailing price of eighty cents a pound. "The boys here just kept hanging around thinking all they needed was one good northeast blow and the mackerel would be here, but they never did get into them thick like they did last year," Bailey said. "You never know when king mackerel will turn up. They usually show up sometime, though, and they didn't. Not this year. The hurricane screwed everything up. That's what it is. After the hurricane there wasn't a fish caught around this village for a month. By anyone. Now we're packing some fish— a hundred forty, a hundred fifty boxes a night—but that's nothing like it'll be, trout ever show up good."

The scarcity of mackerel had kept Risky Business with no

business during what normally would have been one of its best months. As the newest of five packers in Hatteras village, Bailey is discovering constantly just how risky the trade can be. The daily prices Risky Business offers are determined by Bailey's partner, Willie Etheridge III, a Wanchese dealer who places the fish packed by Bailey with wholesale markets in Chicago, Philadelphia, Boston, and New York. The partners have tried to attract fishermen, Bailey said, by offering higher prices than other packing houses as often as they can.

Bailey is a likable man of unusual energy and animation. He arrived in Hatteras village in 1979 with Brownie Douglass, an old college friend. Both men had recently separated from their wives and were looking for an out-of-the-way place where they could settle down and fish. The cape was regaining its reputation as a rich fishing ground, and each year new boats filled the slips of Hatteras Harbor. The two men purchased a forty-two-foot workboat, the *In-Det*, and set out to drop-net, bottom fish, and troll for king mackerel.

Five years later, Bailey quit fishing to run Risky Business. The first winter he survived on two and three hours of sleep a night and worried constantly about equipment breakdowns, undependable crew members, and fishermen who talked of quitting him to pack with someone else. His friends grew concerned that he would drop from exhaustion and the pressures of trying to turn a profit. The stress came not only from long hours and hard labor, but from constant reminders that Bailey had switched sides in the quarrelsome relationship between fishermen and packers. Where fishermen are quietly suspicious of each other, they are vociferous about their distrust of dealers. To hear fishermen tell it, the Wanchese dealers make an easy living by sitting in warm offices, talking on the phone, and cutting deals on fish for which captains and mates have risked their lives. It is a point of view Bailey clearly resents.

"I got into this partly because I think some fishermen do get screwed at the packing house," Bailey said. "I think we can cut these guys a fair deal and still make some money. We do cut 'em a fair deal, but they're not ever going to tell you that.

"I get paid a packing fee, so much money for each box of fish I send to Chicago or Philly or New York. If I pack fish, I know I'm going to make what's mine. But I can go out and fish all week and not come home with much of anything, except money for my expenses. Say you're fishing one day and you get in the trout thick. And Joe and Charlie get in the trout thick too. The price was forty cents when you left the dock, but when you get back in it's ten cents because everybody caught fish that day. It's always the price that counts. And it's the dealer that sets the price, depending on where he can send his fish.

"It's a game, you know what I'm saying? The dealer's got to be sly. If you end up with a glut of trout, you can't call the Fulton Fish Market in New York City and say, 'I've got fifteen hundred boxes of trout; what'll you give me for 'em?' They'll give you a nickel, which means the fishermen don't get much at all. But if you've got fifteen hundred boxes and you call Chicago and say, 'Well, maybe I can get you three hundred boxes,' and you call New York and say, 'Okay, I can probably let you have five hundred boxes,' if you spread 'em out like that the price stays up and everybody's better off."

"Are you glad you quit fishing?"

He nodded vigorously. "I like packing fish, and I'm good at it. If the fishermen bring me fish that aren't pretty, I won't pack 'em. If there's fish to be packed, I'll do it all night. That's what fishing is, you know? You work when there's fish. If there's no fish, you ride to the beach, have a party. There is no 'typical'—typical week, typical catch—and there is no guarantee. There's just fish. If you're lucky."

Luck was not with the Hatteras fleet for the next several days. With the wind still strong out of the southwest, no boats went fishing for the rest of that week and most of the next. When finally the breeze died, the fishermen brought in so many gray trout that the price fell from forty cents to ten cents a pound. It stayed there for two weeks, until enough boats remained in port to ease the glut.

Bailey, meanwhile, had hired a crew of workers that included four women—an unusually high number. ("I want the fishermen to come in here, don't I?" he joked.) Twenty-three boats had signed on to pack at Risky Business. They would likely stay all season, for it is not considered wise for a captain to change fish houses too often. Through February, Bailey packed between twenty thousand and thirty thousand pounds of trout and blue-fish a night, beginning in late afternoon and usually finishing by midnight. Toward the end of the month, the late-winter crab-bers began bringing their catches to the Risky Business docks around 9 a.m.

March 5 marked the middle of Lent, a season when Catholics traditionally consume an unusually large amount of fish. That day the pound price of medium gray trout rose from fifteen cents to sixty-five cents. The fishermen knew the higher prices would probably hold through Easter. And the trout had moved to the south side of Cape Point, the easiest fishing grounds for the Hatteras fleet.

On Thursday, March 13, Bailey was in his office doing paper-work by 7:30 a.m. The drop-net boats had gone out that morn-ing for the first time in four days, and through the static of a marine radio Bailey could hear the captains remarking on the large schools of trout that seemed to be hanging in twenty feet of water just offshore. Shortly before 8 o'clock one captain's voice came across the airwaves loud, low, and smug.

"I am IN. . . THE. . . MEAT."

For a captain to admit he had found fish so early meant that his nets had come up loaded on the first set. It would take all day to pick what he had already caught. And he was not the only one. Judging from the radio banter, the entire Hatteras fleet was sitting atop a school of trout and bluefish worth hundreds of thousands of dollars.

David Wilson had just gotten out of bed when Bailey called him a few minutes after 8:00. A tall nineteen-year-old, Wilson spends most of the year mating on a charter boat run by his fa-ther, Beryl. During the past two winters, though, Wilson had worked for Risky Business. He had frequently bailed fish from boats and stacked cartons past dawn, and Bailey had come to depend on his stamina. It looked like it was going to be a long night, Bailey told him. Could he come in right away and start making cartons?

Analee Gray arrived at the fish house about 1 p.m. to help prepare for the first boats, due to reach the dock around 3:00. Wilson had already assembled several hundred cartons and lids, stomping with relentless energy on a pedal-driven staple gun. Gray, the strong, dark-haired woman with the diamond pendant, was in charge of working the scales, counting cartons of fish, and writing tickets—jobs as important as culling fish. The fish house was quiet, but it would not be quiet for long.

On the radio, captains warned the packing houses to be ready for a large load. Fishermen can estimate the size of their catches by the way their boats ride in the water, and the figures they relayed to shore confirmed Bailey's early hunch. Even boats that had consistently returned with few fish told their dealers to be prepared to receive about seventy-five boxes—7,500 pounds, 150 waxed cartons. Bailey turned to Gray and rolled his eyes. "You know the one big night we have every year?" he said. "This is it."

Just after 3 p.m., the conveyor belt began to roll with the first load of fish. Bailey had assembled a crew of three local men, six men from the mainland town of Plymouth, and three women. Six other workers were on call for later. Two of the women were set to work making cartons. Two of the men were put outside to bail fish. The first boat to reach the dock had seventy boxes of salable fish, mostly medium gray trout. At twenty-five cents a pound, the take before expenses was $1,750. The second boat had a hundred-and-five boxes of trout. The staple gun clattered, the fish rolled off the boat, the forklift carried pallets stacked with cartons to the loading dock. The third boat had ninety-five boxes, mixed trout and large bluefish. The workers groaned. Packing mixed fish meant additional work, since large bluefish must be shipped in wooden boxes instead of cartons. To change over would require a lapse in time, a break in rhythm. And the crew members knew their job would be easiest if they could set a pace and keep it.

By 7 p.m., the workers had unloaded four boats. So far the day had gone smoothly. Bailey went into his office long enough to call a local restaurant. "Can I get an order to go?" he asked.

"Sure."

"Okay, gimme forty burgers and some fries."

Fifteen minutes for supper, and back to work. Sixteen of the boats that packed with Risky Business had gone fishing that day. If the crew could maintain the pace they might finish before dawn. But just after 8 o'clock, the naked bulbs that lit the fish house blinked a single time and died. The conveyor halted; the radio fell silent. Darkness.

"Damn!" someone yelled.

It was a damp, calm night. There was no reason why the electricity should have blown out. But it was out. Risky Business was out of commission until the power was restored. The crew unloaded some boxes that had been trucked from Wanchese and would be filled with bluefish, eventually. Then they sat down to wait. In the cool, wet air their muscles began to tense.

It was past 11:00 when the electricity flicked on and the line again began to roll. The bulk of the evening's work lay ahead. Sighing and stretching, the crew members took their positions and stiffly resumed their tasks. Midnight passed with thirty boxes of bluefish. Two a.m. brought eighty-five boxes of medium trout. Clickety-clickety, the staple guns sounded through the night. Bail the boat, cull the fish, weigh them out, ice them down, stack the cartons. Occasionally Bailey stepped out and returned with a round of Cokes, or looked up from the culling table to urge members of the crew to pace themselves, to keep up the work, but safely.

By dawn the bluefish boxes had all been used, and four crew members with daytime jobs had drifted out. Three fresh workers arrived from Etheridge Seafood in Wanchese to step up the pace. Bailey, Gray, and Wilson worked on. Risky Business had made a commitment to pack every fish brought in, and well over a hundred thousand pounds had already rolled across the table. Bailey had five tractor trailers waiting to take the day's catch to different markets. Ten o'clock passed, then 11:00. At noon David Wilson sat down. After twenty-eight hours he had reached the point of exhaustion.

The last gray trout rolled across the culling table just before 1 p.m. Twelve hundred boxes of fish had been packed, seven hundred of them trout, the remainder bluefish. In a single night Risky Business had packed 10 percent of the fish it would handle all year. It would take four more hours for Bailey to clean up and finish his paperwork, but finish it he would before going home.

Early that morning a few boats had filled their gas tanks and started again for Hatteras Inlet. It mattered little that the captains and mates had gotten no sleep; there were more fish to be caught. The boats had barely reached the inlet before word came over the radio for them to turn back. The packers simply could not handle any more fish. The market had borne the previous day's catch, but barely. Arty trout or bluefish brought into Hatteras for several days would be virtually worthless.

In the dwindling light of afternoon, the boat slips were full of sturdy, white-hulled boats, most of them with four-foot reels mounted on their sterns. The docks were empty, the fish house doors closed. For all appearances Hatteras was a deserted fishing village, a town in hibernation waiting to awaken with the first rays of the warm spring sun.

Epilogue
OLD CHRISTMAS

EVERY JANUARY ON Hatteras Island, a week or so after most families have packed up the duties and indulgences of the holidays, the residents of Rodanthe hold a celebration known as Old Christmas. It is simultaneously a meeting of friends and a curious gathering of people with little in common but their hometown and perhaps their last names.

Old Christmas has been observed in Rodanthe on the Saturday closest to Epiphany for at least a hundred years. It is said to have had its beginnings in 1752, when England adopted the Gregorian calendar and shortened the calendar year by eleven days. According to legend, the towns of Hatteras Island were not informed of the change until decades later, and then they refused to abide by it. Whether or not the legend is true, a tradition

215

has evolved whereby the townspeople of Rodanthe spend Christmas Day with relatives in Waves, Salvo, or southern parts of the island, then throw a party in the Rodanthe Community Center to observe the holiday a second time. The celebration is planned for local families, and although tourists are welcomed, they seldom grasp the significance of the event. Moreover, many tourists are reluctant to attend, for Old Christmas has the reputation of being a drunken brawl.

It once was customary for the men of Hatteras Island to settle their grudges against each other once a year with a fist fight after dinner on Old Christmas. The custom seldom led to anything but a few brief sparring matches, and until recent years the celebration generally was held without incident. In the 1970s, however, it became common for men looking for a brawl to arrive in Rodanthe just before dark on Old Christmas. Frequently the men were not from Hatteras Island but from mainland communities or the northern reaches of the Outer Banks, and they started picking fights as soon as they got into town. The altercations ruined the holiday for some island residents. Even though Old Christmas has been held peacefully for the past several years, a few local families refuse to attend.

On January 4, the day of the 1986 celebration, no one expected any violence. Several weeks before, family circumstances had made it necessary for me to move to Atlanta for most of the winter, but I had managed to return to Rodanthe for the weekend of Old Christmas. Late in the afternoon, I wandered down the gravel road to the community center, a small, white building that once served as the town's single-room schoolhouse. The festivities were to have started at 1 p.m. with an oyster shoot, but it was nearly 2:30 when the first guns began to fire. On the far side of a patio, sheets of plywood had been fastened to a chain-link fence and painted with orange streaks to delineate the target zones. A knot of heads bent over a stack of paper targets that someone had spread on the hood of a car. Several of the targets were untouched; the marksmen had missed them completely. One target had a hole only a quarter-inch from the black bull's-eye.

Maggie Smith, a thin woman with a strong chin and a ski cap covering a crop of dark hair, looked up from the targets and shrugged. "Looks like JoBob gets the oysters again," she said. It was the third time JoBob Fagundes, a local merchant, had won. The men standing around her grunted and moved off.

Beside Smith was a twelve-gauge shotgun and a box of shells. She is Mac Midgett's sister, and she seemed at ease chatting with a half-dozen local men who stood on the fringe of the group. "C'mon," she coaxed. "Who's next? Three bucks for a shot at a half-bushel of Stumpy Point oysters, the best oysters around."

I walked around the community center to where two men— both Midgetts—were stringing fishing net around a patio and stoking an oversized roaster with charcoal and wood. The roaster had been fashioned from a rusty oil drum cut in half and hinged on one side. Long tables with rough plywood tops had been placed around it. As bushels of oysters finished roasting, the men would shovel them onto the tables for the crowd to shuck and eat. The coals would not be ready for a half-hour, and I wandered inside.

The tiny dance hall had begun to fill, and the instruments for a bluegrass band were set on stage. The dancing would come later; now was the time for visiting. At the door Louell Midgett, an Ocracoke native who lives in Rodanthe with her husband, collected money and hugged friends as they entered. She saw many of them several times a month, but it was Old Christmas, after all. I rounded a corner to the building's small kitchen and was enveloped by Virginia O'Neal, the postmistress, before I even saw her. "Merry Old Christmas," she beamed, hugging me tighter. She wore a Christmas-red skirt and jacket, with a holly-green pin on her lapel. Her face shone with a gracious, happy beauty. Around were her friends from the Fairhaven Methodist Church— older women named Midgett, O'Neal, Hooper, and Gray—all in holiday clothes with festival smiles on their bright-red lips.

At a string of tables just off the kitchen, several women supervised a group of young children. These were the wives of the fishermen who congregated in a corner of the dance hall, smoking and leaning back, their crossed arms resting on ample bellies. I scanned the hall, finding scores of faces I did not rec-ognize. It seemed many people had come from towns on the southern part of the cape. I waved to Mac Midgett and pushed my way toward the patio door. As I did, a stout woman with a wide face and large, stylish glasses caught my arm. "Jan." I looked at her blankly. "I'm Joyce Rucker."

Ersie Midgett's only daughter. I pumped her hand and smiled. As a young girl she had slept in the upstairs bedroom I would later use as an office. At the age of twelve she had huddled in-side the yellow frame house as a brutal wind wrenched it from its foundation. Standing behind her were her brothers, Stockton and Anderson, dressed nattily in plaid slacks. "I'm surprised to see you here," I said. It had not occurred to me that Ersie's chil-dren would attend Old Christmas.

"We wouldn't miss it for the world," Rucker said. "This is still home in some ways. But my, it's changed. Every year there are more strangers. There's no way to stop more people from coming here. The island's growing, and in many ways it's good that we have the kinds of amenities we have now. It was hard to live the way we did, with no electricity or roads. We have a movie the-ater in Avon now. I never thought I would live to see a movie theater open in Avon."

A few minutes later I left her to get some oysters. Ersie's chil-dren were among the wealthiest and most controversial figures on Hatteras Island. They had made a substantial portion of their money by selling land. Tonight they would rub elbows with fish-ermen who were slowly losing their livelihoods to pollution and powerful sportsfishing lobbies. During the past ten years the people of Hatteras have divided themselves into two bitter camps, one that wants to preserve the cape's rugged desolation and a second that is working to build a string of glitzy resorts. Among the crowd in the community center were people who had grown up as cordial neighbors, and who now were entangled in disputes over the boundaries of their land. The real estate speculators were winning the fight—or at least were making the most money and gaining the most political clout. But the development of Hatteras was not to be a topic of discussion. Not here, not on Old Christmas.

Outside, a batch of oysters had just finished cooking. A wiry man with curly, brown hair opened the lid of the roaster. Steam cascaded into the night. "Who wants oysters?" he hollered. "You want oysters, you got to make some noise."

A few of us whooped.

"Pretty slack," he said, spreading the oysters across the table in front of me. I picked one up, twisted an oyster knife to pop open the gritty shell, and sucked down the tender flesh. I downed a dozen more and went inside, where the band had begun to play.

The dance floor was filling with people of all ages and physiques, some twisting, some dancing a jerky version of the fox trot. A fisherman with the build of a concrete block held up an arm to twirl his wife, who in her forties still had the figure and toothy smile of a debutante. A thick-bodied elderly couple waltzed in the middle of the floor, bumping buttocks with the people around them. On the sidelines, women leaned their heads close together to talk above the music, and teenage girls shyly watched the dancers. I picked my way through to the other side and halted near Louell Midgett, who was still standing guard at the door. "Interesting party, isn't it?" I said.

"We usually have a good bit of fun," she said, smiling. "If I were you I'd stand back against the wall a bit. Old Buck's getting ready to come in."

Old Buck is a kind of Old Christmas Santa Claus, a mythical wild bull. It is said that many years ago Old Buck impregnated every cow in Buxton Woods and terrorized local farmers until a hunter finally shot him. His spirit lives in the marshes and hammocks of Rodanthe. I had expected him to be personified by a mounted cow head, but the creature that stomped through the door had no eyes, nose, or mouth, just two horns and a piece of cowhide mounted on top of some long, sturdy object, probably a piece of wood. His lumpy back was covered by a green Army blanket, beneath which protruded two sets of legs in blue jeans and men's boots. People crowded into the smoky hall, yelling and clapping, stomping their feet.

A red-faced and jovial man led the cow into the room with a tether. "Look out, Old Buck's wild," he yelled in a gravelly voice. "He's wild tonight."

I pressed myself against the wall as the four legs beneath the blanket kicked and clomped past me. Old Buck was not only wild, he was bent on knocking down as many people as he could. The crowd screamed with laughter and scrambled for cover, some people jumping into the laps of friends who had managed to find seats on the edge of the dance floor. As one man crouched down for a picture, the bull hit him broadside and sent him reeling across stage. Fifteen seconds later Old Buck had jostled his way outside and vanished for another year.

Seldom had I laughed so hard. The crowd caught its breath as the band swung into "Truck Driving Man" for the third time. The celebration had peaked. People drifted outside, calling good-byes into the crisp night air. I had begun searching for my coat when the wiry man who had tended the oysters grabbed a microphone from the band. "Okay, I want all the children cleared out of here," he said, "because this is an adult's night. And us adults are gonna fight."

"No we're not," said a large fisherman standing next to me.

I did not stay around to hear the shouting match that followed. Later I learned that the man had been calmed by friends and that violence had been avoided for another year. Barring hangovers, the town awoke the next day in good spirits. The only apparent casualty was a red pickup that had somehow missed the road and landed on its side in a muck-lined drainage ditch.

By spring I was able to move back to Hatteras Island, back into Miss Ersie's yellow house, which still creaks and moans like an old wooden boat in high winds. In summer the sea oats explode with tawny seeds, the black skimmers glide over Pamlico Sound, the loggerheads heave themselves ashore on silent nights. In fall my neighbors meet in the post office and remark on the weather, the fishing, the hurricanes that may or may not come spinning through.

In a very real sense, Hatteras Island will remain as it has for centuries, a malleable finger of land in a moody, hostile sea. In another sense, just as real and more distressing, its essence vanished with the opening twenty-five years ago of the Oregon Inlet bridge. By moving to the area and settling down with the hope to stay, I myself have chipped a piece from its core. There is a feeling that the island's charm has eroded beyond repair, and that it will only get worse in years to come. To me, Hatteras still seems pristine, yet pockets of shoddy development have so marred it that lifelong residents talk of selling their land and leaving. In Avon and Buxton developers draw up plans for golf courses and exclusive garden homes, to be built as soon as they can find the means to pump enough water and dispose of enough sewage. Such expensive housing would attract a different clientele to Hatteras Island, people with sleek clothes and elegant tastes. Whether or not the developers carry out their plans, Hatteras Island is in the process of being "discovered." Its new popularity is bound to drive up the cost of living and the dearness of land.

In a decade Cape Hatteras may well resemble every other East Coast seaside resort, not only physically but demographically. It is my fear that the independence and self-reliance—the very spirit that has enabled people here to survive storms and shipwrecks and centuries of isolation—will virtually cease to exist. What little spirit remains will be relegated to the rather demeaning category of "colorful" or "quaint." The concept of island time will become one more relic of a discarded past, in league with hurricane oil lamps, hand-woven fishing nets, and bags of yaupon tea.

During the months I was in Atlanta, I lived in a house surrounded on all sides by spreading dogwoods, sweet gums, and loblolly pines. In that sheltered setting I became introspective; I grew oblivious to the direction of the wind, the rise and fall of the earth, the scattering of plants and trees. The light that filtered through my curtains was more white than yellow, the light of an unreflected sun. To soothe my homesickness for Hatteras, I conjured up memories of a fall afternoon I had spent watching birds on the beach north of town. Those images return to me even now, like a recurring dream that is sweet with beauty yet bitter with a fleeting, fragile feel.

I am walking north before sunset. The air is calm, though a short while ago the wind lifted plumes of sand and hurled them against my legs and arms with tiny, painful pricks. Sea oats spill halfway down the dunes and end in crumbling cliffs. Below, the sand is smooth but for tiny mounds of sediment pushed up by burrowing ghost crabs. The beach juts thirty yards to the east, flat as a table, then drops sharply and disappears in sky-blue, shimmering surf. Marbled waves sweep beneath my feet, like clouds sliding against a mountain.

The shorebird migration has reached its height. In front of me sanderlings, turnstones, and at least two types of sandpipers work the beach, chasing mole crabs that fizzle to the surface with receding waves. The birds are in their pale winter plumage; to tell one species from another will take a studious, unwavering eye. Moving carefully, I inch my way closer; I step ten feet toward a flock, bring my binoculars to my eyes, and freeze as the birds skitter a few steps away. They move in and out with the surf, never stopping, the clouds of their numbers dovetailing with the waves. I will never capture everything I want from them, never consume enough to be sated.

The sand is a deep buff, the color of brushed suede. Salty wind blows in my eyes, and I feel the skin on my face tighten from sun. In front of me small white birds startle, fly over the surf in an arc, and light to feed. They spook and again take wing, and again, luminous and white, like handfuls of glitter tossed in the wind.

SELECT
BIBLIOGRAPHY

Barnes, Robert D. *Invertebrate Zoology*. 4th rev. ed. Philadelphia: Saunders College, 1980.

Bearss, Edwin C. "Rescue Operations from Chicamacomico Station, 1874-1954." Unpublished manuscript, 1965.

Behn, Robert D., and Clark, Martha A. "The Termination of Beach Erosion Control at Cape Hatteras." Public Policy Vol. 27, no. 1 (Winter 1979): 99-127.

Bent, Arthur Cleveland. *Life Histories of North American Shorebirds*, part one. 1927. Reprint. Dover Publications, 1962.

Brown, Clair A. *Vegetation of the Outer Banks of North Carolina*. Louisiana State University Studies, Coastal Studies Series, no. 4 (no date or place).

Dolan, Robert, Paul J. Godfrey, and William E. Odum. "Man's Impact on the Barrier Islands of North Carolina." *American Scientist*, Vol. 61, March/April, 1973: 152-160.

Dunbar, Gary S. *Historical Geography of the North Carolina Outer Banks*. Baton Rouge: Louisiana State University Press, 1958.

Godfrey, Melinda M. "An Interpreter's Natural History of the Ghost Crab or The Life and Loves of *Ocypode quardrata*." National Park Service Cooperative Research Unit, University of Massachusetts, Amherst, 1975.

Gosner, Kenneth L. *A Field Guide to the Atlantic Shore*. Boston: Houghton Mifflin Company, 1978.

Jones, Robert A., and Terry M. Sholar. *The Effects of Freshwater Discharge on Estuarine Nursery Areas of Pamlico Sound*. Morehead City: North Carolina Department of Natural Resources and Community Development, Division of Marine Fisheries, 1981.

Lippson, Alice Jane, and Robert L. Lippson. *Life in the Chesapeake Bay*. Baltimore and London: The Johns Hopkins University Press, 1984.

Mager, Andreas, Jr. *Five Year Status Reviews of Sea Turtles Listed under the Endangered Species Act of 1973*. St. Petersburg: U.S. Department of Commerce, National Oceanic and Atmospheric Administration, National Marine Fisheries Service, January 1985.

Matthiessen, Peter. *Wildlife in North America.* New York: The Viking Press, 1959.

———. *The Wind Birds.* New York: The Viking Press, 1973.

McMullan, Philip S., Jr. *Land-Clearing Trends on the Albemarle-Pamlico Peninsula.* Durham: McMullan Consulting, 1984.

Mercer, Linda. *A Biological and Fisheries Profile of Red Drum, Sciaenops ocellatus.* Morehead City: North Carolina Department of Natural Resources and Community Development, Division of Marine Fisheries, Special Scientific Report, no. 41, July 1984.

Parnell, James F., and Mark A. Shields. *Management Plan for North Carolina's Colonial Waterbirds.* Draft Project Report, (no date or place).

Parnell, James F., and Robert F. Soots, Jr. *Atlas of Colonial Waterbirds of North Carolina Estuaries.* Raleigh: University of North Carolina Sea Grant, 1979.

———. *Ecological Succession of Breeding Birds in Relation to Plant Succession on Dredge Islands in North Carolina.* Raleigh: University of North Carolina Sea Grant, 1975.

Otte, Lee J. *Origin, Development, and Maintenance of the Pocosin Wetlands of North Carolina.* Raleigh: Report Submitted to the Natural Heritage Program, North Carolina Department of Natural Resources and Community Development, 1981.

Pomeroy, L.R., and R.G. Wiegert, eds. *The Ecology of a Salt Marsh.* Ecological Studies Series, Vol. 38. New York: Springer-Verlag, 1981.

Pritchard, Peter C.H., ed. *Sea Turtle Manual of Research and Conservation Techniques*. Prepared for Western Atlantic Turtle Symposium, San Jose, Costa Rica, July 1983.

Reiger, George. *Wanderer on My Native Shore*. New York: Simon and Schuster, 1984.

Richardson, Curtis J., ed. *Pocosin Wetlands: An Integrated Analysis of Coastal Plain Freshwater Bogs in North Carolina*. (Proceedings of Pocosins: A Conference on Alternative Uses of the Coastal Plain Freshwater Wetlands of North Carolina; 1980; Duke University Marine Laboratory, Beaufort.) Stroudsburg: Hutchinson Ross Publishing Company, 1981.

Ross, Jeff, and Beth Burns. "Annual Report: Preliminary Investigations on Tagging Red Drum, *Sciaenops oellatus*, in North Carolina." Manteo: North Carolina Division of Marine Fisheries, 1985.

Rudloe, Jack. *Time of the Turtle*. New York: Alfred A. Knopf, 1979.

Saunders, William L., ed. *The Colonial Records of North Carolina*, Vol. 1, 1662-1712, and Vol. 2, 1713-1728. Raleigh: P.M. Hale, Printer to the State, 1886.

Sears, Harold F., Lynn J. Moseley, and Helmut C. Mueller. "Behavioral Evidence on Skimmers' Evolutionary Relationships." *The Auk*, Vol. 93, no. 1 (January 23, 1976): 170-174.

Stick, David. The *Outer Banks of North Carolina*. Chapel Hill: The University of North Carolina Press, 1958.

——. *Roanoke Island, The Beginnings of English America*. Chapel Hill: The University of North Carolina Press, 1983.

Teal, John and Mildred Teal. *Life and Death of the Salt Marsh.* New York: Ballantine Books, 1969.

Terres, John K. The *Audubon Society Encyclopaedia of North American Birds.* New York: Alfred A. Knopf, 1980.

Wolcott, Thomas G. "Ecological Role of Ghost Crabs, *Ocypode quardrata (Fabricus)* on an Ocean Beach: Scavengers or Predators?" *Journal of Experimental Marine Biology and Ecology* (1978) Vol. 31: 67-82.

INDEX

Agriculture
on Albemarle-Pamlico Peninsula, 84, 86-87, 88
Albatross fleet, 197-98, 201-2
Algonkian Indians, 24, 85-86
Amadas, Philip, 22-23
Amphipods, 51-52, 108-9, 112-13, 119, 120
Annelids, 128-29
Army Corps of Engineers, United States, 67-68, 69, 116-17
Austin, Willie and Rachel, 168
Avocet, 75

Bailey, Steve, 193, 194-96, 208-14
Bald Head Conservancy, 136-37, 139
Bald Head Island, 131-32, 136-50
Barlowe, Arthur, 22-23
Barrier island migration, 7-14, 17-19
Bass, striped, 200, 201, 202-3
Beach
erosion, 5, 8, 9-14
nourishment, 10, 12
slope in winter and summer, 57, 157-58
Bender, Jennifer, 139-45
Black needle rush, 82, 90, 114, 116
Bluefish, 27, 194, 200, 202
Bodie Island, 5, 30, 31
Brachner, Arch and Pat, 187-90

Cape Hatteras lighthouse
effects of erosion, 14
Cape Hatteras National Seashore, 5
formation of, 8

Cape Lookout, 5, 8, 11, 13-14, 21-22, 116
Cape Point, 10, 19, 22, 26, 38, 49, 62, 181-82, 183, 192, 196, 201, 202, 205, 211
Caprellas. See Skeleton shrimp
Chesapeake Bay, 5, 23, 25, 103, 178
Chicamacomico lifesaving station, 15, 20, 30, 31-35, 155
Chicamacomico Races, 28-29
Civil War, 27-29
Civilian Conservation Corps, 8, 36
Coast Guard, United States, 15, 33-35, 37, 200, 201
Coquinas, 50, 52, 55, 56
Crabs
fiddler, 107, 118, 119
ghost, See Ghost crabs
mole, 49-50, 52, 55, 56, 57
mud, 51, 119, 128
Croatoan Indians, 19, 22-25
Currituck Inlet, 22, 27

Dare, Virginia, 24
DDT
effect on coastal birds and animals, 75-76
DeMaurice, Wally, 16-17, 156-57, 166-67
Detritus
as food for invertebrates, 109-11, 112, 113
Diamond Shoals, 16, 18-19, 196, 203
Distraction display among birds, 73-75
Dolan, Robert, 10-14
Drop-netting. See Gill-netting
Drum, red 172-90

Hurricanes
   changes in wind direction, 161-62, 168-71
   cutting inlets, 27, 35
   effect on water level in Pamlico Sound, 11, 163, 167, 169-71
   energy in northwest quadrant, 161
   moving houses, 5, 37, 168
Hydroids, 52, 120

Inlets
   cut by storms, 5, 17, 27, 35
   effects of formation on barrier island movement, 14
Intracoastal Waterway, Atlantic, 67, 116-17
Island Convenience Store, 153-54, 156, 160

Juncus roemerianus. See Black needle rush

Killdeer, 75

Lake Mattamuskeet, 87 , 90
Lake Phelps, 86, 88-89, 97, 102
Lifesaving Service, United States, 15, 31-34
Lighthouses
   dates construction completed, 31
Loggerhead sea turtles, 130-51
   conservation programs, 131-32, 135-36, 137-51
   effects of coastal development on nesting, 134-35
   effects of temperature on sex, 135-36, 138
   eggs, 138, 141, 142-43, 144-45

evolution, 132
   hatchlings, 133-35, 146-51
   life span, 133-34
   nest relocation, 135, 138, 141, 143-45
   nesting ritual, 133, 141, 142-44
   overfishing, 134, 135
   predation, 133, 143, 148
   range, 131, 133-34
Lost Colony, Sir Walter Raleigh's, 22-25

Maritime forests
   on Bald Head Island, 132
   establishment on relic dunes, 49
   and freshwater aquifers, 49
   on Hatteras Island, 7-8, 11, 22
McLean, Malcom P., 88-89
McMullan, Philip S., 93-94
Meekins, Cindy, 130-32, 136-39, 146-50
Merilatt, Frank, 181-87
Midgett, Anderson, 36-38
Midgett, Ersie, 34-38
Midgett, Harold, 36
Midgett, Captain John Allen, 33-34
Midgett, Matthew, 30
Midgett, Theodore Stockton, Sr., 34-36
Midgett, Theodore Stockton "Stocky," Jr., 36-38
Midgett Realty, 38, 39
Miller, Todd, 92-93, 103
Mirlo, wrecked tanker, 33-34

Nash, Brad, 168-71
National Park Service
   and relationship with Hatteras residents, 7-10, 12-14

Settlement on Hatteras Island, 22-25, 26-27, 30, 38
Shellfish
   effects of coastal development on, 115-16
   effects of fresh water on, 82-85, 90-92, 93
   primary nurseries for, 81-82, 90-92, 103
Shipwrecks, 15, 30-34
Sholar, Terry M., 90-92
Skeleton shrimp, 51-52, 120
Skimmers, black
   chicks, 65-66
   courtship, 62
   eggs, 63, 65
   nesting habitat, 63-66, 67-71
Snail, salt marsh, 120-22
Spartina alterniflora, 105-6, 109-10, 114, 115, 116-17
Spartina patens, 7, 14, 106, 109-10, 116-17
Spoil islands, 67-71
   colonization by plants, 67-68, 69-71
   effects on birds and marine life, 67-71
   effects on tidal marshes, 116-17
Spring tides, 50, 121
Stilt, black-necked, 72-75
Strathairly, wrecked steamship, 32
Stumpy Point, 81-84, 92-93, 102-4, 204

Teague, Carol, 206-8
Teal, John and Mildred, 109-11, 120-21
Terns
   courtship, 61

defense of nests, 63, 64, 69-70
depletion by millinery trade, 66-67
differences in nests and eggs, 62-65
disadvantages on developed coasts, 67-68
nesting habitat, 68-71
species nesting together, 64-65
Tidal range, 116, 123
Timbering
   on Albemarle-Pamlico Peninsula, 82-84, 86-87, 97
   on Outer Banks, 7-8, 27
Trout, gray, 192, 196, 197, 202-4, 211-14
Truesdell, Hobart, 89-90, 98-102

Verrazzano, Giovanni da, 22
Virginia Coastal Drift, 16

Weske, John, 76-80
West Virginia Pulp and Paper Company, 84, 87, 88
White, John, 23-25
Wilson, David, 211-12, 213-14
Wind
   effect on tidal movement, 21-22, 90-91, 111, 116, 126, 167-68, 169-71
Wirth, Conrad L., 9-10, 12
Wolcott, Thomas G., 55-57
Woodhouse, William W., Jr., 12-13
Works Project Administration, 8-9

Zenobia, 95, 97-98